the
American
Book of
Living and
Dying

the American Book of Living and Dying

Lessons in Healing Spiritual Pain

Richard F. Groves and
Henriette Anne Klauser

CELESTIAL ARTS
Berkeley

*For Mary. The greatest gift God has given me is your love.
You are the life and soul of this work.*
—*Richard*

To Nancy, my soul friend, my lifelong anamcara.
—*Henriette Anne*

Library of Congress Cataloging-in-Publication Data is on file with the publisher.

ISBN 978-1-58761-350-0 (paperback)
ISBN 978-1-58761-238-1 (hardcover)

Printed in the United States of America

Cover design by Chloe Rawlins
Text design by Nancy Austin

10 9 8 7

First Paperback Edition

contents

Preface to the Paperback Edition viii

Introduction 1

Part I. The History

Hospice

The Original Hospice: The Art of Dying Well 13

A Vision from the Past: God's Hotel 14

Our Cultural Bias: Death Is the Enemy 17

Hospice in America: Gift and Challenge 19

Ancient Books of the Dead

The Heritage 21

    ❖ Egyptian Book of the Dead: A Greater Light

    ❖ Celtic Books of the Dead: Spiritual Midwifery

    ❖ Gnostic Books for the Living and Dying:
      Bridge between East and West

    ❖ Tibetan Book of the Dead: Coaching the Soul

    ❖ Monastic Books of the Dying: Prescriptive Care

What the Books of the Dead Have in Common:
Lessons for Us Today 34

Spiritual Pain

Pain versus Suffering: The Human Condition 37

Diagnosing Spiritual Pain: Asking Courageous Questions 39

Responding to Spiritual Pain:
A Psychospiritual Relationship 42

   ✦ Meaning Pain: The Painful-Blissful Encounter with the Truth

   ✦ Forgiveness Pain: The Common Cold of Spiritual Pain

   ✦ Relatedness Pain: Leaving the Familiar Behind

   ✦ Hopelessness Pain: Death as Healer

Becoming an Anamcara 55

   ✦ Ten Commandments for the Anamcara

Part II. The Stories

Annie: the Perfectionist
Will you love me even if I get it wrong? 63

Henry: the Helper
Will you love me even if I can't love you back? 81

Sara: the Achiever
Will you love me even if I am not successful? 95

Heather: the Dreamer
Will you love me even if you know who I am? 111

Park: the Thinker
Will you love me even if I lose everything in life? 125

Maria Elena: the Loyalist
Will you love me even if I break the rules? 143

Andrew: the Adventurer
Will you love me even if I cry? 159

Dorothy: the Asserter
Will you love me even if I am weak? 175

Larry: the Peacemaker
Will you love me even if I disagree with you? 189

Story Archetypes 202

Part III. The Tool Chest

Art Therapy 205

Breath Work 209

Coma Therapy 213

Dream Work 218

Energy Therapies 223

Forgiveness Exercises 227

Guided Visualization 231

Healing and Assistance from Ancestors 236

Healing Religious Abuse and Images of God 240

Intercessory (Nonlocal) Prayer 244

Journaling 248

Life Review Exercises 252

Meditation Practices 257

Music Therapy 262

Religious Rites and Sacred Writings 267

Rituals for the Bedside 270

Rituals of Release 273

Vigil Rituals and Rituals for Remembering 277

❖ ❖ ❖

Bibliography 285

About the Authors 294

Preface to the Paperback Edition

Great Suffering, Great Love

Since its publication in 2005, *The American Book of Dying* has had a profound impact on caregivers and care receivers around the world—far beyond North American audiences. What began as a guide to end-of-life care and a series of real-life stories about healing through suffering has evolved into a worldwide training and education network. Thousands of hospice workers, health care professionals, members of diverse faith-based communities, and the general public have been introduced to the vocabulary of diagnosing and responding to spiritual pain. From Japan, Thailand, and India to Ireland, Austria, and Australia, *The American Book of Dying* has opened windows of insight into the universal nature of spiritual suffering and healing. In Canada and the United States, teachings about the sacred art of living and dying are now featured in many maximum-security prisons, high school classrooms, programs for the elderly, schools of medicine, and seminaries of all denominations.

You might have noticed that the title of this paperback edition has an important addition: the word "living" has been included, so the title now reads, *The American Book of Living and Dying.* This is no small change. No one should wait until the end of life to consider what lies at the foundation of spiritual health and suffering. The soul's yearning and quest for meaning, forgiveness, hope, and healthy relationships measure the quality of every stage of life, and are not just concerns that surface during life's final stage. The stories in this book have a timeless quality and apply to both the living and the dying, transcending age, race, and gender. No one's life is immune from the painful challenges of death and loss. The gift, however, is that we can find meaning and consolation in this darkness.

Now I have to include my own personal story in these pages. Since *The American Book of Dying* first came out, Mary, my wife of nearly twenty years, has died of cancer. Neither the lessons in this book, nor the stories of others, nor a lifetime of working with the terminally ill make it any easier to continue living without my beloved Mary. There is no bypass through the "valley of the shadow of death."

Mary came into my life like a beautiful breeze. With a unique, authentic presence and a remarkable, gentle love, she lit up the dark and lonely spaces in my world and in the lives of many others. It is a strange and incomprehensible thing to lose my spouse, my workmate, and my *anamcara*—soul friend—all at the same time. But my experiences with the dying and their loved ones have taught me an important lesson: people can share a deep connection that transcends physical boundaries and outlives physical form. I've realized that Mary and I are joined by a rare marriage of spirits that continues to be life-giving even after death.

Death is a season that takes away everything that seems sure and consoling. However, Mary's death has also opened my heart to new and previously unimagined ways of living. Rather than merely hope that consciousness survives physical death, I've come to embrace Mary's intangible presence, which I feel almost every day. I'm not an especially contemplative person by nature, but when I take the time to listen to the quiet voice within, I know that Mary is as real now as the day we met. I miss her terribly, but I also realize that it was her *anam* (soul) that I first fell in love with. This new and real presence is becoming deeper by the day. And because there is so much love for me "on the other side" now, death is no longer a fearful fate.

Every ancient book of living and dying views life and death as a continuum, as an unbroken cycle. If we choose to take on the role of anamcara, the journey of our relationship with a loved one does not end with his or her last breath. In fact, we are forever intertwined; they become a part of our existence, and we become a part of theirs. T. S. Eliot, in *Four Quartets*, describes it this way: "We die with the dying: / See, they depart, and we go with them. / We are born with the dead: / See, they return, and bring us with them." Life goes on and is—paradoxically—enhanced by death. And if we can find love and reaffirmed connection in our suffering, we need not fear that life's greatest pains can destroy us.

Richard Groves
June 2009

Introduction

Today will be an ordinary day for most. The sun will rise and set on familiar work and relationships. But for some of our relatives and neighbors, today will not be ordinary. For them, life as they have known it will come to an end. Today they will die.

Since you opened this book, 10 persons have died worldwide, on the average of 1.76 persons per second, to be precise. For every 1,000 persons alive today, 8 will die within the next year. If you live in a midsize American town, that means an average of 3.5 deaths per day. In metropolitan areas the size of Boston, Denver, and Seattle, the daily mortality rate rises to almost 40 persons.

Most people have some warning about impending death. In North America, accidental or sudden catastrophic illness accounts for only about 20 percent of all fatalities—80 percent of Americans die in bed. The majority of us will die a natural death due to long-term disease or the aging process. That means we are far more likely than our ancestors to have ample time to prepare for our own death and the deaths of those we love.

In the face of dying, fears and questions as old as humanity arise. What is a "good death"? How can you best support a dying friend or relative when your own world has been turned upside down? These issues are beyond the measurement of science and stethoscope. Suffering, loss, and grief command our emotional attention when someone we love is dying.

The American Book of Living and Dying hopes to answer those questions. It is written for the nonprofessional caretaker, the one sitting by the bedside in those last days.

America has two trends regarding death and dying. The first is related to the outstanding contribution of the hospice movement. Within one generation, palliative or comfort care has changed the face of end-of-life medicine. Today nearly every community in the United States regardless of size has access to hospice services. And thanks to the "angels" who work and volunteer for hospice, fewer persons die in pain. Nor do families have to bear the burden of caregiving alone. An impressive 91 percent of those served by hospice give a rating of outstanding to this supportive service. Perhaps this is why America's second trend is all the more troublesome to report.

The second trend is the stark assertion that the last two generations of Americans have not, in general, died well. This is no casual opinion, loosely expressed, but a quote from the first president of the American Academy of Hospice and Palliative Medicine, Dr. Ira Byock. Dr. Byock points out that Americans spend more money on medicine and high-tech care at the end of life than any other society in history. Physicians now have an arsenal at their disposal to control physical symptoms like breathlessness, nausea, and pain. Yet for many of us at the moment of death, something essential is missing. An increasing number of hospice professionals are also dismayed.

The underlying premise of *The American Book of Living and Dying* is that there is an answer to the dilemma of this latter trend. The answer is directly related to the soul-sized questions that typically show up in the nearing death experience. For example:

When someone is struggling with emotional or spiritual pain, what kinds of tools might help?

What is the relationship between physical pain and human suffering?

Are there predictable stages in the dying process that call for different responses?

Who are the experts we should consult when a particularly difficult situation arises at the end of life?

What happens during and after a person's death?

How do we prepare throughout our lifetime for our dying?

What can the dying teach us?

The answers to these questions are not something the authors of this book invented or the current society discovered. *The American Book of Living and Dying* addresses each of these concerns through lessons of history found in the ancient books of the dying. For the past three thousand years, our ancestors have left an impressive legacy on the "art of dying." Their collective insights about the relationship between physical pain and spiritual suffering are timeless, as true today as then. It is this wisdom that appears to be the missing link in our modern care of the dying.

The American Book of Living and Dying neither advocates a particular theology nor pretends to be a new system of belief. Rather, it is about our common spiritual experiences at the end of life, drawing from lessons found in every great spiritual tradition. Our ancestors knew that at the end of life answers to these universal questions are accessible. We only have to step out of the way and allow the dying to become our teachers. The good news is that you already know at some level what to do when someone you love is dying. All you need is permission and courage to trust your deepest instincts.

How *The American Book of Living and Dying* Is Organized

This book is divided into three parts. Part I is a historical overview, explaining the hospice movement and tracing the principles of the sacred art of dying back to its ancient roots in monastic, Celtic, Tibetan, and other traditions. Some of the reflections and conclusions here are based on Richard Groves's own translations of centuries-old manuscripts, several of which had been rolled up for a thousand years and never before translated. Part I also introduces the concept of spiritual pain, identifies the four kinds of spiritual pain, and tells you how to become what was known in ancient times as an *anamcara*, or soul friend of the dying.

Part II is the heart of the book: a collection of nine real-life stories illustrating spiritual pain and remedies that helped. This section includes lessons learned from each story, so you can make appropriate choices for your own situation.

Part III is a tool chest, what was known in ancient times as a *vade mecum* (vah-day may-coom) or "take with me." Such handbooks were portable references for traveling doctors and ministers in antiquity. Here, in one easily accessible place, we have gathered together various therapies that you can choose from to ease the pain of the person you are caring for.

A Note on the Stories in Part II

The art of living well and the art of dying well are one.

—*Epicurus*

Attending the death of another human being is a profound privilege. The prospects for growth and transformation at the end of life are second to none. But along with the awesome experience of sharing the intimate journey of life and death with another, our ancestors spoke of a related responsibility. Bearing witness to someone's death reminds us that each of our stories has particular importance. A Jewish proverb puts it this way: "Remembrance is redemption and forgetfulness is exile." When we tell the stories of those who have died, we remember and continue to learn from their experiences.

The nine stories in part II describe persons of different ages, nationalities, and spiritual orientations who are from a variety of geographical locations and variously-sized communities throughout the United States. Their legacies—regardless of whether their last days were spent in a hospital, hospice, or at home—are unique.

Of the hundreds of deaths that Richard has attended, we selected these stories because the people in them illustrate nine archetypes common to human nature. That means you can expect to find characteristics of your loved one in at least one of the accounts related in this collection. The archetypes are based on the model of the Enneagram, an ancient tool for understanding human personality types. For readers interested in more information about this theory, please consult the conclusion of part II, "The Stories."

We are profoundly grateful to the courageous persons and their families who were willing to share their final joys and struggles with us. In order to protect confidentiality, the names and some incidental details have been changed.

Our ancestors believed that the sacred art of dying and the sacred art of living are two sides of the same coin. We invite you to the gift of realizing that we are all teachers for one another as we face our own dyings.

How This Book Came About

A good death does honor to a whole life.

—Petrarch

Several years ago, Richard and his wife, Mary, undertook a pilgrimage to Europe and North Africa with the goal of tracing the early origins of the medieval hospice movement. Generous monks and research librarians from North Africa and Western Europe made available to him hundreds of manuscript pages from the eleventh to the fourteenth centuries, and he spent countless hours translating them from early medieval Latin.

The illuminated texts of these ancient manuscripts, carefully inscribed in calligraphy, detailed what is known as the ars moriendi, or art of dying.

In addition, these old animal skin parchments yielded an exciting bonus: marginalia scratched by contemporaneous doctors, nurses, and monks as they assisted the dying.

Translating these small notations in the margins revealed an intimate look into the personal lives and deaths of our European ancestors from a thousand years ago. The wisdom encoded there shined a light on the missing piece in America's end-of-life care and was the impetus for writing this book. Richard teamed with writer Henriette Anne Klauser to explore the answers to the provocative questions these manuscripts raise, namely, Can we diagnose spiritual pain? And, if we can diagnose it, can we treat it?

The background for *The American Book of Living and Dying* also comes from the Sacred Art of Living Education and Retreat Center located in Bend, Oregon, which Richard and his wife, Mary, founded in 1996. The center offers a unique series of national training programs called the Sacred Art of Dying. The goal is to create a new generation of anamcara, or spiritual companions for end-of-life care.

The Sacred Art of Living Center trains both health care professionals and the general public. More than seven thousand people from the United States and from English-speaking countries all over the world have graduated from these programs. The Sacred Art of Living Center has created a forum for both supporting and acknowledging the essential role of spirituality at the end of life.

How to Read This Book: A User's Manual

In my end is my beginning. —T. S. Elliot

How do you find hope in what may appear to be a hopeless situation? When someone you love is dying, there are unparalleled opportunities in the personal realm for healing. But first, there is the reality of dealing with the emotional fallout. News of a terminal diagnosis of someone we love is like having a head-on collision with reality. Death may indeed be a wise teacher, but it can also be a harsh one. So here are a few ideas about how to read this book in ways that will support you in your specific situation.

The American Book of Living and Dying is a handbook or a resource, something to return to over and over depending on your own changing circumstances. Feel free to read the chapters in the order that best suits your current needs. For example, if you are presently dealing with end-of-life issues in your own immediate world, you need not read *The American Book of Living and Dying* in a traditional, linear way, proceeding from front to back.

Instead, consider beginning with part II, "The Stories." Each of these real-life accounts offers insight into the most common end-of-life concerns. If something from a particular story speaks to your life situation, you can find specific recommendations and practical support in part III, "The Tool Chest," which corresponds with the stories and details special therapies that can help.

If, on the other hand, you are a reader simply curious about this topic, or you want to know the authority and underpinning of these principles, you might want to begin more traditionally with the opening.

Part I, "The History," gives useful background and context for the lessons taught in *The American Book of Living and Dying*. Turn to the pages in part I to explore spiritual pain and learn how the valuable insights of history apply today in dealing with spiritual suffering at the end of life.

The American Book of Living and Dying grew out of two distinct yet interrelated sources: current day hospice experience and historical research. A family member or health care professional at the bedside of the dying has little time for esoteric theories. You can trust that all of the therapies and practices in this book are clinically sound because they are grounded in classical wisdom and contemporary clinical experience.

Please note that the tools you will find here regarding the treatment of spiritual pain are not alternatives to medical treatment. The goal of these pages is to integrate and complement both the physical and emotional-spiritual dimensions of caregiving. The model here is always both/and never either/or.

Caregiving demands unconditional presence. *The American Book of Living and Dying* provides comfort in knowing that others have walked this path before you and paved the way.

A Personal Note from Richard Groves

The dying are the real teachers in *The American Book of Living and Dying*. I was blessed to spend hundreds of hours at the bedside of terminally ill persons. Over a period of twelve years, I personally attended the deaths of five hundred persons. This book exists because early in my caregiving career a mentor encouraged me to keep detailed notes about the lessons I learned from the dying.

I honor and acknowledge the valuable education and life experiences that are the other foundation of this book. Prior to my years of work as a hospice chaplain and executive director of a hospice facility, I served for fifteen years as a Roman Catholic priest. Though no longer working in the priesthood, I am grateful for its opportunities to practice the art of pastoral caregiving. I am also indebted to a seminary education that supported my passion for history, comparative world religions, and foreign language.

For as long as I can remember, languages, both ancient and modern, have been a hobby for me, even though there is little practical use for unspoken tongues like Latin, ancient Greek, and old Semitic dialects. Or so I thought. Then, after years of serving as a hospice chaplain, I made my overseas research pilgrimage. It was there that I learned there is no such thing as a dead language.

The American Book of Living and Dying is also the fruit of a more personal experience. For more than two decades, I worked side by side with my closest friend, colleague, and wife, Mary. There is a peculiar irony that I wrote the first edition of this book in the wake of her diagnosis with metastasic renal cell carcinoma, otherwise known as kidney cancer. Our family friend and oncologist had offered us a sobering prognosis, telling us that this disease would probably take her life. So for the rest of Mary's life, we lived under the uncertain shadow of cancer. Paradoxically, we embarked on the same journey of living and dying that we had traveled with many others. Mary passed away in early 2009, but her valiant efforts to "live with" instead of "die with" cancer continue to be a valuable and bittersweet teacher for me.

A Personal Note from Henriette Anne Klauser

My lifework is about writing, not about how to write, but the psychological aspects of writing and the power of the written word. My previous books treat overcoming writing anxiety and tell how to use writing to manifest goals, build relationships, and heal emotional wounds.

My books are based on a belief in Spirit and synchronicity, and the sense that what holds us back from being all that we can be on any given day is our fear of failure.

I was drawn to Richard's work, his scholarship and his passion, and the tie-in of his ideas with the principles I have dedicated my life to writing about and teaching.

From the start, I understood that *The American Book of Living and Dying* is a message for the living: You don't have to wait for a life-threatening illness to drop the mask and live an authentic life.

There is another, more vulnerable connection. My divorce after a long-term marriage was like a death to me, a profound loss. I questioned my identity, grappled with forgiveness, struggled with the agony of learning to leave the familiar behind, stood frightened on the edge of the cliff of hopelessness. In other words, I faced all four spiritual pains.

For me, working on *The American Book of Living and Dying* was an invitation to celebrate the reality of change, rather than simply to endure and survive. The dictum to lean into the pain rather than run away from it reminded me over and over that there is another side, even if the path to it is not a straight line, but more like a spiral bending back on itself. And I knew that writing about it would help other people.

❖   ❖   ❖

Together we have spent weeks at a time sequestered in a cabin retreat in Bainbridge Island, Washington, or at the Common Ground Retreat House and Hermitage in Bend, Oregon, hammering out these pages with the gift of uninterrupted work and the kindness of those who fed us.

As we worked, we kept reminders on the table in front of us of those whose spirits guided our work: Dorothy's prayer stick, Park's copy of a book by Thich Nhat Hanh, a CD of Henry's song "Wade in the Water," Andrew's autographed baseball, one of Heather's drawings. We felt their presence with us, blessing our work and bringing it to you. They guided our words as we told their stories, not so you would know about them, but so you would know about yourself and the people you love.

Our prayer is that *The American Book of Living and Dying* will be a gift to you with an important legacy, passed on for centuries by our ancestors: we need not wait until our deathbed to discover life's truest priorities.

Part I.
The History

Hospice

The Original Hospice:
The Art of Dying Well

Apply yourself now, that at the hour of death, you may be glad and unafraid.
—Thomas à Kempis

The word hospice comes from the same root word as the terms hostel and hospitality. Hospice conjures up images of Swiss Alpine shelters, complete with a St. Bernard dog wearing his signature brandy cask. These original hospices were indeed places of respite for weary medieval pilgrims. Like early B & Bs, hospices dotted Europe's high Alpine landscape, which followed ancient Roman trade routes. Some of the oldest hospices, created by physician-monks and nuns, trace their lineage back to the year 1000 A.D.

The hospice infirmary was an essential part of an institution where travelers also fell sick and died. Within the relatively safe walls of European monastic communities, the West thus created its first hospital and health care system. A library of records still exists that refer to a larger tradition popularly called the *ars moriendi*, or the art of dying.

Many ancient cultures produced books of the dead. In recent years there has been a revival of interest in writings like the *Tibetan Book of the Dying* and the *Celtic Books of the Dead*. Few Americans realize that, a thousand years ago, the West also produced its own book of the dying. At the turn of the last millennium, early in the eleventh century A.D., a convergence of many great traditions took place in the heart of Europe. The result became an ingenious collection of wisdom with the bold name *Ars Bene Moriendi*, or the Art of Dying Well.

Aspects of this ancient healing art are relevant today. Just knowing that an entire society was once committed to doing whatever it took to support the peaceful dying of its citizens is impressive. The *ars sacra moriendi*, considered a sacred art because of its care for both body and soul, became a blueprint of the original Western hospice that survived for nearly five hundred years.

Our Western ancestors created guides and manuals for their work, but there was no "one size fits all" model to relieve spiritual pain. During the Middle Ages, there was a distinction between art and science. Science was responsible for finding and applying universal principles; art referred to the application of science to a person or thing. At the end of life, the caregiver's art was to find a unique way to relieve a particular person's struggles and fears.

Few places on earth have preserved the spirit of the West's ancient hospice movement like the medieval town of Beaune (pronounced *bone*) in Southeastern France.

A Vision from the Past: God's Hotel

The only measure of a society's greatness depends upon how it cares for the poorest of its poor at the end of life.
—Nicholas of Rolin, Founder of l'Hôtel-Dieu

Approaching the village of Beaune today, the modern pilgrim feels dropped into a dream from long ago. Situated in the famous wine-growing region of Burgundy, Beaune is one of Europe's great trading crossroads. Inside its fortresslike walls is a world-heritage site called l'Hôtel-Dieu, or God's Hotel.

The Hospices de Beaune was conceived in the mid-fifteenth century, prior to the demise of Europe's original hospice movement, only a few years after France's patron saint, Joan of Arc, was burned at the stake. During Europe's bloody Hundred Years' War, the lot of the average peasant was desperate. Roving bands of murderers, rapists, and extortionists spread terror throughout the countryside, as one of Europe's last devastating plagues decimated entire populations. Life and death for the average person was brutish.

In the midst of this despair, the region's chancellor, Nicolas Rolin, convinced both king and pope to exempt the newly constructed Hotel of God from all taxes in perpetuity. The result is a masterpiece of civic Gothic architecture that rivaled the palaces and cathedrals of its day. Rolin and his wife, Guigone, created a prestigious foundation nicknamed "the palace for the poor." They employed some of Europe's great artisans to decorate the roofs with polychrome tiles and emblazon the walls with luxurious Italian tapestries. They commissioned Flemish painters to create one of the best-known altarpieces of the time. Instead of a grim asylum for the dying, this hospice provided luxurious attention for the sick and dying that rivaled the lifestyle of royalty.

Beaune's extraordinary architectural and artistic achievements are only an external expression of the more important work that was housed within. Inside, a small army of nurses and volunteers tirelessly supported the physical and spiritual well-being of the dying. Word was soon out all over Europe about a new standard in health care at the end of life.

A medieval artist's rendition of l'Hôtel-Dieu gives a fifteenth-century vision of the end of life with the creative imagination of an entire community at work. The picture's title, *La Grande Salle des Povres en Dimanche Matin*, translates as "The Great Hall of the Poor on a Sunday Morning." This hospice did not serve the privileged nobility of the day; rather, it was dedicated as a hotel for social outcasts.

Architects still marvel that the elegant hospice complex was built over a river, with a glass floor underneath patients' beds. This unique feature enabled the sick and dying to hear the soothing sound of water, enhancing the environment for patient and caregiver alike. Each private cubicle was furnished with a bed and, more marvelous for the day, clean linens, table settings, a complete apothecary, and aesthetic refinements otherwise available only to royalty.

The artist depicts a flurry of activity, including townspeople providing Sunday brunch, nurses nursing, children playing, musicians singing, and even pets bringing familiarity and solace. The caption could read, "It's Sunday morning, and where is it happening? At the hospice."

In the painting there is a liturgical prayer being conducted at the far end of the building, which was unusual for this period. After all, this was not a house of worship but a secular community hospital. Every dimension of caregiving is interconnected. The core belief of this hospice model was that care for the body necessarily involved caring for the soul.

Standing today inside the floodlight grandeur of l'Hôtel-Dieu, you can still sense the spirit that has eluded the modern hospice movement. Looking upward at the ceiling and rafters, in the same line of sight as it was for countless generations of sick, you can read the mantra of the ancient hospice movement: "*Ars sacra moriendi, ars sacra vivendi.*" The sacred art of dying is the sacred art of living. Here at God's Hotel is a five hundred-year-old image of the West's finest hour in caring for the terminally ill. For the fifteenth-century residents of Beaune, the dying were indeed their teachers.

Completed by the year 1491, the Hospices de Beaune is the last great expression of the original Western hospice model. Its legacy endures only because it was built between the years 1441 and 1491. These dates are more than a coincidence of history. The year 1492, well-known to Americans, marks the end of this great hospice movement. Modernity was about to be born, with all of the benefits that surround us on a daily basis, especially those regarding medicine.

By concentrating exclusively on the physical aspects of caregiving, Western medicine would eventually lose its centuries-old instinct concerning other matters at the end of life. Care for the sick and dying would become institutionalized and professionalized, as family, neighbors, and friends abandoned their own inclination to support others at the end of life. The notion of diagnosing and addressing spiritual pain would become disassociated from the treatment of pain and disease. Since 1492, a crisis management model of illness has become the norm in the West.

Our Cultural Bias: Death Is the Enemy

When someone is born we rejoice,
When someone is married we celebrate
But when someone dies, we pretend that nothing happened.

—*Margaret Mead*

Native Americans and Christopher Columbus discovered each other in 1492. A few years later, a Spanish conquistador by the name of Cabeza de Vaca wrote a letter to the King of Spain with this observation:

> Here [in the New World] the ability to heal is still in the hands of the ailing. Being Europeans we thought we had given away to doctors and priests the ability to heal.

This same letter describes how indigenous peoples treated the dying person. There is a hint here about Europe's shift away from the classical ars moriendi, no longer connecting body, mind, and spirit. A radical change in perspective about something as important as death and dying does not happen overnight. Over the course of five hundred years, cultural beliefs become as familiar as the air we breathe.

A hundred years ago Sigmund Freud questioned whether our so-called civilized attitude about death was not a step backward in evolution, causing us to live psychologically beyond our means. More recently the Pulitzer Prize winner Ernest Becker wrote a challenging and prophetic book, *The Denial of Death*, an insightful study of our contemporary views. Becker analyzed the American phenomenon of the "disappearance of the fear of death" in terms of psychological repression. The apparent denial at the time of death does not mean that we have become fearless about it; rather, it is proof of how effective the power of repression is.

We are all going to die. The human predilection prefers to keep death at arm's length, but no amount of denial can change the inevitable. Bioethicist Daniel Callahan suggests that we have built our medical models on two unquestioned social convictions. First, we have an exaggerated sense of individualism that includes the need to control every aspect of how we live and die. Second, we believe that nature can be brought under human domination and made to do what we want it to do.

The Western perspective on death and dying is the direct result of a medical model that considers death to be the enemy. Science has godlike powers; the cure is within our grasp. It is only a matter of more time and resources. Our unqualified confidence in science creates the illusion that death is an option. In the third millennium world of health care, there is little room for the Angel of Death.

We are beginning to realize the limits of medical progress. The challenge is to strike a balance between the rewards of modern medicine and the human and spiritual context of illness. The goal is to support the chronically and terminally ill in living each day with as much meaning as possible. Our ancestors knew that treating spiritual pain at the end of life was as imperative as treating physical suffering. When spiritual suffering was relieved, physical pain decreased. Meaning, hope, relatedness, and forgiveness were as significant in the dying process as managing disease-related symptoms.

The American Book of Living and Dying accesses a legacy that has brought peace and comfort to generations before us. We may not be able to construct the elaborate hospice buildings of our ancestors, yet a contemporary version of their vision may be emerging.

Hospice in America: Gift and Challenge

Spiritual care is not an optional extra for the dying.

—*Cicely Saunders*

About forty years ago, the phenomenon of the modern hospice movement swept onto the American landscape with lightning speed. Most communities in the United States were about to benefit from the extraordinary work of an English pioneer and physician, Dame Cicely Saunders. In 1967, Dame Saunders established St. Christopher's Hospice in London, challenging the perception that people had to die in agony. As a result of her vision, the modern hospice movement created a realistic hope for a future in which nobody has to die alone or with pain untreated.

Dr. Saunders approaches what she calls Total Pain Management from a psychospiritual perspective, advocating understanding the context of a patient's distress. A bonus is that alleviating emotional and spiritual suffering saves money—good news for a health care system overburdened by skyrocketing pharmaceutical costs. Astounding and verifiable results of Total Pain Management include a decrease in the voluntary use of analgesics.

Following Dame Cicely's approach, care can reach hidden places. Total Pain Management includes looking for vital signs that consider not just the disease but the entire sick person, and it encourages activities like the patient narrative. Many nurses know that pain can sometimes disappear after talking about it because the person is taken seriously. Saunders encouraged doctors to lift artificial taboos about the physician's appropriate scope of treatment and expand their role as caregivers by asking their patients, "How are you within?"

The success of the modern hospice phenomenon in America has been associated with the baby-boomer generation. This generation seems to be taking to heart Carl Jung's admonition that "Death is as psychologically important as birth . . . and to shrink away from it is both unhealthy and abnormal because it robs the second half of life of meaning and purpose."

After only one generation, hospice has been well received by the general public. Palliative care services are an essential part of our communities. The genius of the modern hospice movement was the creation of an interdisciplinary team: doctors, nurses, counselors, and chaplains working as partners in creating a patient's plan of care. But many American hospice workers are frustrated that the management of physical pain and symptoms remains the primary, if not exclusive, focus of care. The challenge for the next generation of hospice workers is to retain sight of Dr. Saunders's wisdom regarding *Total* Pain Management.

The realities of bureaucratic regulations and the reluctance of physicians to refer patients to hospice early enough leave the system burdened with impossible expectations. A dramatic decrease in the length of stay (the number of days a person receives hospice care before their death) means that many of the classical tools for addressing spiritual pain are left untried. In many states, patients spend no more than a week in hospice care, whereas our ancestors consciously journeyed for months with the terminally ill.

For all its undeniable gifts, the modern hospice movement is struggling to preserve its soul. Nevertheless, it has already helped create a conscious dying movement in America. Celebrated advocates, such as Elisabeth Kübler-Ross and Stephen Levine, encourage us to contemplate our own death in advance; we reap unexpected benefits for the rest of our lives. By facing your own ultimate death, you learn to deal productively with each change or small death that presents itself throughout your life.

Ancient Books of the Dead

The Heritage

Fear not. What is not real never was and never will be.
What is real always was and can never be destroyed.

—Bhagavad Gita

Every age has reflected on its relationship with death. There is strong evidence, for example that the remarkable twenty-thousand-year-old prehistoric cave paintings near Lascaux, France, are a record of humanity's earliest hospice sanctuaries. By contrast, American society and culture are young. As we mature and face our fears about death and dying, we do not have to begin from scratch. People die today much as they have always died. The struggles, fears, and concerns at the end of life are essentially unchanging: fear of the unknown, reluctance to leave behind loved ones, and, for all its pain and sorrow, a desire to cling to life. For at least three millennia, societies have recorded these perennial concerns. The Egyptian, Celtic, Gnostic, Tibetan, and Medieval Monastic books of the dead reflect universal themes that transcend culture and spirituality.

Egyptian Book of the Dead: A Greater Light

When the eye of the body is shut by death,
The eye of the soul opens to a far brighter light.

—The Egyptian Book of the Dead

The Egyptian Book of the Dead is the most ancient recorded text of its kind, written in the year 1240 B.C. Copies of the book are found in tombs throughout the region of the Nile. The book seems to be a map for negotiating the perils when passing from life through death. Apparently, people commissioned copies of this text before they died in hopes that it would accompany them on their passage into the Great Light.

A century ago, Sir E. A. Wallace Budge translated *The Egyptian Book of the Dead*, or the ancient Papyrus of Ani, from its original hieroglyphic form. Confident references to the afterlife drawn from Egyptian mythology fill the many esoteric chapters.

The Egyptian Book of the Dead contains an ingenious psychological code to provide a guide for the living as well. Before and after death, the universal riddle in this ancient volume is to learn how to die before you die. The ancients knew that death to ego, to role, and to identity were necessary precursors to the final Great Death, which would only be as painful as our unwillingness to face our Truest Self.

The Egyptian Book of the Dead was radically nondualistic, meaning that matters of the spirit were as important as matters of the body. There is little distinction between the job description for the living and the dying. This advice keeps repeating itself: "Get it now, before you are forced to get it on your deathbed." Curious chapter titles in *The Egyptian Book of the Dead* treat issues such as, "How the Soul Is Joined to Its Body" and "How a Dying Person Achieves Transformation." Each of these brief chapters placed the highest value on the goal of personal integrity. The book's remarkable insights, written over three thousand years ago, seem relevant for our modern ears:

> For if I remain truthful, I am guaranteed possession over my Body and Soul. And if I live and die in integrity, my Spirit-Soul can never be destroyed.

The Egyptian Book of the Dead offers inspiring poem-like prayers that bear a striking resemblance to the psalms of the Hebrew Scriptures. These texts were composed during the same time period as Moses and the Hebrew exodus from Egypt, and there is an uncanny similarity in language. Given the rich cultural stew of the Middle East, scholars have long acknowledged that cultures of this period readily borrowed and adapted both language and theology from one another. For example, in *The Egyptian Book of the Dead* there is a hopeful invocation identical in language and sentiment to the poetry found in the biblical Psalm 116. In the Papyrus of Ani, the prayer addressed to the Lord of Light refers to the patron god of the dying, whom the pharaohs called Ra.

> O Lord of Light, grant that I shall not enter into the place of destruction. I know that I shall never perish nor will my body know the decay of death.

The Hebrew psalm uses the identical words.

The primary focus in the oldest book of the dead speculates on what happens after death. Unlike later books of the dead, the Egyptian version offers little practical advice for the physical well-being of the dying person or the bereaved family. Yet, given the fact that it was written three thousand years ago, it was a remarkable first effort.

Wisdom from Our Ancestors

Die before you die—so that when you die, you will not die.
> —The Egyptian Book of the Dead (*roughly translated*)

Celtic Books of the Dead: Spiritual Midwifery

May I rejoice in the wisdom of the evergreen trees that stand around me.
They teach me how my heart can remain evergreen
even in the winter of doubt and death.
> —St. Columba of Iona

The Celtic Books of the Dead are a tradition preserved, not in the form of an intact book, but through a series of hands-on practices. Emerging out of prehistory, they are an entire school of wisdom passed on through centuries of oral communication. At the core was a remarkable set of teachings from those who called themselves midwives to the dying.

Many of the earliest sources of the Celtic tradition have been lost, but today's growing interest in all things Celtic sheds light on these amorphous Celtic Books of the Dead. There are undeniable connections between so-called pagan practices of two thousand years ago and their embodiment in later Irish monasticism. As late as the early twentieth century, small communities off the stormy coasts of Scotland and Ireland still practiced remnants of this blended tradition. Members of the Celi De, Gaelic for Friends of God, passed on centuries-old practices from an ancient art that sought to relieve both physical and spiritual pain at the end of life. The seasoned end-of-life midwife was called an anamcara, or soul friend.

At the remarkable windswept site of Skellig Michael, off the coast of Kerry, is a unique hospice and monastery, founded perhaps as early as 590 A.D. A special kind of anamcara lived there for centuries in stone beehive-shaped huts. Visitors came to Skellig Michael from great distances to make a unique kind of pilgrimage—a rehearsal for the journey of dying. By overcoming life's "demons of fear," the pilgrims believed they were guaranteed a more peaceful transition on their deathbed.

The Celtic hospice model provided other unique elements of soothing medicine. Midwives used harp music and special prescriptive poetry, together with a wide range of complementary healing modalities. A treasure chest of tools was available to the anamcara, addressing everything from regulating a person's breath and diet to the content of their dreams.

One example of Celtic end-of-life wisdom, well over a millennium old, is attributed to an itinerant monk by the name of Fintan. A quintessential spiritual riddle, this ancient blessing embodies poignant advice for patient and caregiver alike.

> May you have the commitment to heal what has hurt you, to allow it to come close to you and in the end, to become one with you.

At first glance, Fintan's prayer appears to be an Irish curse instead of a blessing. It is, however, an ingenious tribute to a culture that understood the interrelationship of physical and spiritual suffering. The experience of our ancestors was that leaning into, instead of avoiding, pain lessens distress at the end of life, both physically and spiritually. The ancient Celts saw the parallel between the processes of birthing and dying. In their tradition, the ideal hospice employed anamcara midwives who assisted both birthing and dying processes under the same roof. Lamaze classes today teach breath coaching to assist a woman in labor. The Celts used the same breath work to help someone struggling with breathlessness at the end of life.

In the traditional Celtic worldview, what is true in the body is always true in spirit. Similar to the principles of homeopathy, the cure of an illness includes the administration of the very thing you are allergic to. In the spiritual realm, for example, if an issue of forgiveness showed up at the end of life, an anamcara would write a prescription to help you face the cause of your spiritual pain directly. In fact, the job description of these Celtic midwives was to do whatever it took to magnify the very issue that caused spiritual suffering. Today we would say, "Whatever doesn't kill you, makes you stronger." This simple formula worked. The reputation of the Celi De spread far and wide. Hospice patients traveled from across the European continent to partake of the uncanny Celtic capacity to dissolve all types of pain, emotional and physical, at the end of life.

Centuries later, Celtic Christians celebrated their own heroes—like Columba, Patrick, and Brigit—in part, because they inherited extraordinary skills in end-of-life caregiving. Brigit, the daughter of a Druid king, was perhaps the most sought-after spiritual midwife in the history of Ireland. Legend says she had the capacity to bilocate, allowing her to fulfill her vow to be an anamcara with more than one person at a time on their deathbed. Brigit's advice is confident and direct, "A person without an anamcara is like a body without a head." Patrick was considered to be specially blessed because he had ten years to prepare for his death. After a decade of facing terminal illness, no unfinished business was left unattended.

There is evidence that between the ninth and eleventh centuries A.D., this uniquely Celtic style of end-of-life care was exported all over the Mediterranean world. Missionaries like Fintan traveled extensively to monastic infirmaries as far away as Spain, France, and Switzerland. The same institutions exposed to his end-of-life Celtic medicine became the first to bear the name hospice at the turn of Europe's first millennium.

Wisdom from Our Ancestors

The only cure for your suffering is to lean into the source of its pain.

—Celtic Book of the Dead

Gnostic Books for the Living and Dying: Bridge between East and West

This is what dying is like, and life after it.
It is when all distinctions are dissolved . . .
As if even male and the female are one.

—*The Gospel according to Thomas*

The relatively recent discovery of the ancient Nag Hammadi library in 1945 sheds light on a fascinating Middle Eastern perspective previously little known to us. The product of third- and fourth-century monastic communities from Syria to Egypt, these so-called Gnostic Scriptures— meaning that they never became part of the official Bible—possess remarkable similarities with other Asian spiritual teachings, especially in describing how to alleviate suffering at the end of life.

An early text fragment from this tradition, known as the Gospel according to Mary Magdalene, has uncanny parallels to the later *Tibetan Book of the Dead*. Its chapters describe the stages of dying and the predictable challenges faced during the life-to-death transition. In this tradition, the spiritual companion's job was to help the dying person negotiate universal perils that show up at the end of life.

In the Mary Magdalene text, there is a powerful passage written as a dialogue between a dying person and the temptations at the end of life. In the following verse, Ignorance, one such temptation, approaches a dying person with doubts and taunts:

> And where do you think you are going? How dare you expect to find peace? Don't you realize that you are all bound up in wickedness?

The universal temptation at the end of life is to doubt the essential goodness of one's nature. The person of Mary Magdalene, who represents every soul, turns to Ignorance with the following advice, which she has learned "from the Savior":

> Why do you judge me, when I judge not? . . . Don't you realize that all things are good and eventually meant to go free, things both on earth and in heaven?

The same gospel then describes in detail how the soul will have to contend with seven specific demons or obstacles in the dying process; *The Tibetan Book of Dead* outlines a list of similar trials.

> The first daemon to contend with is darkness, the second is desire, the third ignorance, the fourth, confusion of bodily existence, the fifth is the kingdom of the material, the sixth is foolish wisdom and the seventh is wrathful wisdom.

Stories of contemporary near-death experiences corroborate what our ancestors realized: the dying person sometimes faces fierce spiritual obstacles before being able to release their spirit. Chief among these temptations is to think of oneself as evil or unworthy at the end of life. Parts of Gnostic scriptures read like an ancient map for finding peace at the end of life. The consistent advice is to directly face one's mortality and embrace the indestructible nature of spirit.

Mary Magdalene proposes her strongest piece of advice for the person who is in the last stages of dying: simply, rest in the power of the present.

From the heart of all spiritual traditions is the belief that *now* is the only place where healing and transformation can take place. The proof that such a therapy might actually work for the terminally ill is seen in their loss of distraction and human desire.

> And when the final moment has come, rest only in this moment and remain in silence. Then you will finally declare victory by knowing, "O Ignorance, for once and for all you are the one who must die."

Even though these writings never made it into the official Bible, they nevertheless give us fresh insight into our ancestors' attitudes toward death and dying. Ironically, here in an early Christian text, is a core Buddhist teaching that all human suffering is due to attachment, although *The Tibetan Book of the Dead* would not appear for another three hundred years.

Wisdom from Our Ancestors

In the face of temptation, trust your own essential goodness.
—*Gospel According to Thomas*

Tibetan Book of the Dead: Coaching the Soul

Hey, Immortal one, your time has come! There is nothing to fear.
Cling only to the freedom of peace and compassion.
—*Bardo Thodol*

The ancient tradition that has attracted recent, popular curiosity among Westerners is *The Tibetan Book of the Dead*, also known as the *Bardo Thodol*. This eighth-century A.D. Buddhist scripture can be traced back to the legendary Padma Sambhava. For many centuries, monks carefully copied and handed down these teachings from one generation to another. Full of detailed instructions for the dying and their coaches, this text was traditionally read aloud as a means of helping the dying during what was called their life-to-life transition. The ideal was to repeat these teachings for a full forty days following a person's death.

The deathbed guide received detailed instructions on how to assist the dying person, including how to support the actual physical process of dying. The *Bardo Thodol* suggested verbal cues for the death coach to use. They include psychospiritual therapies, such as visualization exercises. The book even contains details regarding the optimal physical posture for the dying person. Here is a sample from the opening lines of the *Bardol Thodol*, which the death coach was to repeat while gently massaging the arteries in a person's neck.

> O nobly born, [here you would mention the person's name] the time has come for you to seek the Way. Your breathing is about to cease and your teacher is here to set you face to face with the Clear Light. Your job now is just this: to know your true Self. Let me assist you in staying steady in this state.

Like similar formulas found in the Celtic tradition, this Buddhist text proposes advice that is ancient, yet universal. At the end of life, what matters most is personal connection, touch, breath, and the ability to maintain clear consciousness, that is, to focus on what is real instead of illusion.

A number of passages from *The Tibetan Book of the Dead* bear an uncanny resemblance to a much earlier Chinese text, the *Tao Te Ching*. In both cases, the dying person was given powerful images to help neutralize the anxiety and fear that often precede death. The following passage from the *Bardo Thodol* echoes the same words of encouragement found verbatim in the 34th chapter of the *Tao Te Ching*:

> The Way to which you are traveling is not unknown to you. All things derive from this One Way. Now it is time to let all things dissolve back and return to the Source.

Aware that emotional pain can exacerbate physical pain, another job of the death guide was to minimize the fear of dying by reminding terminal persons of their true nature in an ever-changing universe. The prescription against fear was simple, echoing a sentiment of many aboriginal peoples: Because there is no death in the circle of life, only great change, it follows that fear itself is an illusion.

By breaking the cycle of projection, neurotic patterns of thought, and unconscious influences, the death coach helped to dissolve suffering with a healthy dose of reality. The purpose of reading the *Bardo Thodol* to a dying person was to remind that person of what he or she had practiced in life; *The Tibetan Book of the Dead* thus also shows us how to live. Similar to the advice given in other books of the dead, the caregiver is reminded that no matter how much the dying person may appear to be suffering, it is possible to live happily in the present moment because it is the only moment we have.

Wisdom from Our Ancestors

When the journey of my life has reached its end
And I wander through places of confusion,
May I stay awake so to transform fear and suffering.
—The Tibetan Book of the Dead

Monastic Books of the Dying: Prescriptive Care

Grant that my last hour might be my best hour.
—*English Book of Hours*

The Monastic Books of the Dying are not so much a distinct textbook as part of a larger library called customaries. These centuries-old records preserve the daily life or customs of the same monasteries that housed Europe's earliest hospices. Written a thousand years ago, they detail an amazing range of holistic modalities for treating the sick and dying, including a generous use of music and ritual, morphine, acupressure, and aromatherapy.

In the Middle Ages, the term *prescriptive care* described a unique plan of care tailored to the specific needs of a person. Instead of a cookie-cutter approach, these early hospices dealt with the individual. The directions found in The Monastic Books of the Dying indicate that at the end of life, nothing took priority over supporting someone through his or her spiritual pain.

Records from the West's earliest hospices still exist in monastic libraries. There we find references to the rich polycultural heritage of southern Europe, including influences from Sephardic Judaism and Islam. Other manuscripts document the work of the ancient hospices in Europe's heartland of Switzerland, southeast France, and the Rhineland of Germany. In the Celtic lands, bits and pieces of the end-of-life midwifery traditions are still preserved through songs and poetry.

High in the remote Alps, medieval monastic customaries refer to a curious blending of health care and spiritual practices, some of which are suspiciously Celtic in origin and Middle Eastern. An ancient library in the tiny Swiss mountain village of Engelberg still houses remnants of the hospice tradition. The Benedictine abbey of Mount Angel was established there more than a thousand years ago. Its oldest manuscripts prove that Mount Angel was a "franchise" of the earliest hospice movement in Europe.

The monks who ran the Engelberg infirmary, as well as other hospices throughout the neighboring parts of Germany and France, preserved a critical link between the ancient Irish and medieval European hospice movements. They frequently mention the out-of-place Gaelic name, Fintan— proof of the itinerant missionary's presence. Together with countless unnamed others, Fintan brought Celtic hospice medicine to the heartland of Europe.

Medieval libraries preserve animal skin parchments with hand-calligraphied prayer books, legal records, and all sorts of medical documentation. Some of these records contain curious, handwritten marginal notes known as *glosses* or *marginalia*, much as a modern book might contain a highlighted passage. This medieval graffiti closely resembles the chart notes that a doctor or nurse might write for a patient today. These scriblings offer insight into the kinds of diseases persons suffered from at the time and which therapies were most useful.

A set of observations found in Germany, for example, concerned a certain Brother Odo who, sometime in the twelfth century, overcame an acute condition of breathlessness through the use of music and chant, lowering both his level of anxiety and his heart rate. Other marginalia refer to psychospiritual distress. Such was the case of a young fourteenth-century woman known only as Benedicta. Her chart notes indicate that she eventually died in peace but only after months of intense struggle with an undisclosed issue of forgiveness. We can only guess why the curious use of lemon juice was prescribed as a tonic for this lady.

Our ancestors of a thousand years ago created something remarkably holistic for end-of-life care, with a unique art of first diagnosing and then responding to spiritual pain.

We also get a glimpse into a medieval patient's plan of care from some amazing Spanish sacramentaries, or prayer books for the dying. In one book, alongside a phrase of Gregorian chant, is a ritual prescribed for a dying man named Pedro de Compostella. The words of the psalm prayer are moving, especially because they were sung to a mode of chant meant to mimic a lullaby.

> *Memento mei Deus, quia ventus est vita mea.*
> (Remember me, O God, for your very breath is my life.)
>
> —Based on Psalm 104, vs. 29–30

Apparently the ailing fellow had been struggling with some kind of lung-related disease, perhaps akin to a modern diagnosis of chronic obstructive pulmonary disease (COPD), lung cancer, or asbestos-related mesothelioma. The nature of his illness created an understandable anxiety about suffocating to death. By repeating the same musical phrase, the caregiver monk was prescribing a kind of breath-work technique that worked. The creative visualization eventually lowered Pedro's anxiety. The book records the outcome: "A marked reduction in both (the patient's) physical and emotional suffering." There is even a chart note that adds how the man died, "with a prayer of thanksgiving and a sweet smile on his lips."

Such observations became the foundation for The Monastic Books of the Dying. These books of the dying were unique in other ways. For one thing, they contain far less text than music. Like a choreographed symphony, the musical settings of the monastic Book of Hours matched the changing moods and times of the day and seasons. The so-called Western modes of music were created during this same period of the eleventh century by the women and men who ran the original hospices. To support their use at the bedside, each of the seven musical modes of our familiar Western musical scale correspond to the seven traditional moods of the human spirit.

At this particularly contentious time in world history it is worth noting that during the early part of Europe's second millennium, in places like Spain, Portugal, and parts of Italy and France, Jews, Christians, and Muslims often lived and died side by side in peaceful coexistence. A particular genius of some monastic customaries was their inclusive, interfaith character. Quoting texts and sentiments common to all three monotheistic traditions, such as the Book of Psalms, respected the dying of all faith traditions. The earthy nature of the particular scriptures chosen encouraged the terminally ill to express a full range of emotions—despair, anger with God, perhaps even cursing—under the rubric of prayer. No wonder the end-of-life medicine of these monk physicians was so highly prized.

Wisdom from Our Ancestors

Unless you find paradise at your own center
There is not the slightest chance you may enter.
  —*Monastic Tradition of the Dead*

What the Books of the Dead Have in Common: Lessons for Us Today

It is the nature of all things that take form to dissolve again.
—*Gautama Buddha*

Many of the ancient texts focused on a person's journey into the afterlife, yet also taught lessons about how to deal with the process of death and dying. During the final phase of dying, called the death vigil, our ancestors believed that it took an entire village to help someone die well.

There are remarkable connections between the Egyptian manuals for the dying and the Hebrew Psalter, as well as parallels among Taoist, Buddhist, and early Christian writings. Similarities found in ancient Celtic, Middle Eastern, and Western Monastic traditions are too specific to be coincidental. Such cultural cross-pollination points to a collective wisdom among our ancestors about what brings peace at the end of life. Parallels extend to rituals for grieving that include the Mexican Dia de los Muertos, the Native American potlatch, and the annual August Japanese O-Bon festival.

Our ancestors had a relentless commitment to the elusive thing we yearn for in the West—a peaceful death. Through centuries of careful observations, they created an entire language to name the gradations of the dying process. In hospice circles today we refer to a patient's final stage with a single phrase: active dying. The ancients on the other hand found a detailed vocabulary to describe the many and distinct stages at the end of life. Both the Western monastic and the Tibetan Buddhist traditions include *forty* or more stages in the life-to-death transition. Each of these phases is associated with a particular set of tools to support both patient and caregiver.

Because the books of the dead span diverse spiritual and cultural traditions, not to mention distances of centuries and geography, we would expect differences in content and philosophy. More surprising are the similarities.

Here are key underlying points that show up consistently. In other words, this is the common ground of our collective human experience at the end of life.

+ IT IS A PRIORITY THAT HUMAN BEINGS ASSIST EACH OTHER AS COACHES OR MIDWIVES THROUGH THE STAGES OF DYING. To be proactively involved in the death of another human being is the ultimate act of love. The ancient books of the dying were not just for an esoteric few. There was an overriding desire to disseminate the knowledge of these traditions among average laypersons. And it was essential to include both family and friends throughout the death and dying process.

+ THERE ARE CERTAIN OBSERVABLE AND UNIVERSAL PATTERNS OR STAGES IN THE LIFE-TO-DEATH TRANSITION PROCESS. Human beings have always died in essentially the same way. Our common experience has been documented for millennia. The good news is that these patterns can help us to anticipate and support the various changes that body, mind, and spirit inevitably seem to face in the process of letting go.

+ THERE IS A CLEAR RELATIONSHIP BETWEEN PHYSICAL AND EMOTIONAL PAIN. Relieving suffering at the end of life requires a holistic approach that acknowledges both dimensions of body and spirit. There is a difference between healing and curing. It is always possible to be getting well in the midst of serious illness.

+ IT IS NECESSARY FIRST TO DIAGNOSE SPIRITUAL PAIN BEFORE ATTEMPTING TO RESPOND TO IT. The records of antiquity point to certain universal experiences or names for spiritual pain and suffering. Helping the dying person to identify spiritual pain gives the caregiver important clues as to appropriate means of support.

+ A "GOOD DEATH" IS DEFINED AS OUR ABILITY TO MAINTAIN A SENSE OF CLEAR KNOWING OR CONSCIOUSNESS AT THE END OF LIFE. Medicine is effective when it controls pain without compromising clarity of consciousness. The unfinished tasks at the end of life often hold the key to spiritual suffering. Other cultures insist that the goal of dying well is to help a person die—*con los ojos abiertos,* in the Latino tradition, or "with our eyes wide open," in the Buddhist tradition.

+ SOME FORM OF CONSCIOUSNESS SURVIVES THE DEATH OF OUR PHYSICAL BODY. What is death? For most of human history death was not the opposite of life, but the opposite of birth. In ancient times, theological language provided the primary answer to this question. Nearly fifteen million Americans who have survived a near-death experience describe similar phenomena, regardless of their belief systems.

+ WE PREPARE THROUGHOUT OUR LIFETIME FOR OUR DYING. Standing before the mystery of death had the same impact on our ancestors as witnessing the mystery of birth. In such a twilight place, it is as if time itself stands still to allow the survivors to reflect on life's bigger questions. Death has the power to heal because it has the power to put life into perspective and to bring forth life's important priorities. The art of dying can become the art of living.

Spiritual Pain

Pain versus Suffering:
The Human Condition

I am not a mechanism. And it is not because the mechanism is working wrongly that I am ill. I am ill because of wounds to the soul, to the deep emotional self.

—D. H. Lawrence

Pain in life is inevitable. Suffering is optional. Today we often use the terms *pain* and *suffering* interchangeably. The ancients knew there was an important distinction between these two concepts, and that at the end of life, this distinction was more than semantics.

Pain is the hard truth of disease, old age, and dying; however, our response to pain—called suffering—is highly subjective. Our ancestors understood that, especially in the case of spiritual pain, once it is diagnosed, it can always be treated thereby mitigating suffering. They also observed that when mind and spirit are cared for along with the physical self, most fears—suffering—about the end of life vanish.

Spiritual Pain

The presence of pain, whether physical or spiritual, causes us to feel helpless or motivates us to find a way to end the suffering.

One definition of pain is, "any unpleasant sensation occurring in varying degrees of severity as a consequence of injury, disease, or emotional disorder."

Rarely do people choose pain. An involuntary instinct takes over when pain is present to do whatever it takes to stop it. Yet when we are taken to an emergency room, the physician will not prescribe an analgesic until the cause of the pain is clear. Otherwise, the antidote could exacerbate the pain or even be toxic. Experts in pain management clinics call this *purposive pain,* meaning that the pain is a symptom pointing to an underlying cause. Once the source is identified, the pain can be adequately addressed. The same is true of spiritual pain. Once its origin is known, there is hope for relief.

Suffering is often a choice. It is a particularly human capacity to tolerate or even consciously bear painful realities. Parents, for example, willingly choose to suffer for the good of their children; soldiers endure hardship and suffering for their country; we may make a resolution to suffer through a diet or exercise regime in order to reverse heart disease. The unique capacity for human beings to choose, rather than to avoid, suffering is the true meaning of compassion.

What of suffering and illness? American physician Dr. Larry Dossey says, "Bodies do not suffer; people do." This implies a shift in modern medicine from a basic concern with disease to a greater focus on the total human person. In the wake of a serious diagnosis, dealing with the impact on the emotional and spiritual self is as critical as managing the physical symptoms. When hospitalized, we do not check our psyche and emotions at the door. Even the most sophisticated pain clinics concur that when our inner state is relaxed, the body has a greater capacity to heal.

To determine whether a person is in a state of spiritual pain or spiritual suffering, the ancients spoke about taking a spiritual pulse, asking the sick person, in the language of Cicely Saunders, "How are you within?" The response of patients to this simple question can provide a useful key to their spiritual or inner dimension.

The distinction between pain and suffering becomes critical in the practice of the sacred art of dying. Spiritual suffering is a subjective response to pain and not in itself destructive. Many persons come to recognize times of suffering and illness as opportunities to get to know their soul. Carl Jung said, "If you get rid of the suffering before you answer its question, you get rid of the self [that is, the psyche or the soul] along with it." Disease is a language that offers data about our inner as well as our outer world. Suffering does not have to end in hopelessness. When curing is no longer an option, healing is always possible.

Spiritual pain calls for diagnosis and sometimes intervention. Words that signal inner pain include *alienation, loneliness, separateness, abandonment, despair, meaninglessness,* and *fearfulness.* Untreated, spiritual pain exacerbates physical pain and can lead to the terminal illness of the soul—hopelessness. Diagnosing spiritual pain has not been part of our recent experience in Western medicine. We need to relearn these skills from our ancestors through the sacred art of dying traditions.

Diagnosing Spiritual Pain: Asking Courageous Questions

Let me not beg for the stilling of my pain but for the heart to conquer it.
—*Rabindranath Tagore*

Nurses tell about patients who lived far longer than what was thought to be physically possible—without food, water, or even an appropriate level of oxygen intake. There are stories of people in extreme physical anguish who resemble living skeletons. Some persons seem unwilling to let go even after the attending physician predicted their deaths months earlier. Then closure takes place on an item of unfinished business—the visit of a long-awaited relative, release of withheld forgiveness, the disclosure of a long-held secret—and the person dies. How do we know when such a critical issue may be keeping someone from a peaceful death?

Hospice professionals sometimes describe spiritual pain as a "crawling out of your skin" pain. In the face of such agony, our ancestors knew that no amount of analgesic could numb or cure the inner cause of a person's distress. It was the job of the end-of-life midwife to discover and ask courageous questions that could help the dying person identify his or her deepest spiritual wounds. A core belief of the ars moriendi is that healing and peace are possible only through this hole in the soul.

In the sacred art of dying tradition, a family member or even close friend is often not the appropriate midwife to deal with extreme spiritual pain. Good intentions get in the way, or worse, we use clichés or pills to circumvent what is screaming for attention. Instead, someone who has walked through other dark nights is often needed. In the presence of emotional and spiritual anguish, it is hard to step aside and do nothing.

Regardless of who is called to the bedside, it takes both intuition and courage to ask what is going on beneath the skin of things. In the sacred art of dying traditions of antiquity, only two consistent ground rules were required for the caregiver in the art of diagnosing spiritual pain.

1. DIAGNOSING PAIN IS ABOUT HOLY LISTENING RATHER THAN COMPULSIVE FIXING. Trust that, at some level, the patient already knows the cause of their spiritual pain. The caregiver's job is to listen deeply and help their companion to articulate what may be happening within. In that simple process the role of the spiritual midwife is to become a mirror of compassion back to the patient.

2. SPIRITUAL SUFFERING AND PHYSICAL PAIN ARE ALWAYS INTERRELATED. Many wisdom traditions provide maps where the energies of body and psyche, or matter and spirit, intersect: chakras in Indian Ayurvedic medicine, chi and acupressure points in Chinese medicine, or the Sephirot of Adam in Hebrew Kabbalism. Any imbalance in body, mind, or spirit affects the entire organism.

While our ancestors lacked the marvelous diagnostic tools of modern medicine, they were adept at knowing how to take the spiritual pulse of those who were sick and dying. Even in an altered state of consciousness such as coma, for example, simply paying attention to a person's breath can reveal much about that person's inner world. Imagine the advantage of having both physical and spiritual diagnoses working in tandem. No one would feel abandoned in the face of terminal illness because the community of caregivers would never abandon the possibility of healing.

Even without formal training in the sacred art of dying traditions, there are simple mechanisms you can use as a starting point for diagnosing or measuring spiritual pain. We are accustomed to evaluating the nature and degree of physical pain; it is just as possible, regardless of whether or not a person belongs to a formal religious or spiritual tradition, to ask a fundamental spiritual question like Dame Cicely Saunders's query, "How are you within?"

Here is a simple scale for measuring spiritual pain that has met with success in both acute care as well as hospice settings.

SPIRITUAL PAIN SCALE

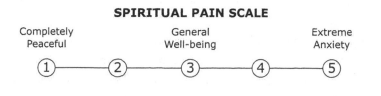

Completely Peaceful	General Well-being	Extreme Anxiety
①——②——③——④——⑤		

Responding to Spiritual Pain:
A Psychospiritual Relationship

Pain which is not transformed is always transmitted.

—*Father Richard Rohr*

Modern understanding of the relationship between healing and spirituality is incomplete. The impulse to do something in the face of sickness is understandable, but spiritual pain is a normal part of living and dying. Often you have to just walk through it.

Spiritual pain needs to be received, listened to, and heard. There is no pill or quick fix. It requires a witness. But as spiritual pain becomes more acute, intervention can be appropriate.

Those who practiced the sacred art of dying observed inseparable connections among physical, emotional, and spiritual pain and in the way each pain was managed. The truths learned in the body apply to nonphysical distress as well. The antidote for all pain is the same: always lean into, rather than avoid, the pain.

In childbirth, the pain lessens as the mother relaxes into the situation when coached to ride the waves of pain instead of fighting them. It is the same with emotional distress. Leaning into the suffering is the key to moving though it. Once we have learned why the pain is trying to get our attention, everything should be done to transform it.

Modern medical science confirms this ancient piece of wisdom. Emotional distress clearly exacerbates a patient's physical symptoms. Stress compromises the body's immune system, hindering its natural capacity to heal. Even an exercise as effortless as meditation or breath control can yield immediate relief.

Chronic physical pain creates a negative state of mind and spirit leading to a vicious cycle of distress. Symptoms associated with chronic or terminal illness can be managed when you understand suffering in a multifaceted way. Once we understand the social, emotional, and spiritual factors integral to human suffering, the use of narcotics decreases and the quality of life increases.

In all the books of the dead, regardless of time, place, or culture, the experience of spiritual pain is related to one of four timeless qualities:

1. Meaning

2. Forgiveness

3. Relatedness

4. Hopelessness

In the spiritual realm, these are the only four illnesses that require diagnosis. Understanding something about each of these four classical categories may be the key to a peaceful death.

Meaning Pain: The Painful-Blissful Encounter with the Truth

Meaningfulness makes us well;
Meaninglessness makes us sick.

—*Matthew, Sheila, and Dennis Linn*

There is ultimately only one great spiritual question: Who am I? The answer to this question is rarely known except in the dark night of the soul. Terminal illness has the power to silence us and create a crisis of meaning. Whether it is through personal chaos due to a recent cancer diagnosis or a public social catastrophe like September 11, few experiences have the power to awaken our Truest Self like a brush with mortality. These liminal moments have the potential both to create and solve a painful crisis.

The contemporary person is intolerant of mystery. Ambiguity irritates us. That is why we are novices in the face of unfixable illness. Twentieth-century American mystic Thomas Merton expressed the mystery of sickness in the following way:

> True love and faith are learned in the moment when prayer no longer seems possible when the body aches and the heart has turned to stone.

Such is the paradox of human meaning. It gives us life and yet, when lost, can be a powerful agent of transformation into something better.

Meaning is a particularly human quality that enables us to have direction in and for life. Whatever has significance or connotes purpose in life also defines our reason for existence. A crisis in meaning can come in many forms. It is normal to wonder in the midst of serious illness, Why should I go on living when everything I value is slipping away? If there is no longer anything that gets us out of bed in the morning, depression or anxiety are bound to set in.

Our ancestors understood that a crisis of faith or identity at the end of life constitutes Meaning Pain. The sacred art of dying traditions observed that, in spite of such distress, the dying potentially have an advantage. In the midst of a meaning meltdown, the spiritual midwife or companion to the dying can invite courageous questions such as:

What is it that I am still willing to live and die for?

How do I make sense out of illness and death?

Is there something beyond the familiar world that I know and love?

In many religious traditions, those whom we call saints and mystics have discovered the sweet quality of surrender that enables a person to live more fully in the midst of dying. The same spiritual pain that regularly creates an identity crisis also suggests a plan or way out. Paradoxically, as one secure view of the world is dissolving, another vision emerges out of the chaos.

One of the noble truths of Buddhism teaches that cessation of suffering occurs only when the thirst of desire is extinguished. When the "I" dies, the illusion of who "I am" ceases to exist. In Judaism, the Passover encounter between the "I" and the "Thou" takes place precisely at the threshold of the Angel of Death. In Christianity, the Mystical Body is an experience where it is no longer "I live" but the "Divine lives in me." In every example, the response to an identity crisis is a kind of ego-ectomy.

One does not have to speak a theological language to understand the valuable lessons of doubt and ambiguity. Today's quantum scientists concur that, as Albert Einstein put it, "We are all caught up in the movement of the universe that is constantly luring us from chaos to surrender."

A crisis in meaning can be a wake-up call, a realization that the "I" has become alienated from the Truest Self. American synthesizer Ken Wilber suggests that all the lessons of contemporary science, psychology, and spirituality lead to the same cryptic conclusion: "The more I go into I, the more I fall out of I."

We return to the same courageous question that began this discussion, Who am I? The painful-blissful encounter with the mystery of life and death cannot be avoided. Our ancestors knew that these were precisely the times when a coach or midwife needed to propose an appropriate spiritual remedy.

The lessons learned sections after each story in part II present tools related to crises of meaning at the end of life. The following spiritual pain scale could be a starting point in helping a caregiver determine whether a diagnosis of Meaning Pain is involved.

MEANING PAIN SCALE

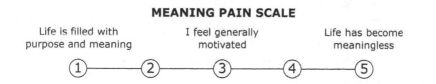

Life is filled with purpose and meaning — I feel generally motivated — Life has become meaningless

① ——— ② ——— ③ ——— ④ ——— ⑤

A Spiritual Riddle: When Meaning Has Been Lost

If there is anxiety, let it reign.
A calm successor will eventually arrive.

If there is anger, let it reign.
A peaceful successor will eventually arrive.

If there is doubt, let it reign,
The truth of its own accord eventually makes itself known.

Every steadfast witness experiences resolution.

—The Tao of Dying

Forgiveness Pain: The Common Cold of Spiritual Pain

The one who opts for revenge digs two graves.
—Chinese Proverb

It has been well documented that at the end of life, most spiritual pain is related to forgiveness. Therefore, Forgiveness Pain could be called the common cold of spiritual pain. All great healers speak of forgiveness in terms of a condition for healing. Every spiritual tradition believes that we are forgiven to the extent that we can release others. This is the sentiment expressed in one of the most beloved prayers in the world, "Forgive us our faults as we forgive the mistakes of others."

Today it is possible to measure the benefits of forgiveness on the human body. As the brain's limbic system squirts beneficial neuropeptides into the body, along with a release of negative emotions, the act of forgiveness has a salutary physiological effect.

Forgiveness takes practice. For someone who has spent a lifetime harboring anger or hatred toward self or others, the challenge of "forgiving," that is, handing over an issue or grudge, is no small struggle at the end of life. Human nature defends the wounded ego, and the temptation to take revenge can be strong. Stories from hospices show that more often than not, the most challenging person to forgive at the end of life is not another but oneself. The good news is that such a release even at the twelfth hour of life brings peace of mind and lessens physical agony.

The cardinal principle of leaning into one's pain applies in a particular way to the work of forgiveness. Every event of our lives is buried deeply in our nervous system. We need to return to the "scene of the pain" for healing and release.

Our ancestors knew that there was no such thing as an emotional or spiritual bypass when it came to forgiveness work. While it is hard to admit the wounds we have inflicted on others as well as those done to us, doctors of the mind and soul like Carl Jung knew that "to cherish such secrets is a spiritual misdemeanor for which nature will visit us with sickness."

Near-death-experience survivors have given us another reason for moving forgiveness work to the front burner at the end of life. There is an almost universal occurrence during the dying process called the life review. The life review is an opportunity to see one's entire life without edit or rationalization. The sacred art of dying traditions knew of this experience, and they encouraged a predeath review to prepare a person for the inevitable. Similar to the process recommended by Twelve-Step programs, the result was something like a deathbed confession. Verbalizing, or even admitting on paper the wounds of a lifetime, can cause a noticeable change in a person's state of mind as well as immune system.

Most of us know that there is power in releasing guilt. We think we should be able to forgive those who hurt us. But sometimes there are sincere reasons why we might not be able to, or do not want to, forgive. Even on our deathbed, it is understandable that *not* forgiving certain situations in life can appear reasonable, if not noble. Sometimes there is power in hanging on to life's betrayals. Can anything be done when a person has tried to forgive and is stuck?

This may be a time when it would be useful to define what forgiveness is *not*:

+ Forgiveness is not condoning or excusing ignorant or evil behavior.

+ Forgiveness is not denial of our own hurt.

+ Forgiveness is not about inviting an abuser back into our lives.

+ Forgiveness is not forgetting real wounds and betrayal.

The fact is that all of us have been let down, dishonored, abused, lied to, cheated on, and diminished in body and spirit. We have also been accomplices in the same behaviors toward others. But we can be healed from these wounds to our soul. The reality is that as long as we hold onto these hurts, they poison us emotionally and physically.

A simple definition of forgiveness might be "the willingness to let go of another person's jugular." Perhaps the most we can hope to surrender from the painful past is the right to get even. Our ancestors created effective tools to address the pain caused by not being able to forgive. You can learn about these in part II and part III of this book. But the first step for the dying person or their caregiver is to identify whether Forgiveness Pain is the primary source of distress. The following spiritual pain scale can be a helpful starting point where forgiveness is involved.

FORGIVENESS PAIN SCALE

I feel a deep sense of reconciliation toward myself and others	There are no outstanding issues that are calling for forgiveness in my life	I feel a strong sense of unforgiveness toward myself and/or another
①————②	————③————	④————⑤

An Extreme Prayer When Forgiveness Is Difficult

O Lord, remember not only the men and women of good will,
But also those of ill will.
Do not remember all the suffering they have inflicted on us.
And when they come to judgment,
Let all the fruits we have borne be their forgiveness.
>   —*An Unknown Prisoner in Ravensbruck Concentration Camp*

Relatedness Pain: Leaving the Familiar Behind

Hold onto what is good, even if it is a handful of dirt.
Hold onto my hand, even if I have gone away from you.
>   —*Pueblo Blessing*

Many people fear death. Even if they are suffering, the familiar world can be hard to leave behind. A good definition of healing found in many Native American traditions is to "live in right relationship," that is, to see the beauty and harmony in everything. There are natural cycles to the seasons of life. Every day requires a balance of darkness and light. And while it may be painful to trust that there is a season for everything, including death, it is more painful to resist this reality. Relatedness Pain is about such resistance.

Some people can accept life as it comes. In a rare and powerful book, *Six Months to Live*, a twenty-two-year-old young man by the name of Matt wrote this personal testimony: "I wouldn't trade my life for anyone else's. If I could choose not to have cancer, and continue my life as it was, I wouldn't do it."

Such people become teachers for the rest of us. Notes left on Matt's casket by his friends tell us why.

Matt, your life disturbed me in a good way. Love you man, Luke

Matt, thank you for being real and not trying to be someone else. Suzy

Matt, your death showed me that God is real. Thanks, Cathy

When something or someone we love is lost, it is impossible not to hurt and not to grieve. We feel Relatedness Pain to the extent that we loved. Grief is like a badge of honor, proof that we have loved. But the ancients did not describe this pain in terms of personal relationship alone. Relatedness encompasses our relationships to things, roles, or identities. Whatever matters to us has the potential of creating pain in its absence.

In the sacred art of dying traditions, the solutions for Relatedness Pain lead us to trust that, as an anonymous poet put it:

> Beyond the absence there is presence
> And beyond the pain of loss
> There can be love.

Such sentiments rarely occur before walking though the agony of loss. Perhaps that is why our ancestors assure us that after leaning into instead of avoiding the pain, there is always the possibility that something new and life-giving is waiting.

An American athlete was stricken in her prime with a degenerative muscle disease. To family and friends, Jeri's Relatedness Pain had to do with her inability to compete in the Olympics. She was understandably angry at the unfairness of her disease. During a televised interview a few months before her death, Jeri surprised herself when she broke down in tears and said, "The same competitive sports that brought me fame and fortune have also ruined my life. Because of sports, I lost my marriage, my daughter, and the things that really matter most in life."

No one except Jeri could have known that the anguish of her life had nothing to do with disease or her inability to compete—that was only the symptom of her real spiritual pain. The result of Jeri's breakdown was worthwhile. Her daughter, who was watching the interview across the country, reached out to reconcile with her mom before she died.

Every great loss is like a divorce, and every divorce is certainly like a death. At the end of life, we bring emotional bruises from both loved and unwanted parts of life. The gift of a good friend is to listen deeply and trust that on the other side of pain may lie greater and undiscovered treasures. It takes courage to trust that it is never too late to heal.

RELATEDNESS PAIN SCALE

I feel a strong sense of connection with the persons and things that matter most to me   The most important areas of my life seem balanced   I feel seriously alienated from someone/thing that is important to me

A Meditation for Those in Relatedness Pain

People who cannot let go of their egos
Who can't look death in the eye, can't live either.
You are me and I are you.
Is it not obvious that we are inter-we.
You cultivate the flower in yourself
I transform the garbage in myself
So you will not have to suffer.
We are in the world
To bring peace and joy to each other.
     —*Thich Nhat Hanh*

Hopelessness Pain: Death as Healer

There is only this mystery . . . that one can contain death, the whole of it
and hold it to one's heart gently and not refuse to still go on living.

—R. M. Rilke

How is it that the same set of circumstances in life can turn one person to hope and another to hopelessness? If our ancestors considered Forgiveness Pain to be the common cold of spiritual pain, then Hopelessness Pain is a terminal illness for the human spirit. In some Latino traditions there is an expression for this condition called susto, soul dead. Regardless of whether the body is still functioning, to be afflicted with susto means that one has lost all reason for living, similar to what Dante said was written over the gates of hell: "Abandon all hope ye who enter here." To live without hope would be a kind of hell wherever you are.

Hope is an exclusively human characteristic. It comes from our ability to imagine what could be life-giving. When such a desire is sustained by an expectation of fulfillment, hope is the result. We are hopeful as long as something we consider important is not mere illusion.

How would you diagnose the spiritual pain of hopelessness? It can be tricky. Sometimes loss of hope is not connected so much to a particular event as to a set of cumulative losses. Imagine, for example, someone who has been dealing with long-term, chronic illness. One day it dawns on her that, as poorly as she feels today, this is the best she may ever feel again. Hopelessness may be the result.

On the other hand, the family friend or caregiver may misinterpret what they see as Hopelessness Pain. The sacred art of dying traditions give us an edge in recognizing the natural processes of dying. As the body shuts down, more attention is given to inner awareness. What might appear to be a diminished expression of character and personality could indicate a radical shift in priorities, which is not necessarily bad.

Dr. Marlene Halpin, counselor, caregiver, and Dominican nun, expresses in her poetry the paradox that patients often experience at the end of life. Hope and hopelessness are common themes:

> As my mind and heart roam around my life now
> I see that different things were important to me at different times
> Once, this was important. At another time, that.
> I gave a great deal to succeed in those then-important things
> Which I can hardly remember now.
> So what is important now?
> This minute.
> Maybe, the next minute—my being.
> I may not be as I was
> But I still am . . .

What once sustained hope may no longer matter. In the language of the Japanese poet, Basho:

> Oh hope be still.
> For to hope would be hope
> For the wrong thing.

At either end of the spectrum of life, it is not uncommon to hear about a diagnosis called failure to thrive. Often unrelated to any medical condition, nurses know that this same mysterious "illness" shows up among newborns and nursing home residents. At its core is a loss of the will to live, so a person's life force simply saps away. The ancients recognized this illness as *terminal hopelessness*. They knew its symptoms were emotional and spiritual in nature. Death, for all of us, ultimately involves an ending and a yielding, a recognition that our old familiar life is no longer sustainable.

In the presence of Hopelessness Pain, words are rarely effective. Sacred art of dying traditions recommend simple gestures, like using physical touch, enhancing the environment with light and beauty, or bringing the sick person in contact with nature. Rituals like lighting a candle or massaging the body with scented oil also appear to alleviate this kind of pain. Sometimes caregivers report that the sounds of repetitive, nonintrusive music can help to lift the heavy mood that accompanies the agony of hopelessness.

The good news from our ancestors is that even when recovery from illness is no longer an option, it is always possible to support people who are struggling with Hopelessness Pain. The degree to which persons have a sense of hope or feel guidance beyond themselves is related to the willingness of others to remain unconditionally present.

If you sense that someone you love is struggling with hopelessness, the following spiritual pain scale might be a starting point for conversation or reflection.

HOPE PAIN SCALE

I feel hope-filled and optimistic		I generally trust what the future holds for me		I am experiencing deep depression and hopelessness
①———	②———	③———	④———	⑤

A Poem of Hope

Come, come whoever you are
Wanderer, worshipper, lover or drunk
It doesn't matter.
Ours is not a caravan of despair.
Come even if you have broken your vows a hundred times.
Come, come again to hope.

    —Rumi

Becoming an Anamcara

There is no greater honor than to be with another as they journey Home.
A person who dies without an anamcara is like a body without a head.

—*St. Brigit of Kildare*

When someone in your world is approaching their final weeks or days, choosing to be truly present is one of life's great privileges. It takes courage to make such a commitment, and it can be overwhelming, but you can trust the perennial wisdom of our ancestors that it is the dying who are our teachers, not vice versa.

There are many names for those who journeyed with the dying: midwife, spiritual companion, death coach. We propose here the ancient Gaelic term *anamcara*, because of its continuity with the great Celtic tradition, whose remarkable school for the dying helped to create the West's first great hospice movement. *Anamcara* means soul friend. Perhaps that simple translation will encourage anyone who finds himself or herself in this role by chance or by design. We invite you to wear the name as a mantel of comfort and support.

Our ancestors took the anamcara's role seriously. The role presumed an unconditional covenant between persons who believed that a peaceful death was the reward and climax of a good life. In ancient times, the best way to ensure peace at the end of life was to have cultivated a lifelong anamcara relationship. Then you were guaranteed both a spiritual mentor in life as well as an insightful personal coach at the time of death. In other circumstances, the wisdom of the ages simply trusted that those who most needed to be present would always show up the bedside. The old Celts said it well: "There are no accidents in life especially about death."

We invite you not to pass up the opportunity to journey with others through the dying process, should this be your call. If you become an anamcara early in the disease process, you may have the opportunity to assist in diagnosing and responding to the person's spiritual pain. *The American Book of Living and Dying* is here to help you. For many, the invitation to become involved at the end of life may not occur until the final stage, the vigil. By this time, many of the concerns regarding spiritual pain may already have been resolved or the person may no longer have the strength to process these issues.

No matter at what stage you enter the scene, as anamcara you can make an enormous contribution to your loved one's end-of-life process. You already have what it takes to be a supportive companion. In addition, here is a summary of practical advice from the world's great sacred art of dying traditions to bring with you to the bedside.

Ten Commandments for the Anamcara

> Death is the only real and wise advisor that we have.
> An immense amount of pettiness is dropped
> If you catch a glimpse of it as your companion.
> —Carlos Castaneda

1. BE PRESENT

The first and most important "rule" is just to show up. Making a commitment to be available to a person who is terminally ill should not be done lightly. Know what you can and can't do—don't promise the impossible. When you do show up, take several moments to ground yourself before spending time with your friend—that is, become present by letting go of your own past and present concerns. Your friend will immediately sense whether you are emotionally available to them.

2. TRUST THAT WHO YOU ARE IS ENOUGH

It is normal to feel inadequate at times like this. Try to be natural—just be yourself. Be aware of any tendency to pretend you are comfortable—it probably means that you are not. Simple gestures to offer assistance and casual conversation cannot go wrong. The greatest gift you have to offer now is yourself. A simple rule of thumb is, when in doubt, trust your instincts. Generally, it will be a relief to your companion that you are not assuming an artificial role.

3. SHARE WITH YOUR FRIEND AS AN EQUAL

One of the main complaints from people who are chronically or terminally ill is that friends and family treat them differently. There can be a tendency to coach or give advice, or, in moments of uncomfortable silence, to bombard your companion with questions. Good conversation is give and take. Don't presume that you know what is needed. When in doubt, just ask what your friend needs.

4. LISTEN RATHER THAN BE CONCERNED ABOUT DOING

Remember that you and your companion are living in different "time zones." Your world remains vertical, busy with "doing" and activity, while theirs has become horizontal, where "being" at rest is more natural. Slow down and allow yourselves the gift of patient listening. You will still hear the words with your mind, but try to listen with your heart. Sometimes what is *not* said is important. Holding someone's hand or just being together in silence may seem unproductive, but it may eventually evoke deeper and more meaningful conversation.

5. PAY ATTENTION TO CHANGING PRIORITIES

Changes in personality can be disconcerting to friends and family. Such changes, however, are a natural part of the dying process. As a person becomes more contemplative and drawn inward, their priorities shift. Former conversations about routine concerns like the house or the job may no longer hold interest for your companion. Sharing memories and nostalgia may be ways of avoiding new and more pressing issues. Take your cues from your companion and, above all, tell the truth. Most dying persons are no longer concerned with putting a spin on their circumstances. Instead, they may be trying to protect *you* from the truth. This is a time for both of you to learn from the situation. It may even encourage the dying person to hear that your own priorities are being affected by your new relationship.

6. PAY ATTENTION TO YOUR NEEDS AND FEELINGS

Taking care of yourself physically and emotionally is the best way to ensure quality time with your companion. Don't be afraid to tell them when you are tired or distracted; they already know it. Perhaps the sound of sooth-ing, ambient music or a trickling water feature would be appreciated by both of you during a visit; check it out with your companion. If you see your visit as an obligation, it will drain your energy. If the time spent with your com-panion is a respite from the hassles of everyday life, you are likely to return more often and with available energy. Consider the care and nourishing of your own soul with supportive stories, including the ones found here in part II, and those in classic books like *Final Gifts* or *Tuesdays with Morrie*.

7. JUST KEEP BREATHING

As long as there is breath, there is life. In some cultures, paying atten-tion to our breathing is also a prayer, just as the word *respiration* literally means "to take in spirit." If your companion is conscious, inquire whether you may join them in the simple act of supportive breathing. Additional information on this technique is available in part III, "The Tool Chest." The beneficial effects of breathing in sync with someone who is suffering have been well-documented. Depending on the belief system of your com-panion, you can also use this profoundly supportive time as a period of quiet prayer. Recent Gallup Polls show that 93 percent of Americans pray regularly or occasionally, and an astounding 96 percent say that they would have no objection to others praying for them. Most people are not opposed to a spiritual exercise, as long as it respects their integrity and belief. When in doubt, ask.

8. PAY ATTENTION TO THE CLUES

Human beings are always giving either positive or negative feedback to each other. Paying attention to small kinds of nonverbal communication is an important guide for the anamcara. Normally we first focus on a person's physical needs: a drink of water, attention to hygiene, a change of pillow position, or an added blanket for comfort. Remember that your companion may not be able to open or close a window or change the environment with light or sound. But also pay attention to your companion's emotional or spiritual body. Does your friend seem restless or at peace? Has there been a change since your last visit? Ask how you can best be a support in this moment.

9. REMEMBER THAT YOU ARE NOT ALONE

During the dying process, death becomes the greatest teacher when it's no longer an enemy to be resisted. Our ancestors spoke of death as a natural friend who will eventually bring relief and welcome us home. Common occurrences have been recorded at the deathbed experiences of many thousands of hospice patients. In the nearing death process, appearances of angels and deceased relatives and friends are commonplace. Regardless of your belief about such phenomenon, realize that for many dying persons, distinctions between the past, present, and future become blurred. In the bittersweet moments of dying, other dimensions of life, including the spiritual dimension, may become magnified. Consider allowing significant mentors and friends in your own life, past or present, to become a virtual support system for you and your companion. In a moment of doubt or fear, turn to your higher power, however you understand it. As the door opens between time and eternity, know that you are not alone.

10. GRIEVE AND KEEP REMEMBERING

It is not uncommon to experience a mixture of both relief and sadness when your companion has died. This is a sacred moment. Resist the temptation to move back into normal life too quickly. While you may have masked some of your feelings in order to support your companion's process of letting go, it is important to give yourself permission to feel deeply after the time of death. Be aware that some traditions discourage extended periods of mourning in the presence of the body. In some cultures, for example, as in the *Bardo Thodol*, there is advice that wailing near the body holds the person's spirit back. But all sacred art of dying traditions support, in fact require, a significant period of reflection and inactivity after the death in order to tend to the important task of grieving. Our culture has few ways to support grief work, so grieving is critical for the healing and support of the anamcara. Dying is part of the natural cycle of a changing universe, but your life goes on and is enriched by this awesome experience. Savor its lessons and trust that someday you may have the blessing of dying in the presence of your anamcara returned.

A Blessing for a Peaceful Death

I pray that you will have the blessing of being consoled and sure about your own death. May you know in your soul that there is no need to be afraid. When your time comes, may you be given every blessing and shelter that you need. May there be a beautiful welcome for you in the home where you are going. You are not going somewhere strange. You are going back to the home you never left. May you have a wonderful urgency to live your life to the full. May you live compassionately to transfigure everything that is negative within and about you. When you come to die, may it be after a long life. May you be peaceful and happy in the presence of those who care for you. May your going be sheltered and your welcome assured.

May your soul smile in the embrace of your anamcara.

—Contemporary prayer based on an ancient Celtic text

Part II.

The Stories

HOSPICE | PATIENT CHART

NAME
Annie

AGE 47 | **GENDER** ☐ M ☒ F | **RACE / ETHNICITY** Caucasian

BORN IN
St. George, Utah

MARITAL STATUS
DIVORCED

CHILDREN ☒ Y ☐ N (2) Daughters

VOCATION
Volunteer Work

SPIRITUAL / RELIGIOUS ORIENTATION
LDS ~ Non-practicing

DIAGNOSIS
Ovarian Cancer

PROGNOSIS
SERIOUS

OBSERVATIONS
Annie is a divorced mother of two adult children. She remains involved in life despite her cancer. There is concern that her busyness is a distraction keeping her from facing ghosts from the past.

Annie: the Perfectionist

Will you love me even if I get it wrong?

Annie lived in a tight-knit rural community. To all appearances, she was one of its model citizens. A dedicated mother and a tireless volunteer with the local school district, she was also a major force behind a community arts center. Yet she was carefully hiding a secret that haunted her. The spiritual pain Annie was dealing with was Forgiveness Pain. The tools that provided the breakthrough were journaling, life review, and confession.

Annie's Story

The dominant cultural force in the town where Annie lived was the Mormon Church. Annie's father was a respected bishop in the church. She was an only child who had adopted the best values of her faith and community: an unquestioned commitment to family, a willingness to sacrifice and give to others, a deep generosity, and a comfort in sharing the spotlight. She was particularly sensitive to the people in her community who were in need; it was her defining trait.

One day, Annie collapsed while on a volunteer job. She was taken to the hospital where they did an emergency hysterectomy. Tests showed she had ovarian cancer. Richard was a chaplain in the hospital, and he met Annie post-surgery, right after she received the news from the doctors that she probably would not outlive the cancer. One of her daughters was there, processing the conversation with the doctor about the gravity of her mother's case.

Richard's First Meeting with Annie: A Woman with a Plan

My initial impression of Annie was that she was a no-nonsense, action-oriented woman. In spite of her crisis situation, from her bed she was orchestrating a plan for all the practical things that had to be done.

I noticed on her chart that there was a second daughter. When I asked conversationally about her, Annie became angry. "Kathy is the last thing in the world we need to be dealing with right now."

When Jody, the other daughter, offered to take Kathy to her own home for a few weeks while Annie was recovering from her surgery, Annie answered, "You wouldn't know what to do; she's my problem." I found out later that Kathy, age twenty-two, had Down syndrome.

Annie was fit, trim, prim, and proper. Her daughter Jody, age twenty, was just the opposite. Jody, a vibrant spirit, had a weight problem. You could tell her mother had the upper hand in their relationship. Here was a woman who had just been diagnosed with stage IV ovarian cancer telling her daughter, "Tuck your blouse into your pants." Jody dutifully did so.

The other thread immediately apparent in this scene was that Annie did not want her former spouse around. She told Jody that under no circumstances was she to tell her dad about her mother's illness. Annie was like a teakettle that had reached the top of its boil and was getting ready to shriek.

Next Meeting: Wonder Bread Lunch

The next time I encountered Annie, she was at home, recovering from her extensive surgery. The house was immaculate, with a slight scent of Lysol. The rooms were nicely appointed, with a few scattered pictures on the walls. Everything was cream and beige and matching, as if she had seen each room in a showroom and ordered it whole.

Jody was there and I met Kathy. I commented to the girls how clean the house was. Jody responded, "A germ couldn't live here for thirty seconds." The way she said it, it was not a compliment.

Since it was almost noon, Annie headed toward the kitchen counter. Would I stay for lunch?

I was embarrassed; I was there to support her. Jody waved my protests aside. "Forget it, you are going to eat here whether you like it or not."

The plate of sandwiches arrived: Wonder Bread with the crusts cut off. I had not seen that since I was a small kid.

Kathy started to sit down at the table, when Annie confronted her. "Did you wash your hands?"

Kathy looked down at her hands nervously. "Yes," she said.

After we ate, we talked for a while, and then I asked if it would be all right if I came by once a week.

Annie replied, "Why not come every Wednesday for lunch? I insist."

Jody smiled a knowing smile, "You are a marked man."

For the next few weeks, I showed up on Wednesdays and ate Wonder Bread crustless sandwiches. Jody and I began to warm to each other. I felt stung whenever Annie made comments about her daughter's weight problem in front of me. Annie pointedly left the mayonnaise off Jody's sandwiches and criticized her when it came to dessert. "Do you need a second serving of that?" Or, "Do you have to take the biggest piece of cobbler?"

Sometimes Jody answered back; sometimes she grabbed another piece of cake or licked the mayo off the knife in defiance. Mostly she did the same thing Kathy did; she lowered her eyes and said nothing.

Meeting with Jody Alone

After several midweek meetings, one Wednesday Jody followed me out to the car. "Do you want to meet me for coffee?" She was reading my mind. If I knew some background, maybe I could be more helpful to her mom.

We met at an offbeat coffee house in town. When we met, I found out that Jody was close to her dad, who lived in the same community. She described him as the salt of the earth, whereas she saw her mom as a rubber band wound as tight as could be before breaking.

Jody's take on their relationship was that her dad, Dan, loved her mom, but Annie was so hard on him, and on herself, that one day he packed up his stuff and just left. Annie was infuriated. After that, she would have nothing to do with him and had cut him off from contact with Kathy. Jody suspected there was some kind of guilt driving her mom, but she did not know what it was.

According to Jody, her mother's one outlet, the one thing she did for herself, was to write. Over the years, she had amassed quite a collection of journals.

Jody suggested that I stop coming by for Wednesday lunch and come instead at a time when she and Kathy were not there.

"Next week I am taking Kathy to a dentist appointment in the morning. Show up at that time and we will both be gone. You and Mom could have a real conversation."

Annie Alone

When I arrived, Annie seemed flustered at first to see me. We went into the living room, which immediately shifted the energy of the visit. She was no longer able to fuss over food. "I am here to help you," I told her, "not to have you prepare lunch for me."

She was guarded. "What will we talk about?"

"Whatever you want to talk about," I answered.

There was a crack of emotion. "Do you have about twenty years?"

"No, but I can give you an hour every Wednesday. Jody will get Kathy out of the house on Wednesday mornings so you and I can have a chance to talk."

Over the next few weeks, even as the cancer began to take its toll, bit by bit Annie started to open up. She spoke with great respect of her mom and dad and their deep involvement in the Church of Latter Day Saints. However, she thought that she had not lived up to their expectations.

"I am their only child. They gave me a good home and a good education, and in return, I give them a broken marriage and two grandchildren who are lost souls. Kathy and Jody are the only grandchildren my poor parents will ever have. Kathy is not normal, and Jody wastes her time with weird friends. My dad offered to pay for her college, but she was not interested."

It sounded like Annie was most worried about displeasing her parents. "What about you?" I asked. "Where is your disappointment?"

This was a topic worth exploring.

Defenses Down, Getting to the Heart of It

Over the next few weeks, the disease and the treatment started to make Annie more uncomfortable. She was undergoing chemotherapy, and her defenses were down.

One day, Annie talked about her anger, starting with her frustration at not being able to vacuum. Then she got to the core of it. She said bitterly, "Look how my life turned out. I am the laughing stock of the community. My husband abandoned me, and I know everybody takes his side.

"This is what you get; you give up your life for your family, you do everything right. And now I am going to die without any of my own dreams fulfilled. I could have been a principal in this town. What did I do instead? Make chocolate chip cookies for PTA meetings.

"Once that one was born, my fate was sealed," she said, pointing to Kathy's room. "I couldn't even get my teacher's license because I was taking care of her. Other kids grow up and move out; parents are given a second chance. I am stuck with a preteen-ager until the day I die."

Ironically, the pain meds and her weakened state were helping Annie open up. She had no energy. She could not fret over household details. That helped. She was no longer distracted by everything else.

Journaling, the Healing Power of Writing

Jody had said that Annie kept journals, so I suggested that she write about her disappointment, her anger, her hurt.

"You don't have to share what you write, but just putting it on paper will get it out, and it might help you not feel so bound up inside."

The next time I went to see Annie, she was weaker, but she told me she had been writing in her journal. The results so far were less than satisfactory.

"This is a bad joke," she said. "I am writing about my lost dreams. A life that could have been. Writing about all the things that might have been; how does that make me feel better?"

Rereading Journals as a Life Review

Some people like to look through old photo albums. Annie's journals were equally or even more revealing. I suggested that she go back and reread her old journals and mark anything that was a disappointment. She was to pay attention to what came up around those times and also to note what was joyful, playful, and memorable.

There was a shift in Annie's attitude after I asked her to review her journals. Before, whenever I visited her, we were constantly interrupted by the phone ringing off the hook. The various committees she was still involved with were demanding, and they counted on her for solutions to problems big and small.

Now when I came, Annie took the phone off the hook. She did not want to be distracted from this inner work.

Listing Life's Disappointments

As Annie went through the journals, she noticed the theme of disappointment underlining everything: people disappointed in her, her disappointment in others. Using this theme as a foundation, she began to unfold the story of her life.

She came to the realization that a lot of her letdowns had to do with expectations, her own expectations and the expectations of others. Telling her story helped her understand that setting high standards was an integral part of her nature. It made her a hard taskmaster in her relationships.

I suggested that she make two lists: people in her life she had disappointed and those who had disappointed her.

It took pages and pages of paper. Many people were on both lists.

Forgiveness

Anger, disappointment, and judgment are all related to forgiveness. The next step for Annie was to move from the disappointment lists to a forgiveness list. Annie examined both columns and highlighted those names where she felt there was unfinished work, where forgiveness needed to happen.

She bracketed and put aside those people who were not at fault. For example, Kathy was a disappointment, but Annie could not blame her daughter for it. Kathy's disorder was not an issue that warranted forgiveness.

Even though her cancer was progressing, Annie had a renewed spark, an interest. A friend introduced her to the popular book called *A Course in Miracles*. A particular sentence moved her deeply, though she found it scary:

> The holiest ground is where an ancient hatred has become a present love.

Annie wondered whether that were possible and wished that it could be.

In reading *A Course in Miracles*, she had an insight. Where she couldn't forgive, it felt like a prison.

People often thought Annie was angry with them, when in reality, she was angry with herself. She talked about guilt a lot. That was her prison.

"I can forgive anybody else, but no matter how many times I try to forgive myself, it never makes a difference. I am so irresponsible."

Guilt Is the Teacher

A classic book on forgiveness is Joan Borysenko's *Guilt Is the Teacher, Love Is the Lesson.* Annie no longer had the energy to concentrate on the printed word, so a friend read passages from Borysenko's book into a tape recorder, for Annie to play. She listened to Borysenko's methods for going beyond unproductive guilt to guilt that could lead to love and healing. She heard Borysenko explain what got in the way of that transformation. *Guilt Is the Teacher, Love Is the Lesson* has a heavy emphasis on the need for confession, that is, to say out loud to another what is driving our self-incrimination.

Annie was getting worse, and she was confined to bed. Jody arranged to have the bed brought into the living room, a more pleasant atmosphere, and so her mom could be involved with the family and any visitors who came.

One day, I saw a tender interaction between Annie and Kathy. Kathy was bringing a glass with a straw to her mom. She tripped and spilled the water all over Annie and the bed. Kathy started to shake and apologize. Annie took Kathy's head and brought it next to her own and said, "It's okay. It's okay. It's not your fault. None of it is your fault."

Then Annie started to cry, the tears flowing freely. It was one of the first times I had seen such deep emotion, and it opened something up.

When Kathy left the room, I asked, "What is going on?"

"You know that forgiveness list I made? There are only three names left on it. I can live with everything else, but not these three."

"Can you tell me who they are?"

"You already know one: me. The second one is Dan, and the third one I can't tell you. The problem is, I can't forgive me because the other two can't forgive me."

She was reluctant to contact Dan, however, and was not comfortable writing or dictating a letter to him. Could we find some other way to get in touch with him, maybe let Jody help? At that, Annie got emotional and broke down. She realized that she needed to express to Jody how much she loved her in the same way she had just given that message to Kathy.

Annie's health continued to disintegrate. Her physical condition was very weak, and her pain more difficult to control. Her nights were fitful and sleepless.

I met with Jody privately and told her what was going on. "You have the key," I told her, "to connect your dad with your mom, the key that will enable her to forgive herself. Do whatever it takes to bring them together."

The following Sunday was Annie's forty-eighth birthday. We talked about having a birthday celebration at the house. Jody would put it together and invite Annie's parents and a few close friends. Jody had the idea that this would be the appropriate time for Dan to show up. I told her to use good judgment and promised to pray up a storm.

The day of the birthday arrived and it was rough. Annie was in a lot of pain; her mom and dad were there, trying to make everything okay. Her mother was upset that Annie wasn't eating. She went into the kitchen, made a peanut butter sandwich and cut off the crusts.

There were long uncomfortable periods of awkward conversation. We were waiting for Jody to come with the balloons.

Then Jody walked in with her dad.

Annie's father blew up at the sight of him. "You have got your nerve, mister, to show up in this place when my daughter is dying, after all you've done."

Annie was so weak she could hardly talk, hardly lift a finger, yet she sat up in her bed, absolutely alert, turned to her father and mother, and reamed them.

"You don't know the kind of hell I've been through. I'm the one who should be asking *him* for forgiveness."

There was a stunned silence. Annie took a gulp and said, "When I was sixteen years old, I had an abortion. This was the man who stuck by me and married me in spite of it, and he gave you two wonderful grandchildren. I am sick and tired of apologizing for my life because it did not meet your expectations."

You should have seen the look on Dan's face.

Dan went over to the bedside. Annie grabbed him with a strength we did not know she had left in her. She broke down sobbing, "Dan, can you ever forgive me?"

Dan picked her up out of bed—she was nothing but a bag of bones—and held her. He started to cry and said, "This is the bravest woman in the world."

With that, he carried her out of the living room, back into their bedroom. Her father and mother were flabbergasted. The rest of us just stood there in a state of shock.

Kathy repeated, "My mom is the bravest mom in the world."

Jody hugged Kathy, and then Kathy said, "I miss my daddy so much."

About a half an hour later, Dan walked out of the bedroom.

"She's gone.

"Don't be sorry. It was just perfect.

"She died in my arms."

Annie's Spiritual Diagnosis: Forgiveness Pain

Believe that Forgiveness Is Possible

Not being able to forgive can forge a prison of unfair pain. Annie was stuck. Her life script did not fit with her expectations of the world, so she condemned herself for being a disappointment as a wife, mother, and citizen. Annie teaches all of us that forgiveness is possible, but it requires hard work and honesty.

Understand the Shadow Side

Annie's nature was to be a perfectionist. Her family members experienced her as harsh and demanding. The lesson is that we tend to project onto others the shadow side of our own broken selves. In other words, if you are picky, unrelenting, and judgmental toward others, chances are that's how you treat yourself. In the end, Annie was able to break through the wounds in her personality to find healing.

Experience the Ripple Effect

The conclusion of this story included a transformation that went far beyond Annie. Her release enabled other family members to experience healing as well. Forgiveness not only frees the forgiver, but it has a ripple effect that extends to others.

Forgiveness issues after a divorce are especially tricky. Families tend to rally around the person who was left. In Annie's case, Dan was demonized as the initiator of the divorce with no opportunity for reconciliation. Annie's "confession" turned the tables, which instantly rehabilitated Dan's reputation, much to the surprise of her parents.

Be Patient

Annie's secret haunted her for decades. But human nature cannot be programmed to change. Stories of deathbed confessions abound; however, trust the ancient wisdom that there is a time and season for everything under heaven.

Guilt can be counterproductive. But at the end of life it can motivate dramatic change. In Annie's case, the disease process allowed her to slow down and reflect on the regrets of her life. It takes time and courage to listen deeply to oneself, but the fruit of such reflection can break the unhealthy patterns of a lifetime.

Cut Out Distractions

Annie's personality created a predictable rhythm in her life. Being responsible for others' needs defined her days. Changing routines can help support a person's inner work. For Annie, unplugging the telephone and television was essential. This is when Annie did her best work.

Spiritual Reponses to Annie's Pain: Journaling, Forgiveness Work, and a Life Review

The Healing Power of Writing

Keeping a journal can be a powerful opportunity for self-reflection at the end of life (see "Journaling" in part III, "The Tool Chest"). Through writing, Annie could look at the pattern of disappointments in her life—and how she thought it was her job to fix everything. Through writing, Annie found a path to forgiveness.

Ovarian cancer can be painful. Anger makes the pain more difficult to manage, but writing about the anger and resentment releases some of the pain and toxicity. Writing makes sense of confusion and gives voice to the wisdom within. Writing brings you face to face with your own truth and reality. The lesson here is that the simple act of putting pen to paper can initiate a profound healing process.

Looking over a Lifetime

The outcome of Annie's willingness to keep a journal and reread her journals was a life review process (see "Life Review Exercises" in part III, "The Tool Chest"). Survivors of near-death experiences unanimously speak about some form of life review as an integral part of the dying process. Basically, a life review is the opportunity to see the whole of our life—unedited—without judgment or blame. Through her journals, Annie came to see what everyone around her already knew. She had spent a lifetime trying to be perfect, she held herself and others to impossible expectations, and she harbored bitterness and disappointment with the world. But instead of creating more guilt, Annie's life review helped to set her free.

The Hurt Lists

As Annie gained the courage to express herself more candidly, she engaged in a traditional forgiveness exercise (see "Forgiveness Exercises" in part III, "The Tool Chest"). Making lists of everyone she had ever hurt and who had hurt her revealed a terrifying reality: Annie risked going to her grave unable to reconcile with three key relationships in her life. This realization created both a crisis and an opportunity. The scene was set for an encounter with Annie's ex-husband.

Admission and Responsibility

Ultimately, it was not enough to acknowledge a lifetime of hurt on paper. Annie realized that she had to take responsibility for her own part in failed relationships. Through Jody's astute mediation, Annie's admission to her family was the final act in setting her troubled spirit free. Annie made amends and even found meaning in her pain. She confirmed the ancient psychospiritual dynamics of finding peace at the end of life: confession is good for the soul.

Presumptions Surrounding Annie

It is rare when even close family members know all that is happening at the deepest level of a person's soul. Assumptions are based on our experience of someone's life. These suppositions need to be tested to provide the best support for a loved one at the end of their life.

- We presumed that Annie was a person in control of her environment. We did not know that her inner world was in such turmoil.

- We presumed that Annie would never be able to let go of her routine long enough to allow herself to be ministered to.

- We presumed that Annie was too busy and involved with others to spend time keeping a journal.

- We presumed that Jody would not be able to mediate a breakthrough for her mother.
- We presumed that Dan was going to remain completely out of the family picture.
- We presumed that Annie would never stand up to her parents in defense of her former husband.
- We presumed that Annie, the perfectionist, had no deep, dark secrets from the past.
- We presumed that Annie's admission of "imperfection" would cause anxiety, whereas it became the source of her relief.
- We presumed that Kathy's role would be negligable in the breakthrough for Annie's healing.

Lessons for the Anamcara: Supporting the Perfectionist Personality

Perfectionist personality types appear to be idealistic and in control. They pride themselves on being rational, on being orderly, and on holding the highest moral standards. But life is rarely perfect. When life circumstances are chaotic, Perfectionists have a choice to make: either move to anger or learn from the blessings of imperfection. At the end of life, it is helpful for the anamcara to understand the unique way that Perfectionists deal with their spiritual pain.

Meaning Pain

Challenge: The desire to do what is good and right in the world sometimes meets with the reality of failure. Perfectionists are empowered by a strong sense of mission. But when their hopes are dashed, these persons can become disoriented, irritable, and excessively critical. The helpful anamcara knows not to take this personally, though it can feel like they are the object of the Perfectionist's irritation.

Opportunity: Perfectionists often possess an extraordinary talent for self-discipline. Once their beliefs have been tried in fire, the Perfectionist considers them worth living and dying for. The anamcara needs to take a Perfectionist's priorities seriously while helping them not to take themselves so seriously.

Forgiveness Pain

Challenge: Perfectionists place high demands on themselves and others, hence they can appear intolerant and unforgiving of failure. Realize that in times of crisis, Perfectionists suffer from extreme self-criticism measured against impossible expectations.

Opportunity: Do whatever it takes to help relax the Perfectionist's nonstop inner critic. Help them to see that everything in the universe is a process of order and chaos. They are not an exception.

Relatedness Pain

Challenge: A Perfectionist personality does not take any relationship casually. Therefore, things and people can be the source of terrible disappointment for Perfectionists. Feelings of anger, judgment, and resentment regarding what is wrong can simmer for years, causing no small amount of stress for all involved.

Opportunity: At their best, healthy Perfectionists continue to hold high ethical standards while letting go of the need to fix everything else. An anamcara can measure a Perfectionist's inner state of balance by his or her sense of humor. Support Perfectionists in relating to life out of a sense of joyful freedom.

Hopelessness Pain

Challenge: Eventually the burden of living with too many "musts and shoulds" creates an impossible set of obligations. A guilty conscience can exasperate the Perfectionist's feelings of despair and worthlessness.

Opportunity: Coming to realize that zeal for perfection is itself a fault can be a paradoxical source of relief. Here is a possible new commandment for Perfectionists: Thou shalt not should on thyself.

Overarching Advice

A Perfectionist could fall into the trap of making "dying well" a final test of character. At the end of life, the only work left is to accept life as it is. Support the Perfectionist in trusting that life is unfolding exactly as it is supposed to. Gentleness and forgiveness are the only virtues worth cultivating now. Serenity comes from letting go of mistakes and replacing anger toward self and others with compassion.

HOSPICE	PATIENT CHART

NAME Henry

AGE 46 **GENDER** ☒ M ☐ F **RACE / ETHNICITY** African-American

BORN IN Yazoo City, Mississippi

MARITAL STATUS Widowed **CHILDREN** ☐ Y ☒ N

VOCATION High School Teacher

SPIRITUAL / RELIGIOUS ORIENTATION BAPTIST

DIAGNOSIS Brain Damage due to Drowning Accident

PROGNOSIS CRITICAL

OBSERVATIONS Henry has been in a coma for seven months due to a car accident; he is rarely responsive. A decision has just been made regarding removal of life support.

Henry: the Helper

Will you love me even if I can't love you back?

Henry was a high school music teacher. Because of a car accident, he was in a coma. His caregivers did not understand Henry's internal crisis. A hospital cleaning lady provided the catalyst to unlock his deepest struggle. The spiritual pain Henry was dealing with was Hopelessness Pain. The tools that provided the breakthrough were music therapy and coma work.

Henry's Story

Widowed five years after his marriage—his wife was killed in an airplane accident—Henry poured himself into his career as a Mississippi high school music teacher. He had no children, and he swore he would never remarry because he had lost the love of his life. Henry's students were his children; he had that kind of love and sense of responsibility toward them. The students called him Uncle Henry.

Henry had an amazing ability to bring different worlds together and keep students interested. He believed that all American music could be traced to African American roots, starting with the Negro spiritual. The Negro spiritual combined elements of melody and sentiment from Africa with the experience of slaves and their newly adopted religion of Christianity. These hymns used passages from scripture as a kind of code language among the slaves that helped make sense out of their misery. When the slaves sang "Steal Away to Jesus," for example, the slave masters thought they were talking about heaven. They were also singing about stealing away to freedom.

The next step of the lineage evolved the blues, and from the blues, jazz, and from jazz, rock, and from rock, rap. Henry used modern music as a teaching tool. That was one of the reasons why he was so popular among the kids. Mixing rap with black spirituals and philosophy, he loved to quote Martin Buber: "The world is not divided between the sacred and the profane, but between the holy and the not-yet-holy."

The Accident

The accident happened in January. Henry was driving his prize voice student to a Martin Luther King celebration in Atlanta, where she was to perform. The soloist's name was Maggie, short for Magnolia. Maggie was the great-granddaughter of a slave from Mississippi, and part of the ceremony would honor that. The other two students in the car were her backup singers; one of them was Henry's nephew.

Henry was afraid they would not make it to Atlanta in time so he decided to drive through the night. He knew he was pushing it, driving long hours, but he did not want Maggie to miss this chance to sing before this special audience.

During the early-morning hours, there was a bad storm. They were going across a bridge in Alabama when they hit a patch of black ice. The car skidded out of control and crashed over the barrier into the cold river.

Maggie, in the front seat, was killed instantly. Henry was trapped behind the steering wheel. His nephew tried to free him but couldn't. The two boys got out and swam to safety. They ran to the road and waved down a passing car. The men in the car jumped into the water and managed to pry Henry loose. Fortunately one of the men knew CPR, and Henry began to breathe again, although close to ten minutes had passed. Because he had gone so long without oxygen permanent brain damage would have normally occurred. In effect, Henry had already drowned.

The Good Samaritans who stopped took Henry to a nearby hospital. He was placed on artificial life support.

When the attending physician examined Henry the next day and heard what had happened, he shook his head and said, "Poor fellow, it would be better if he had died. He will never resume consciousness." It turned out later that Henry heard him say that.

Removing Life Support

Over the next few months, Henry's friends and caregivers employed extraordinary means in an attempt to rehabilitate him. They consulted experts from other parts of the country. But aside from an occasional shudder, there seemed to be no response, no conscious communication.

Because Henry was a musician, his family and caretakers had constant music playing in his room, tunes they thought he would like: BB King, jazz, black gospel music, anything they thought would appeal to him. In hopes of providing a healing environment, they even invited a professional harpist to visit weekly, based on the theory that maybe Henry needed non-rhythmic music, which has no set beginning or end.

Henry had an occasional positive response to the recorded music and what his caretakers perceived to be a blank reaction to the harp music. There was little hope. At six months, the medical ethics board discussed the appropriateness of removing Henry's life support. The brain damage was extensive, and the prognosis for recovery was nil. After much discussion, his family and the medical staff came to a painful conclusion. They removed the life-support respirator. But Henry did not die.

Coming out of the Coma

Shortly thereafter, very late one night, a black cleaning lady was working in Henry's part of the hospital. She had a radio with her, tuned to a Montgomery, Alabama, Christian station. She was supposed to use earphones but had forgotten to bring them with her. She kept the volume low, hoping she would not disturb anybody. She did not want to miss her favorite program.

The woman set the radio down in the hallway and came into Henry's room to pick up the garbage. The song on the radio, with its rich baritone solo, was the old spiritual "Wade in the Water."

Henry spoke to the cleaning woman: "Would you mind getting me a glass of lemonade?"

Happy to oblige, she went down to the kitchen to get the lemonade. A nurse intercepted her. "Where are you going with that drink?"

The woman told the nurse which room she was taking the refreshment to.

"He can't drink lemonade."

"Oh sorry; he asked for it."

"He asked for it?!"

The nurse hurried down the hall and into the room, where she found Henry awake, with his eyes wide open.

Richard met Henry during the two weeks that he was lucid after he came out of his coma. Doing rounds as chaplain at the Alabama hospital, he followed the sound of a saxophone and poked his head into a room at the end of the hall.

Richard's First Meeting with Henry: The Sound of Music

"Are you the one making all that racket?" I asked by way of friendly introduction. Henry laughed, put down the instrument, and invited me in.

Truth is, there was a lot of buzz about this patient, and I had wanted to meet him. Henry had celebrity status. They were calling him The Miracle from Yazoo.

In the room, Henry was holding court, surrounded by family and friends. The saxophone was on the bed. I was immediately brought into the conversation.

In the next two weeks, I got to spend some time with Henry, hearing his firsthand account of what it was like to be in a coma.

Henry Waits on the Roof

During the visits that followed, Henry shared with me that while he was in a comatose state, it was like being suspended in time, where there was no past, present, or future, only now. There seemed to be no boundaries. Henry recalled that sometimes he felt as if he was in his body and could hear what was being said in his room, and sometimes he could hear conversations or situations happening down the hall.

One day, he said, a patient in the room next to him "coded" with a cardiac arrest. A loud signal alerted the nurses and doctors. When you are in coma, everything is amplified; smells, sounds, bright lights, and body sensations are exaggerated. The noise of the alarm was so piercing, it hurt Henry's ears. He could hardly stand it.

Henry's solution? He left his body, went through the roof, and waited.

While he sat there, he saw the woman who had just died come up to the roof and then leave. Although he had been brought to the hospital unconscious, and at this point had not yet awakened, he described her with accuracy.

"She was an older woman with extremely curly long gray hair."

He greeted her, but said she seemed to be in a hurry, as if to say, "I've really got to get going." Henry told this story like a person relating a dream.

One of the most incredible tales he told was that he had gone to Atlanta for the Martin Luther King celebration that Maggie was supposed to sing at. He described the young woman who took her place in great detail.

His nephew who had been in the car with him when the car crashed, thought this was too weird. "What did she sing?" he asked, challenging Henry.

Henry answered forcibly, "She sang Andre Crouch's 'Nobody Knows the Trouble I've Seen.' And they gave a tribute to Maggie and told what had happened on her way to sing that night." Henry then described the singer's outfit as a colorful African gown with a matching head wrap.

It checked out. That is exactly what took place in Atlanta.

Other "Travels"

"They do their travels" is the language of coma therapists.

Henry said that when he knew he was in his body he felt trapped, as though he were still drowning, in a state of suspended animation.

When he seemed to be asleep, he had little awareness. Every now and then something jarred him "like that harp music."

The harpist came every Thursday. "I know they had good intentions, but I decided on Thursdays I was going to leave. Then I decided that I would leave for Thursday *and* Friday because every Friday they served catfish, and the smell of it made me sick. I decided that I needed to leave every Thursday by noon and make sure I did not come back until late Friday night, so that is when I would go traveling."

Next Visit: Henry Tells His Dreams

The next time I came to visit, Henry was reflective. He wanted to talk about two "dreams" he had while he was unconscious. He believed the second one contributed to his coming out of the coma.

The first was a dream about his grandparents, who had a citrus grove in New Orleans. He was a child again, walking with his grandfather. The lemon trees were in blossom. The reenactment seemed so real, it was like being there. He picked a lemon and took a bite, as he would eat an apple. He made a funny face, surprised that it was bitter.

The second dream was about Maggie.

There is no consensus reality time sequence capacity in the coma state, but there can be awareness. Henry was aware that it was a hot, humid, Southern day. He remembered feeling physically uncomfortable. In fact, there was a breakdown in the hospital air conditioning system in July for two days. That was what he was recalling. At this same time, they were considering withdrawing Henry's life support. Henry could hear their discussions.

All these events were concomitant: the heat, the breakdown of air-conditioning, the decision to remove him from life support. Henry remembered wanting badly to communicate that he was thirsty, but he could not say anything. He was feeling trapped and desperate and frustrated, suddenly back in the water drowning. He was trying to make sense out of why this had happened, when Maggie appeared to him. She approached him, looking like an angel. In her hands, she held an incredible bouquet of lemon blossom twigs with tiny citrus flowers. She never spoke.

Henry looked into Maggie's eyes and said how sorry he was. She communicated back to him nonverbally that the tragedy of the accident was a bittersweet gift for both of them and that all was well.

Henry became very emotional when he recounted this dream. In his vision, Maggie dissolved into the water, but instead of the water being a state of hell and drowning, the water was transformed into a pool of lemon blossoms and he could breathe again. This mental picture released him. He cried tears of joy.

"I was just waiting for that angel to tell me that she was okay." Henry remembered specifically hearing the voice of a nurse saying, "Oh look, he's crying. He must be upset." And he remembered them wiping the tears.

"I wanted to say, 'No, I am so happy. They are tears of joy, not sorrow.'" Henry said there was amazing synchronicity in the vision of Maggie. The shift from water to lemon blossoms and the hymn on the cleaning lady's radio.

A few weeks after recounting his experiences, Henry died of cardiac arrest.

Henry had been stuck in a drowning state for seven months. To him the coma was like being underwater, in a state of suspended drowning.

"Wade in the Water" was the song that pulled him out.

Henry emerged from his inner world to finish up business and connect with friends and family before leaving.

The baritone solo hit his resonant tone, and the lyrics of the hymn spoke to him of Maggie.

Henry as a Teacher

Henry had spent his career helping students see connections. The accident and Maggie's drowning were personal tragedies that he could not reconcile. The coma became a resting place to do that work, a place for him to process his deeper beliefs.

Maggie was the instrument that helped him decide to come back to consciousness and stay for a while. Not for long, but long enough to tell his story. Long enough for the teacher who loved his students to give one more lesson.

Henry's Spiritual Diagnosis: Hopelessness Pain

Watch What You Say

Henry's whole way of life came to an end with the drowning accident. But even while in a coma, Henry continued to hear what was being said around him, including plans to remove his life support. Everyone in Henry's world considered his situation to be hopeless. The lesson is that our attitudes and conversation still impact a comatose person—for good and for bad.

Know that Inner Work Is Going On

Henry described his experience in coma like being suspended underwater. He also continued to carry a burden of concern for Maggie's wellbeing. Stories are plentiful from coma survivors who continued to do their inner work. Our job is to support them and avoid laying our expectations on them. Remember, once Henry was assured that Maggie was okay, he spontaneously came out of his coma.

Observe Responses

Although a comatose state may appear hopeless, Henry later related that he enjoyed numerous "out-of-body" experiences. An important lesson for family and caregivers is that—even though not always responsive—the patient may be doing their travels on some other level. A careful observer of Henry, for example, might have noticed reduced response rates on Thursdays and Fridays.

Be Sensitive to Helplessness

Helper personality types like Henry feel helpless when they are unable to provide support to those left behind. It is frustrating to have spent life serving others and then to be cut off from normal relationships. Hopelessness Pain is the final result of extreme helplessness.

Allow the Patient to Lean into Their Pain

Henry's story confirms the wisdom of the ancients that says leaning into our pain is the only way out of it. The accident and Maggie's drowning were a personal tragedy that Henry could not resolve. The coma came to be his resting place to do that work. Maggie was the only person who could give Henry permission to regain normal consciousness and stay long enough to tell his story.

Take All Evidence into Consideration

There is no easy solution to ethical issues surrounding artificial life-support systems. Family members, health care professionals, and ethics committees must work together based on the best evidence available. Stories like Henry's, however, demonstrate how difficult it is to decide whether to resuscitate a person who appears to be brain dead or when extraordinary means of prolonging life are no longer reasonable. Preparing advanced medical directives can help us articulate our personal preferences from our normal state of consciousness. What we might want in coma is situational and will have to wait to unfold. An advanced medical directive calling for coma communication therapy would provide for this eventuality.

Spiritual Responses to Henry's Pain: Music Therapy and Coma Therapy

Resonant Tone

Music was a natural connection to Henry's inner world. Ultimately, it was the synchronicity of a familiar song that brought Henry back to normal consciousness. The baritone hit a resonant tone for Henry, and the lyrics became a bridge between Henry's inner world and outer world. But for Henry, other musical styles including traditional harp therapy were not effective (see "Music Therapies" in part III, "The Tool Chest").

The Right Solution

Trapped in a watery state of drowning, Henry remained stuck for seven months. The song "Wade in the Water," a metaphor for his connection to Maggie, pulled him out. But it would have been impossible for friends and family to figure out such a solution. Ultimately, it was the unconscious synchronicity of the cleaning lady's radio program that made the difference. The lesson here should relieve caregivers of the anxiety to discover the right solution. The best we can do is to support the patient in finding what they need.

Working with People in Coma

Very few traditional coma therapy techniques (see "Coma Therapy" in part III, "The Tool Chest") were prescribed for Henry. However, through this extraordinary story, we learn a great deal about persons in altered states of consciousness.

- Sensory experiences continue in the comatose body, including hearing, vision, movement, smell, and feeling.

- Though limited by the body's suspended state, there seems to be opportunity for nonlocal travel and experience.

- Simply paying attention to the breath of a coma patient can yield important information about which channel of communication might be useful.

- Persons in altered states of consciousness are always providing some form of feedback to caregivers. Subtle signals include movement, sounds, or changes in breathing. Coma therapy techniques teach us how to read whether a person's feedback is positive or negative.

Presumptions Surrounding Henry

We learn from Henry's story how our presumptions, though well intended, can get in the way of providing appropriate support at the end of life.

- We presumed that Henry's situation was hopeless and that there was no possibility of him returning from the coma.

- We presumed that because of the accident, Henry missed out on the Martin Luther King celebration in Atlanta.

- We presumed that once taken off life support, Henry would die.

- We presumed that those who could help Henry most would be family or medical experts, but after seven months of trying, it was the cleaning lady who "brought him back."

- We presumed that Henry's tears were of sadness, not joy.

- We presumed that harp music would help him, not annoy him.

- We presumed that environmental influences like sound and smell didn't bother Henry.

Lessons for the Anamcara:
Supporting the Helper Personality

Helper personality types possess an uncanny ability to know what others want while ignoring their own personal needs. Consequently, their experience of spiritual pain is often in proportion to the pain they encounter in others. If you are dealing with someone who has spent his or her life primarily helping others, here are some general guidelines about how they may experience spiritual pain.

Meaning Pain

Challenge: A Helper's world is defined in terms of who needs him or her. Helper personality types are likely to lose a sense of purpose and meaning when they are disconnected from the significant others who have been at the center of their universe.

Opportunity: Find a way of supporting the Helper to turn inward. In silence or contemplative practice, for example, Helpers can discover their own innate sense of worth and purpose.

Forgiveness Pain

Challenge: Helpers are highly intuitive and may experience a particular kind of anguish when they perceive that someone else holds a grudge against them or is unwilling to talk about or process a misunderstanding.

Opportunity: Support the Helper in separating their unhealthy need for approval from an authentic need for forgiveness.

Relatedness Pain

Challenge: For the Helper it is all about relationships with other human beings. Therefore the Helper's identity is threatened when their role as father, mother, teacher, mentor, or whomever is threatened.

Opportunity: Support Helpers in discovering their own inner worth. Help them to cultivate a deeper sense of identity based on their own merits, aside from past badges of honor.

Hopelessness Pain

Challenge: Not to be of service makes the Helper feel useless and unwanted. Recognize that Helpers may be depressed because they cannot do what they feel loved for. If prolonged, this sense of helplessness can lead to depression and despair.

Opportunity: Realize that a Helper's prolonged mood change may not necessarily be a bad thing. It could be the precursor of newfound hope and more mature relationships.

Overarching Advice

The goal should always be to assist the Helper in discovering his or her own truest needs, which have often been neglected in service to others. This personality type may find it especially difficult to accept help from others. Simply reassure the Helper that you are okay and don't need their help. Then encourage them to stay faithful to some form of contemplative practice, though it may not feel natural or comfortable at first. Ultimately, unplugging from life may provide their best chance for real inner healing.

HOSPICE · PATIENT CHART

NAME SARA

AGE 53 **GENDER** ☐ M ☒ F **RACE / ETHNICITY** CAUCASian

BORN IN Brooklyn, New York

MARITAL STATUS MARRIED **CHILDREN** ☐ Y ☒ N

VOCATION SURGEON / Opthalmologist

SPIRITUAL / RELIGIOUS ORIENTATION Jewish

DIAGNOSIS Congestive Heart Failure

PROGNOSIS 6 months

OBSERVATIONS
Sara is an opthalmologic surgeon, blind from rapidly advancing medical condition. Husband Sam is attentive and frustrated by her depression.

Sara: the Achiever

Will you love me even if I am not successful?

Sara was a nationally recognized eye surgeon until she became terminally ill, and then, gradually, in a cruel irony, lost her sight. Her husband, Sam, at his wit's end, affirmed her past accomplishments, but that offered little solace. He was surprised to learn that what she needed was to know that she was loved for herself, not her deeds. The spiritual pain Sara was dealing with was Relatedness Pain. The tools that provided the breakthrough were breath work, dream therapy, and religious ritual.

Sara's Story

Sara's childhood and upbringing shaped her life in a significant way. Her mother, Sara Jane, was a New York Broadway theme artist, set designer, and choreographer immersed in theater as a profession. Although she was good at it, Sara's mother felt that her occupation was lightweight. She did not want her only child to do anything like it. Growing up, Sara was given a strong message: anything to do with the arts is taboo, a waste of time. Her mother wanted Sara to become something important and practical, like a doctor.

To please her mother, Sara suppressed her creative side, her desire to be artistic and theatrical, and got on an early track for medical school. She became a respected surgeon and scientist, yet she was always attracted to the Bohemian life of dancing and theater. The contradiction of the two worlds warring within her showed up in a series of anxiety attacks and a recurring dream.

Sara had a close friend, Joan; Joan was the only person who understood her. Joan was both friend and mentor. Her mantra to Sara when she had a panic attack was, "Just keep breathing. Just keep breathing." Joan's reassurance and reminder was the only advice that ever helped Sara when she had high anxiety.

Sara had a returning dream: She is in her scrubs, preparing to operate, and instead of being in a normal surgery room, all of the doctors, all of her colleagues, and even the students watching, become actors on a Broadway stage. They sing and dance, and all their movements are choreographed in unison. When Sara lifts the sheet off the patient's face, the patient is blue and has stopped breathing. Then Sara realizes she is staring at her own face; the patient is herself. She would wake up from this dream hyperventilating in hysteria. Joan was the only person in Sara's life who knew about this dream.

Sara believed that hard work is the answer, and with an unstoppable investment of time and energy, she achieved high status in her field. She became a famous eye surgeon. She was internationally recognized for her talent, her surgical skills, and her cutting-edge research. Everything seemed perfect in Sara's life. She was at the top of her game professionally, and she was married to Sam, a man who adored her and was unconditionally there for her. Then Sara developed congestive heart failure. Ironically, she also began to lose her eyesight through macular degeneration.

Richard was asked to visit with her as part of the hospice team assigned to her. Sara was Jewish and Richard, being an avid student of Judaism, knows Hebrew. Richard knew very little about Sara until he walked in during this last chapter of her life. Later, her husband shared Sara's many achievements with him.

Richard's First Meeting with Sara: A Museum of Awards

You can walk into anyone's home and without knowing anything else, know her by her trophies. Whenever I go into a person's house for the first time, I can tell what they care about by looking for their altars: what mementos do they enshrine?

What I observed when I arrived at Sara's house were indications of someone honored for being competent, honored for all she had done in her life. The hallway was a memorial wall of plaques and distinguished citations. The living room was like an office—diplomas and awards dominated the décor. There was very little artwork and few family photos; the house was a shrine to Sara's success. *How could someone be this brilliant?* I thought, and then I wondered who she was underneath these honors.

Over the next six months, I visited with Sara and her husband once a week. It was difficult for Sara to access her own needs or to know what was important to her; her time and talents had been entirely invested in medicine.

She seemed to be at a crux. She felt that she had nothing more to give, nothing ahead to look forward to. She felt bereft but did not want anyone else to know—that was part of her image. She was working hard to cover up her feelings and project a confidence she no longer felt.

After visiting with Sara several times and after talking with her husband, I was convinced that Sara's pain was Relatedness Pain, mostly in her relationship to herself. She had put her life energy into becoming the best that she could be professionally, and her identity was solely connected to her performance as a surgeon. This ambitious professional track alienated her from her deepest self.

One day, Sara told me about her recurring dream, which she was still having. It was coming up more frequently the more ill she became. I asked her if she would be willing to do some dream work, and she was open to it. In dream work, the first and most important thing to do is just to try to remember your dream. Sometimes details come back in the telling of it. I encouraged Sara to talk about her dreams in the present tense; better yet, she should write them out. The next best thing would be to draw them out. I suggested to Sara that she keep a journal to monitor her dreams. With her limited vision, she had to use a huge magnifying glass and a bright light.

As she got increasingly sick and her eyesight failed even more, Sara recorded her dreams on an audio recorder. Finally, she lost her strength to do even that, so I asked her if she would be willing to tell Sam each morning whatever she remembered from the night before. Then Sam could retell it to me, and she and I could work with it. It wasn't easy for Sara to let go and trust, but she agreed to do that.

High Holy Days and Memories of Girlhood

In mid-September, two weeks before Sara died, there was a shift in the weather. First it was very hot; then there was a cool spell. The changing weather reminded Sara of growing up back East. When it got chilly and the humidity went down, her mother would say, "Ah, the Jewish holidays are coming." The Jewish New Year, Rosh Hashanah followed by Yom Kippur, coincided with autumn.

One night in September, Sara had an incredible variation on her recurring dream. The people in the dream watching her in the operating room were all playing rams' horns, trumpets of different shapes and sizes and colors. At first Sara wanted to turn her back on all this noise and these people. She headed toward the operating table. Then she stopped. This time, she didn't pull the sheet back. Instead, she sat down on the floor and started weeping.

Describing this scene to me, Sara began to sob as hard as she had cried in her dream. I asked her what feeling was making her cry, and she answered, "God, I've always wanted to play the shofar; I want to do that, just once." Sara did not have much use for theology; her desire to be part of the celebration seemed to be a metaphor for something more.

Because of her grandmother, she had a fondness for one particular part of the Jewish New Year. Once a year, the whole family would go to temple for Rosh Hashanah. The reason that Sara always went was because her grandmother told her this story: Every New Year's, when the ram's horn is blown, Hashem (God) opens the Book of Life. In it are all the names of all the people who are going to get sick and die the next year. But if you pray hard enough, and make a good contribution for the poor, you may be able to change God's mind.

Sara told Richard, "I know it sounds superstitious and simplistic, but I think I believe that. If I can make it to Rosh Hashanah, then I can beat this game, and I can have another year of life."

It was significant that in this version of the dream, instead of going to surgery, Sara had sat down and cried. Instead of turning her back on the others in the dream, she was one with the choreographed music group. They all seemed to be in a temple rather than an operating arena. And when she got up, she had made a decision: to walk out of the operating room and not perform the surgery. She glanced back and saw the sheet where the patient was, and there was no body under it.

Dream Work and Good Grief Work

Clearly the patient in the dreams was Sara herself, and the others who were watching, playing instruments, and singing were an aspect of who she wanted to be. In the last dream, she wanted to blow a shofar; she wanted to be on stage. When she could finally collapse in tears and not fight that, she no longer had to perform surgery; in fact there was no patient there. There was no work to be done; she had done the work in her grieving.

By leaning into her pain and allowing herself to feel deeply through her dreams, Sara was able to symbolically walk away from the obligation of her life as a surgeon and to mourn what she had never had. It was good grief work she was doing.

Sam Draws Sara's Shofars

When Sam heard about Sara's dream in the temple, he asked if he could draw it for her. As she described the scene, he drew an incredible sketch of shofars blowing in all positions and colors. It was beautiful.

Drawing Sara's triumphant dream was healing for Sam, too. He was her number one cheerleader, and this gave him a way to connect with her and be the one helping her.

The End of Sara's Life

Sara died on a very hot day, the week between Rosh Hashanah and Yom Kippur. She was too sick to go to temple. The day she died was stifling and sultry.

She had been having difficulty breathing all week, which is a sign of water in the lungs. Her heart was not pumping sufficiently, and heart failure was setting in. For a person who had had panic attacks all her life, being breathless made her anxious, and it was hard to keep her comfortable.

Her friend Joan would have been a great comfort to her at this stage, but she had died several years earlier. Since Joan meant so much to Sara, in a way she was still around. With guidance, Sara could imagine hearing Joan's voice telling her to keep breathing.

This helped for a while, but soon Sara was so restless that there was little that brought her peace. Not the presence of other people, nothing; no matter what medications she took, no matter what the hospice team did or did not do, she seemed uncomfortable day and night.

Physical symptoms indicated that Sara's body was starting to shut down. She was not taking in adequate food or liquid to sustain her, and her skin color was changing. The skin is an important indicator of what is happening inside the body. Edema, an accumulation of fluids, sets in when the heart is no longer able to pump the blood efficiently.

Psalm 104: Your Breath Is My Life

In the middle of the week, Sam called. "You should come. Sara is a goses" (a Jewish expression meaning "close to the end").

I went immediately to their house and climbed the stairs to the second story bedroom. It was sweltering. The open window gave no relief. The air was still and heavy. Sam and I looked at Sara and we talked to her, and I said, "I think this is it, Sam."

There are some prayers Jews traditionally recite at the time of death, and one of them is based on Psalm 104. Sam and I chanted this prayer in Hebrew. We got to the line that translated in English is, "Remember me, oh God, my life is only a breath and your Breath is my life."

The Hebrew word for breath is "ru-ach," which is an onomatopoetic word. It has a guttural resonance and sounds like the breath it is: ru-ach. As we got to that word, suddenly the curtain stood on end, and a rush of air came into the room. To our astonishment, Sara momentarily became conscious and fluttered her eyes.

Sam stopped praying, startled. "Did you see that?!"

Sam said, "Let's try that again."

We went back and reread that line of the psalm, and another gust came into the room. This time Sara spoke. She said, "Oh, do that again. Do it again, honey."

It was an incredibly intimate, precious moment. The look on Sam's face was beatific. I stepped out of the room to let them be alone with each other.

Those were Sara's last words, her last communication with the world.

When I went back into the room, Sara seemed to be asleep. A calm had come over her. Instead of the thrashing and restlessness, the labored breathing and discomfort of before, from this point on, between now and her death, she moved to a deeper coma, tranquilized almost. When she finally breathed her last, it was not the anxiety-ridden gasping that sometimes happens at the end. It was a gentle, gentle, letting go. We almost could not tell when she stopped breathing. Reciting the psalms and a coincidental breeze brought her comfort and guided her to a place of letting go.

Memorial Service One Year Later

The Jewish tradition is to light a memorial candle on the anniversary of death. I bought a Yahrzeit candle for Sara in Jerusalem, and called Sam a year after her death, suggesting that we get together for a short memorial service in her honor.

The idea of coming together and lighting a candle was almost perfunctory. We said some prayers and reflected on Sara's life. Sam lit the Yahrzeit candle. A breeze came and blew the candle out.

We looked at each other, astonished. Sam pondered the curious happening for a moment and then said, "I don't know what I believe about what happens after people die. It doesn't matter to me." He paused a moment, then added, "But to have the candle blow out when we were praying for her could make a person almost believe."

"Believe what?" I asked.

"I don't know," he answered. "Believe that she is still around."

Sara's Spiritual Diagnosis: Relatedness Pain

Affirm What Matters Most

In many ways, Sara's story is the story of our culture. We see our worth in what we produce. Hard work is the answer. But at the end of life, when it is no longer possible to do whatever it is we do well, many people encounter a deep sense of loss and despair. Sara's Relatedness Pain was predictable. Her commitment to career and work left little time for herself or other relationships. Her caregivers trusted that as her image was melting down, it was important to help Sara see that she was much more than the sum of her accomplishments.

Observe the Environment

Walk into anyone's home and you will find altars honoring their life's priorities. Sara's home was a shrine to her professional accomplishments. But at the end of life, it is not our possessions that matter—home, car, status, and degrees become secondary. Paying attention to a patient's trophies can be a helpful icebreaker to initiate conversation, and they also give important clues as to what has been missing in a person's life.

Watch for Cues

The dying person gives us all the cues we need; it is up to us to pick up on them. There was nothing that Sam or the caregiver could offer Sara except to take her seriously and support her in doing this work. It would have been easy to conclude that Sara was going to die the way she lived and should just be kept physically comfortable. Instead, picking up on cues about the realities of her inner world helped to name and alleviate her spiritual pain.

Learn from Regrets

Sara carried regrets from her childhood that were crying out for attention. Her dreams were filled with important metaphors for the unlived parts of her life. When dying, it is common for these issues to demand our attention. In Sara's case, a repeating dream held clues about her regrets, as well as a way out of her pain. Family and friends should not be afraid to ask about regrets. Chances are, life was just too busy to pay attention to our dreams. But it is never too late to learn from our regrets and teach others in the process.

Slow Down

Both Sara and Sam were stuck. Then, because of her disease, life quieted down enough that they could, in slow motion, observe little things that they might have missed in the fast pace of life. They paid attention to dreams and a wind that blew the curtain. Sam noticed a candle that went out. In our normal consciousness, at such a moment we would just strike a match and light the candle again. The sick live in a different "time zone" where every little thing is magnified. Things do not take on more meaning; the meaning is always there, we just do not pay attention. Heightened awareness is part of the gift.

Spiritual Responses to Sara's Pain: Breath Work, Dream Therapy, and Religious Rites

Stabilization and Direction

Sara's friend Joan gave her simple advice. In the face of anxiety, our only job is to keep breathing. Breath work (see "Breath Work" in part III, "The Tool Chest") is one of the most ancient spiritual practices in end-of-life care. Breathing is a way to stabilize and direct the energy of the entire body. Slowing down the breath and moving it to a deeper place has a beneficial effect on the body's nervous system, our internal organs, and the mind. Sara dealt with anxiety attacks all of her life. By breathing with Sara, friends and caregivers could help her relax and go with the flow.

Metaphors for Life, Spirit, and Love

As Sara was dying, breath and wind became powerful metaphors for life, spirit, and love. The words of a psalm prayer referring to breath brought Sara back to consciousness and left an invaluable gift for Sam. A year later, the "coincidence" of an extinguished memory candle provided confirmation and solace to the bereaved husband.

Diagnostic Tool

Paying attention to dreams is one of the most direct ways to diagnose spiritual pain. Sara's career life was too hectic to give heed to her inner world. But the masks of role and accomplishment drop away at the end of life. Once the old tapes ran out, Sara could listen to deeper voices that asked, "Do you love me only for what I produce, instead of for who I am?" For Sara, dreams became a useful way to listen to her soul. In the final months and weeks of life, dream therapy (see "Dream Work" in part III, "The Tool Chest") can be a profoundly supportive spiritual practice for both patient and caregiver.

The Power of Ritual

For Sara, a nostalgic time of year coupled with an ancient ritual from her faith tradition were significant. Many persons are not able to verbally communicate at the end of life; ritual has the power to express deeper feelings and beliefs. We live in a deritualized society, and not everyone relates to traditional religious rituals. Nevertheless, the art of creating healing rituals (see part III, "The Tool Chest") only takes a little imagination and effort, with tremendous potential payoff. The ancients expressed it this way: When you can't say it with words, have a ritual.

Presumptions Surrounding Sara

In the face of death and suffering, we want to help. But sometimes, our good intentions are clouded by assumptions that may not be accurate. It is important to encourage caregivers first to acknowledge their presumptions, which are usually based on the best evidence available. Then they should test them. In Sara's case it would have been easy to draw several incorrect conclusions.

- We presumed that because Sara was a high achiever, her greatest accomplishments were related to her outstanding medical practice.

+ We presumed that Sam and Sara's relationship was mediocre.

+ We presumed that since Sara considered herself only culturally Jewish, the rituals surrounding high holy days would hold little meaning for her.

+ We presumed that Sara's lifelong struggle with anxiety and compromised breathing would cause her significant physical distress at the end of her life.

+ We presumed that once Sara became nonresponsive, final prayers and rituals were performed more for the caregivers than for the patient.

+ We presumed that the one-year memorial ritual, performed out of duty and tradition, would be no more than a casual remembrance.

Lessons for the Anamcara: Supporting the Achiever Personality

Like everyone else, the Achiever personality type spends part of his or her life's energy developing a role or image of who they wish to be in the world. This image is not necessarily bad, but it is tragic when they come to believe it is all that they are. At the end of life, Achievers can be confused when they no longer are able to sustain these images. The challenge then is to remove the masks and to see oneself more directly. Regardless of the source of spiritual pain, an anamcara can help the Achiever to feel loved for who he or she is rather than for their accomplishments.

Meaning Pain

Challenge: For an Achiever, failure feels like death. When much of life has been spent producing, it can be terrifying to find one's face in the mud of one's limitations. The anamcara can assure the Achiever that she or he still has worth beyond all previous goals and tasks.

Opportunity: A crisis of meaning can also provide the impetus to revisit priorities. For an Achiever, success is purchased at a very high price, personally and emotionally. Help the Achiever examine failure as an opportunity to take care of long-neglected needs and relationships.

Forgiveness Pain

Challenge: In the wake of an Achiever's accomplishments, there can be a trail of corpses—not literally, but in terms of relationships. A life review is a painful but necessary exercise for persons who have focused on developing their professional goals to the exclusion of other priorities. The dying Achiever needs to forgive him or herself for a relentless pursuit of achievement.

Opportunity: At the end of life, forgiveness has less to do with taking things back than with the honesty to admit our shortcomings. The anamcara should know that Achievers often beat themselves up for not following their heart. Forgiveness work draws on that very capacity and eventually feels more rewarding than any professional accomplishment.

Relatedness Pain

Challenge: Because Achievers are extremely competent, driven, and accomplished, many people do not realize that they can be challenged in their relationships. The problem is that while their energetic ambitions are focused on career, other more important relationships become sidelined. Allow the Achiever to mourn lost dreams; it can be the key to their transformation.

Opportunity: Efficiency and effectiveness are valued in the workplace, but they do not create meaningful relationships. Invite Achievers to invest themselves in the relationships that matter most. While it may feel like they need emotional training wheels at first, Achievers become endearing when the need to perform is set aside and they can just be.

Hopelessness Pain

Challenge: When Achievers drive themselves too hard, the result is an emotional and/or physical breakdown. If they are feeling condemned as a failure, Achievers can come down so hard on themselves that they land in a hopeless pit of depression. Do not abandon Achievers at this critical time, though their inclination will be toward shame and isolation.

Opportunity: As Achievers let go of feelings of worthlessness, they can tune into the real desires of their heart. Often it is in times of extreme illness or breakdown that the Achiever will discover what has been eluding their grasp. An anamcara will watch for those opportunities and encourage the Achiever not to put their mask back on.

Overarching Advice

The Achiever has spent a lifetime cultivating the persona of a superhero, believing that this is what others expect of him or her. The paradox is that we usually get exactly what we invest ourselves in, and it may taste like ashes in our mouth. Achievers become exhausted from pushing too hard in life. When facing death, there is nothing more to accomplish except being. The best support we can provide for this personality type is to cultivate regular contemplative listening. Our dreams do not lie. Trust that an Achiever's dreams have the seeds of their heart's deepest truth.

HOSPICE	PATIENT CHART

NAME Heather

AGE 4 **GENDER** ☐ M ☒ F **RACE / ETHNICITY** CAUCASIAN

BORN IN Cedar Rapids, Iowa

MARITAL STATUS N/A **CHILDREN** ☐ Y ☐ N N/A

VOCATION Daughter / Artist

SPIRITUAL / RELIGIOUS ORIENTATION Non-specific

DIAGNOSIS LEUKEMIA

PROGNOSIS One Year

OBSERVATIONS Heather is struggling for her life and also for her Mother's attention. Socio-economic problems complicate this case including her Mother's incarceration.

Heather: the Dreamer

Will you love me even if you know who I am?

Imagine being a little girl in a world where you felt different from children your own age and felt separated from your mother. Now imagine being such a child, and diagnosed with incurable leukemia. This was the world of Heather at the age of four.

The spiritual pain Heather was dealing with was Relatedness Pain. The tool that provided the breakthrough was art therapy.

Heather's Story

Heather collected miniature cereal boxes. She cut the dotted slits and opened the little doors on them carefully, keeping each box intact, then dumping the cereal into a bowl or plastic bag and removing the waxed paper lining. She would not pour milk into them or eat directly out of the boxes because she was saving them to make tiny houses.

Heather was at Children's Hospital, and Richard was assigned as her chaplain. The first time he went to visit her, he found the little girl on the floor, with her brow furrowed, painting one of her small boxes.

Richard's First Meeting with Heather: Cereal Box Homes

Heather was bashful, but when I asked her what she was working on, she answered, making up a name, "This is Blue Fox's house."

Bending down, I said, "It is so pretty. Do you have any more?" When she nodded yes, I asked if I could see them. She thought this request over for a moment and then, shrugging her shoulders slightly, she revealed her treasure: a fantastic village, a world made of two dozen single-serve cereal boxes. "I paint them and put my things in them. I close the doors at night so everyone is okay," she said.

I saw at once that these decorated cereal boxes were almost sacred to Heather. For a little girl dying of blood cancer, life can be scary. In her hospital bedroom, the little colorful condominiums created a world of safety, a miniature world where life was not frightening. When it was time for me to leave, Heather had a gift for me. Timidly, she offered me one of her painted boxes.

Heather's Mother, Angie

Heather was being raised by her aunt because her mother, Angie, a drug addict, had effectively abandoned her. Now Angie was in jail, serving a six-year sentence for check forgeries and drug trafficking.

Heather's feelings about her mother were ambiguous. In her short life, she had seen her mother only sporadically. There was little communication. As a liaison between them, I went to the prison to visit with Angie and talk about Heather.

Angie confided that she did not understand her daughter. "She's always been an odd kid. She's not interested in what other kids are interested in. I don't know how to relate to her. For instance, I bought her a Barbie doll, but she didn't care about it. She just wanted to play with her dumb cereal boxes. Go figure. I thought, *Gee, my mother never bought me a doll like that.* I would have been thrilled when I was her age if anyone bought me a dress-up doll.

"She makes her own toys—and God help you if you mess with her stupid boxes. She's obsessed with them. I don't get it. It costs a lot to buy cereal that way in individual servings. I think you should buy cereal in bulk."

Once, when Angie wanted to take Heather on a camping trip, Heather packed her suitcase with cereal boxes. "There was no room for her clothes. We had quite a fight about it. So I didn't take her camping."

Angie told me that she wrote to Heather in the hospital, but Heather was too young to write back. "And it's hard for me to make outgoing calls, and then she does not want to talk to me on the phone anyway. What can I say to her?"

The issue here was clearly Relatedness Pain and that pain was on both sides, both the daughter and the mother. The challenge was to find a way to breach their separateness, to open up the communication lines. Over the next two months, I continued to go back and forth between the prison and the hospital, searching for a way build a bridge between Heather and her mom.

Heather Draws a Picture

It was Heather who provided the first opportunity for connection. Heather was always drawing or painting. One day she made a drawing for her mother. The drawing was quite dark, but there was a rainbow across the middle of the paper. To the left, in the upper corner, she pasted glitter. Pointing, she explained, "That's where I live."

Below the rainbow, she colored the picture pitch black. "That's where Mummy lives. Mummy's place has a flower in the corner."

I bought Heather's picture to Angie in jail and told her it was a hopeful sign; Heather was reaching out to her. Angie took the picture and looked at it long and hard. At first, she said nothing, then she started to cry. "What can I do?"

We talked about her little girl in a hospital bed, surrounded by her paints and cereal boxes. Heather was a visual learner; maybe the way to reach her was for Angie to draw a picture in return, depicting her life, what was going on where she was. There was one problem with that suggestion—for Angie, a major drawback. "She sure didn't get that artistic bent from me. I hate drawing. I can't draw."

"That's easy," I said. "Draw like a four-year-old."

So Angie let go of making pictures that were perfect. She just let the crayon move across the page and record her life in a primitive way. The first picture Angie drew was a picture of herself on KP duty. She was a stick figure in the kitchen, peeling a mountain of potatoes.

Heather laughed and laughed when she saw that drawing. She drew a picture back in return, and soon mother and daughter were exchanging drawings regularly. Heather's themes in her drawings were rainbows and flowers, light and darkness. Sometimes she drew pictures of storms or of the sunlight right after a storm.

Heather, with a depth beyond her years, seemed to sense that this was their way of writing to each other. Her artistic ability was matched by uncanny psychological insight. She was a sensitive little soul who could pick up on her mother's moods. "Oh look," she would say. "Mum's picture has more green and yellow today; she must be happier inside."

Angie, for her part, began to see her life differently. Drawing pictures for her daughter expanded her confined and limited world dramatically. Now she was on the lookout for subjects to draw. Her crude but colorful sketches gave meaning to the trivia of her life. And drawing made her happy. She was communicating with her daughter.

Angie had fun drawing like a child. After the potatoes, she drew a flowering tree that she could see through her window. Playfully, she exaggerated the flowers and made it a tulip tree, with giant tulips sprouting every which way. Heather loved the joy expressed in that picture.

Occasionally now, they could even talk on the phone. During one conversation, Angie asked Heather, "For your fifth birthday, what kind of cake do you want?" Heather answered, "For my birthday, I want french fries. A french fry cake, with french fry candles."

Before, such a silly unconventional answer would have unnerved Angie. But now it made her laugh. She was learning. This time, the mother did not disregard her daughter's eccentricity, but celebrated it. She drew her a wonderful crazy drawing—just what Heather ordered—a wild cake like no one had ever seen before, covered in french fries jutting every which way.

Sunflowers Point toward the Sun

Heather's favorite book, *People Should Be Like Sunflowers*, which her aunt had given her, had a special message: Sunflowers turn their back on what's scary. They keep turning their faces toward the light, toward the sun. As the sun moves across the sky, the sunflower turns to follow. The message was to be like a sunflower when you are scared or worried. Don't be afraid; just turn to the sun.

What could be scarier than getting radiated? What could be scarier than having cancer cells eating up your body? After rainbows, Heather's favorite thing to draw was sunflowers.

One day, Heather had an idea. Using the oils kit she carried with her everywhere, she bent over in front of a mirror in the bathroom and painstakingly painted a bright yellow sunflower on her bald head.

Once it was done, it made her feel merry. She wore a plastic cap when she showered so the bright yellow image would not wash off. The sunflower on her head was her signature, her special mark. She was so proud of her new look that she drew a picture of herself with the sunflower head to share with her mom. And I took a photo of her, as well, to bring to the prison.

When Angie saw the picture of Heather's head with no hair and the flower on it, her response was negative. "There she goes, being a little weirdo kid. Who would think of that? Get her a hat; get her a wig. Why does she want to call attention to her difference?" In fact, Angie decided that she would knit Heather a hat, and she was determined to give it to her in person.

A Visit from Prison

Angie applied to prison authorities for permission to visit her daughter and relentlessly kept after them. It took weeks of processing. Meanwhile, Heather was getting sicker and sicker. Finally, authorization came through;

under heavy guard, escorted by prison security in uniform, Angie would be allowed a one-time visit to her little girl in the hospital.

Heather had to be prepared; she hadn't seen her mother in quite a while. Neither of them knew what to expect or even how to act with each other.

Heather's aunt and I met Angie at the hospital entrance. The guards and prison escort watched Angie like a hawk as we all went up the elevator to Heather's room.

Angie said hello to Heather and held out the hat she had made for her. Heather glanced at the hat and said nothing. She was trying to be gracious, but she did not want the hat. Her aunt tried to smooth things over. "Aren't you going to say thank-you to your mom? She made this for you. Here, let me put it on."

"No." Heather had her boundaries; she would not put on the knitted cap. She did not throw a tantrum, but she set the hat aside. Angie's face dropped. She felt rejected by her daughter, and hurt.

Then Angie glanced at the wall and her eyes widened in astonishment. All of her drawings, from the crude to the carefully drawn, were displayed in Heather's room. Heather had put every one of her mother's drawings up on her wall. So they did not talk about the hat or Heather's lack of hair; they talked about the drawings.

This was one of Heather's last good days. After this visit, she went quickly downhill.

Breakthrough

Angie went back to the prison. At last, she was beginning to realize an important truth: her daughter was a brave girl, facing her own death with courage and creativity. One day Angie took out her paints. She shaved her head and painted it with a sunflower.

She asked me to take a photo of her sunflower head and take it to Heather. When I arrived at the hospital several days later, Heather was sleeping.

"Wake up," I said softly, kneeling by the side of her bed. "I want you to see something."

Heather looked at the photo in my hand and beamed. By that time, she could not say anything; soon after she slipped into a coma. This was a few days before she died.

Angie's Transformation

I went to the prison to tell Angie the news that her daughter had died. I told her that when Heather saw the picture of her mother's head, her face lit up, radiant with joy. Then I told Angie what her drawings had communicated to Heather and how much they had meant to her. Angie broke down sobbing. She never thought that her simple drawings could have that much impact. This was the beginning of Angie's inner healing; she was on her way to becoming a changed person.

When the time came, I went before Angie's parole board to tell them about Heather and the art exchange. I showed them the last picture Angie drew for her daughter. Black bars totally covered the frame of the picture; in the middle was a bird in flight with one wing behind the bar and one in front. The bird was not stuck in the cage, but free—coming at you. This picture marked a major shift; Angie had moved out of self-absorbed attention. "Fly away little one!" she had written on the bottom.

I told the parole board about the sunflower on Heather's head and showed them the photo of it. I talked about how Angie had reached out and affirmed her daughter, then I showed them the picture of Angie's shaved and painted head, at one with her little girl. One woman on the parole board was a tough, no-nonsense person. When she heard the story about the sunflower, she shed a couple of tears. The parole board commuted Angie's six-year sentence to four years, of which she had already served two.

Angie began to realize that, in fact, she could be a good artist. By drawing every day, she had developed a personal style. The bird in her last picture for

Heather was not bad. This last picture was not like a four-year-old's any-more. She continued to draw and paint while she completed her sentence.

Today, Angie works at a senior center teaching art therapy. She paints watercolors and uses different mediums, including crayons. She shows the seniors Heather's last picture. She was a very sick little girl when she drew this picture, and she knew that she was dying.

When Heather painted her final rainbow she reversed the corners where she had always put herself and her mom, putting herself in the lower-right corner. She covered this corner with a thick layer of many colors, then scratched out big white letters in the middle of it. The letters read, "HI"! Her last word to her mother, "HI," declaring them forever connected.

People come to Angie's classes for healing. When they say, "I can't draw." or "I hate to draw," she smiles at them and gives them the easy answer, the answer that changed her life. "Draw like a four-year-old."

Heather's Spiritual Diagnosis: Relatedness Pain

Be Open to Learning from the One Who Is Dying

Heather is the teacher in this story although she was only a little girl. A young child illustrates the important lesson that, regardless of age or cir-cumstances, the dying are our teachers.

Celebrate Uniqueness

At the end of life, the caregiver needs only to accept the patient and allow her to be herself. Heather had to know that it was okay to be differ-ent and that her mother accepted her for who she was, not for what she wanted Heather to be. When Angie moved from a place of trying to change her little girl to celebrating her daughter's uniqueness, Heather's idiosyn-crasies became not just endearing but signs of her incredible depth.

Pay Attention to Clues

Heather needed to create and live in her own world in order to survive. Facing unusually challenging life circumstances, Heather's extraordinary creative talents also provided important clues about her fears and isolation.

Consider Intervention

Since time was running out for Heather, an intervention was called for, though it is always scary to step in the middle of a dysfunctional relationship. The recommendation to communicate through drawing worked because it drew on Heather's core strengths. The result was a creative solution that invited both mother and daughter to find common ground for communication.

Spiritual Responses to Heather's Pain: Art Therapy

Revelation of the Inner State

Art therapy was the primary vehicle for healing between Heather and Angie. Particularly for a small child, or for someone who has limited verbal capacity, any form of creative expression can reveal a picture of their inner state of being (see "Art Therapy" in part III, "The Tool Chest"). A deep burst of spirituality can sometimes come from children who are ill. Through her painting and her cereal boxes, we get a view of Heather's heart and soul.

Healing Goes Two Ways

Art also unlocked Angie. Drawing and painting became a new kind of language that dissolved old barriers of misunderstanding between mother and daughter. Painting became a way for Heather to write to her mother and for Angie to write back.

At the end of Heather's life, Angie's painting of a sunflower on her head became a picture worth a thousand words. With this final gesture Angie went further than acceptance. Heather's unconventional ways stopped being a source of upset, and Angie could show that she was on Heather's side. Through the simple act of drawing pictures, mother and daughter became united.

Presumptions Surrounding Heather

In the face of a difficult situation, it is impossible to remain totally objective. We inevitably form judgments and presumptions about people. Naming these can free us to discover creative, out-of-the-box solutions. In Heather's case, there were several erroneous assumptions.

+ We presumed that because of Heather's introverted personality, she did not want to let others into her world.

+ We presumed that Angie would never have a comfortable relationship with her extraordinary daughter.

+ We presumed that the obstacle of incarceration made significant communication between Heather and Angie impossible.

+ We presumed that a lifetime of hurt, misunderstanding, and alienation could not be overcome.

+ We presumed that Angie would remain a hardened person because of tragic life circumstances.

Lessons for the Anamcara: Supporting the Dreamer Personality

Dreamer personality types are not immune from any of the four dimensions of spiritual pain at the end of life. Here are general guidelines for the anamcara that can help to identify which area of spiritual pain is primary.

Meaning Pain

Challenge: Above all, Dreamers want to distinguish themselves from others and from the parts of life that seem ordinary and unimaginative. Dreamers find superficial relationship and conversation frustrating. Without depth or intimacy, this personality type tends toward withdrawal, self-absorption, and melancholy.

Opportunity: Dreamers place great value on creating a world that is deep, beautiful, and meaningful. Provide support by listening deeply. Trust that they possess a natural ability to find creative solutions and a renewed sense of purpose when engaged and encouraged.

Forgiveness Pain

Challenge: Dreamers are among the most emotionally astute personality types. Their naturally intuitive nature, however, can get them in trouble when they overly personalize the responses of others. In the face of personal failure, this hypersensitive type can also be extremely self-critical and unforgiving.

Opportunity: Being a clean mirror back to a Dreamer is a great gift. When a Dreamer becomes excessively identified with his feelings, the anamcara may help to move the person from resentment to compassion.

Relatedness Pain

Challenge: Conflicts arise when Dreamers lose a sense of objectivity. Jealousy and envy sometimes sabotage the very relationship or thing that a person most desires.

Opportunity: When Dreamers focus on life's missing elements of happiness, support them in appreciating relationships and things as they are.

Hopelessness Pain

Challenge: Dreamers become trapped by wasteful fantasies and impossible expectations. Feelings of shame and being defective can lead to dark episodes of depression and despair.

Opportunity: The prayer of gratitude can be a powerful antidote to the paralysis of hopelessness. Help the Dreamer to see how his or her small hopes and dreams sometimes stand in the way of finding real hope and fulfillment.

Overarching Advice

When emotional balance is achieved, the Dreamer's behavior changes from reactivity to creativity. This personality type finds it difficult to remain focused on the reality of the present. The trap is either to remain stuck in past, unfulfilled expectations or to develop anxiety and dread about the future. The anamcara can remain sensitive to this suffering while encouraging any spiritual practice that supports what is real instead of what is fantasy.

HOSPICE | PATIENT CHART

NAME PARK

AGE 37 | **GENDER** ☒M ☐F | **RACE / ETHNICITY** Asian-American

BORN IN Seoul, South Korea

MARITAL STATUS Separated | **CHILDREN** ☐Y ☐N

VOCATION Computer Technician, Inventor

SPIRITUAL / RELIGIOUS ORIENTATION Buddhist / Presbyterian

DIAGNOSIS ALS (Lou Gehrig's Disease)

PROGNOSIS 3-4 months

OBSERVATIONS Park is a hardworking entrepreneur who values his independence above all else. His physical condition is deteriorating ~ He seems to be a loner.

Park: the Thinker

Will you love me even if I lose everything in life?

ALS—a rare and progressive degenerative disease—ravages the nervous system but does not touch the mind. The ALS patient eventually loses the capacity to speak or move. The tragedy is that while people with ALS may appear to be like vegetables, they still have all their mental faculties. Park's mind was as sharp as ever inside a body he could not control.

The spiritual pain Park was dealing with was Hopelessness. The tools that provided the breakthrough were spiritual geographying and a meditation practice called centering prayer.

Park's Story

Park was a young man in his late thirties. He was born in South Korea and educated there in American schools. Fluent in English, he moved to the United States in his twenties and married an American woman.

Park had a background in chemistry, computer science, and business, especially the dry-cleaning industry. He had invented a technologically brilliant computer system for cleaning clothes, a system where the chemicals used in the process would be less harmful and carcinogenic to the workers.

With a strong work ethic, Park was on his way to being a successful businessman, regionally and nationally, with the potential for being a wealthy man. Then he was diagnosed with ALS (amyotrophic lateral sclerosis), also known as Lou Gehrig's disease. When Park was diagnosed, his wife abandoned him. She did not have the stamina to face his deterioration.

Three Chaplains—Fired

Growing up in Korea, Park was exposed to two different backgrounds: his father was a Buddhist and his mother was Presbyterian. He was avidly interested in both spiritual traditions, though he leaned more toward Christianity, even considering becoming a minister at one point. Along with his scientific bent and study, he had gone to a Baptist Bible College in Korea. Jokingly, he called himself a "Ba-Bu" (Baptist-Buddhist).

Park had a reputation in hospice even before Richard met him. There were four spiritual caregivers at the hospice where Richard was working; Park had "fired" three of them. Though one of the chaplains was a Baptist, none of the chaplains could pass Park's scripture test. Richard knew that, with his Roman Catholic background, being unable to quote biblical chapter and verse, he might not even make it through the front door.

Richard's First Meeting with Park: The Book of Ester

As fate would have it, the day I first visited Park, in my briefcase, with my Bible and other things, I had a book by Thich Nhat Hanh, a Vietnamese Buddhist monk, entitled *Be Still and Know: Reflections from Living Buddha, Living Christ.*

As usual, I looked for the altars. When I saw Park's stark surroundings, I was convinced that he was a rugged individualist. He lived in the back of a cleaning establishment in a meager storage room. There were no pictures on the walls, no homey touches. The feel was Spartan, and the place had an old closet, musty, thrift shop kind of smell to it.

As soon as he saw me, Park came right to the point. "So, what would you do for me?" I was surprised; that was the first time anyone had asked me that question so directly. I answered that I would want to know about Park and how I could support him.

Park was clipped in his response. "What does that mean?"

I understood that Park enjoyed the study of scripture, so I told him that I would bring my Bible and we could talk. Saying that, I opened up my briefcase and began to unpack it. Putting aside the Thich Nhat Hanh book, I took out my Bible.

"Turn to the Book of Ester. Read chapter four verses twelve through fourteen," Park instructed.

I began to read.

> Taking off her splendid garments, she put on garments of distress and mourning.
>
> Help me, who am alone and have no help but you, for I am taking my life in my hands.

"Stop," said Park, holding up his hand. "What does that say to you?"

I answered that Ester's prayer was the prayer of someone about to commit suicide. Ester was contemplating ending her life, and she was crying out for help. What would bring a person to that kind of despair? This answer apparently showed Park that I would be willing to sit there without judging, and that it would be safe to explore depression together.

"I think we might get along," he said. "Come by next week."

At this point, Park could still speak, although some of his words were slurred. He knew that soon he would not be able to talk. Abruptly, he asked me, "Do you know about ALS? Do you realize that it is just a matter of time, and I won't be able to talk, to eat, to go to the bathroom? It will get so bad I won't be able to do anything without help, and I will be here watching the whole thing happen?"

In other words, if ever there were a reason for a human being to feel the despair of Queen Ester, this would be it.

Continued Visits

As I continued to visit Park, I found a man of few words with a complex interior, the proverbial still waters running deep. In place of anxious or frenetic energy, he was observant.

Park was a scientist with an inquisitive mind; he was looking for a spiritual caregiver who would journey with him.

Each time I went to see him, I noticed subtle changes in Park's condition. I also found that Park wanted to talk about what was different from last week to this week. In the beginning, he was still able to get around; he could go to the refrigerator and drink the shakes that had been prepared for him. But his nervous system was shutting down, and his scientific mind was trying to figure out how to stay independent.

East versus West: Buddha and Christ

One visit, Park finally told me why he kept me on as his chaplain. I thought it was my commentary on Ester, but it was not that at all. Rather, Park had noticed the copy of Thich Nhat Hanh's book that I had set aside. "When I saw you were reading that book, I knew we could talk," Park said.

An amazing conversation unfolded then that continued until Park's death, about the nature of his illness, the meaning of life and death, the differences between East and West, and what it meant to be a disciple of Jesus and a son of Buddha.

Park not only had an extraordinary mind for chemistry and computer science, but a staggering appetite for philosophy and theology as well. As a person born in Korea now living in America, he had remarkable insight into both worlds.

In the dingy room where he lived, the beauty was not in decoration or creature comforts but in a most incredible library of great thinkers. Anticipating the degenerative nature of his illness, he had collected on his computer the philosophy of Wittgenstein, the complete works of Thomas

Merton, along with Buddhist sutras, and an exhaustive collection of Bible commentaries. He had disks with translations; he had scanned texts of entire books in preparation for the time when he could not turn pages. The computer was something he could control.

Everything he treasured, he downloaded to his hard drive. He could access page after page of text, with an equally large library of philosophy, theology, chemistry, and other scientific works. He was able to weave in and out of the liberal arts or the scientific worlds effortlessly and draw out various insights and connections.

Park was completely comfortable living in his own head. His intention was to have information available for as long as possible; but it was more than knowledge for knowledge's sake. The questions that he was asking were coming out of a deeper place. His concerns and preoccupations were not, "What is going to happen to me next? What will I do when I can't walk?" Rather, they were couched in terms of larger questions, philosophical questions about what was happening to him.

When he asked me to consider Ester's story and wondered whether suicide is a legitimate option, he was not looking for an answer but exploring the question for himself. At what point would he not want to live anymore? Would it be when he was no longer able to feed himself? Or when he had no control over his bowel functions? What would constitute a quality of life that was finally unacceptable?

Breakthrough Moment: Truth Has No Boundaries

What appealed to Park about the Buddhist monk, Thich Nhat Hanh, was that he recognized a kindred spirit in him, someone else grappling with the larger questions.

He explained, "In South Korea, for my mother, a Christian, you had to make a choice. For my father, it did not matter, as long as I was on a spiritual path. So I became a Christian to please my mother, but for me, I kept the part of my father where to become a Christian was not a matter of subtraction (losing my Buddhist background) but an addition. Christianity was something I added *to* what I already was."

Park saw America as a land of bifurcation, this *or* that. In Thich Nhat Hanh, he found a mentor who could see that every part of the truth belonged. When you are a happy Christian, you are also a Buddhist, and vice versa. Park would refer to certain teachings in *Living Buddha, Living Christ* and want to talk about them. A critical point in Park's discussions came one day when he came across a particular line from Thich Nhat Hanh: "Most boundaries are artificial; truth has no boundaries."

Park did not believe as some do that nothing matters; he had the passionate commitment of a deep seeker, and he knew truth could be found in both traditions. If you knew spiritual traditions deeply, you saw how they complemented each other and led in the same direction. It was important for him to connect East and West. The challenge was to find a way to bring the traditions together. In a way, to bring his mother and father together.

Buddhist and Christian Mystics

Another key insight came from reading Thich Nhat Hanh:

Everything you say about God is a lie.

This did not mean that Park was indifferent. In fact, he was upset when he heard that some people think Buddhists are atheists. He explained that Buddhists only say what the mystics of all traditions say. He quoted Christian mystics like Meister Eckhart and Thomas Aquinas: "If it can be thought of, it's not God."

Being in Park's presence was humbling. He never put down another way of thinking; he would just say, "Oh that's sad." He had a powerful lesson to teach: Most of what concerns us about manmade religion is nonsense and immature. His Buddhist heart saw that body and spirit were not good or evil, they were not about life or death; rather, both were part of the same mystery. He could sit in the presence of a question like suicide and, rather than condemn it as immoral, could consider it in a larger way.

A spiritual tool or therapy to help him had to be able to hold the container of "both/and" instead of "either/or." An ideal tool was spiritual geographying.

Spiritual Geographying

Spiritual geographying is a way of understanding your life story in terms of ebb and flow. In its simplest form, spiritual geographying is a good workshop icebreaker. Participants are asked to list the three greatest moments of their life, and then the three worst moments. Making these two lists holds a surprise: people gain an instant insight into the most significant aspects of their life, what is important, and what needs to be healed.

Interestingly, after people do this easy exercise and reflect upon what they have written, a remarkable fact becomes clear. There is often a correlation between the high and low points; often the lowest point in life was just before a great blessing.

Spiritual geographying was an attractive tool for Park because it allowed him to look at the difficult things he was facing and not judge them as bad, but rather see them as a personal opportunity. This spiritual perspective resonated with his Eastern beliefs and also echoed the message of the beatitudes in Christ's Sermon on the Mount.

Park's philosophy of death was profound: "I am losing, one by one, the physical aspects of myself, but I am not losing myself." In this scheme of things, loss contained a potential freedom. The challenge was to frame it that way, to see the larger picture of his gradual deterioration.

> We are afraid of death, we are afraid of separation, and we are afraid of nothingness. In the West, people are very afraid of nothingness. When they hear about emptiness, people are also very afraid, but emptiness just means the extinction of ideas. Emptiness is not the opposite of existence. It is not nothingness or annihilation. The idea of existence has to be removed and so does the idea of nonexistence. Emptiness is a tool to help us.

—Thich Nhat Hanh, *No Death, No Fear*

Thich Nhat Hanh uses an analogy with waves to explain human nature. Waves can be big or small, high or low, but it does not matter; they are all water, they are part of the ocean. The mistake is when we think of parts of life as small waves, rather than as parts of the reality of human existence. Park believed that Jesus taught the same thing.

Detachment and Desire to Be a Thinker

Park had very little bitterness about his wife leaving. For one thing, since she was gone, he did not have to watch her struggle. He thought it would devastate her to see him so debilitated. For another thing, being alone gave him more space to figure out the impact of his illness without worrying about its effect on her.

He harbored a desire to be a thinker, a philosopher. Disease gave him both the opportunity and the time to reflect; there was nothing else to do. His illness forced him to focus on what was physically happening to him and to process what it meant. What opened up to him was a depth of understanding that he would not have had if he had continued working in the cleaning business.

One by one, Park began to lose control over his bodily functions, and he applied the rules of spiritual geographying to each step. Spiritual geographying became a game. The key was not to define a loss as "good" or "bad," which is the Western way. The Eastern way is to ask instead, Can I hold all of this as one? Is there a way of being slammed down and seeing the opportunity in it?

Losses and Corresponding Gains

The first stage of Park's physical deterioration was his loss of the ability to have an erection. In telling about that, Park smiled ruefully and said, "One thing has gotten easier; without a hard-on, I don't have to worry about women anymore."

Erectile dysfunction, in a strange way, was helping to cure the pain of losing his wife. Once and for all, it resolved the issue of her abandonment.

Passion no longer defined who he was. In some ways, he saw it as a relief, a letting go; impotency opened up more space to his interior search.

Park's larynx got weaker and weaker until finally he was no longer able to speak. The curse of losing his voice meant that he could no longer carry on the philosophical dialogue that he loved. But through spiritual geographying, he could explore a corollary.

Anticipating the loss of speech, he had already installed a synthesized voice system on his computer that could speak the words that he typed. Today entries on such software can be done with eye motion, but that development was not available to Park. He had to use a long stick in his mouth to hit each letter on the keyboard. The synthesizer could only "speak" a sentence at a time, and it took a long time to get each phrase down. I realized that our days of stimulating questioning and reasoning were over. The first thing Park typed was, "You look sad." I answered frankly, "Well, I am, Park."

Park smiled and worked hard to get the next sentence out, "I have it." I looked over Park's shoulder, watching him type, reading what he wrote. Park did not want me to do that. He wanted the program to talk. He motioned me to sit down in the chair.

While I sat waiting, I told Park that I would miss our longer conversations, but I was glad that he could manipulate the keyboard so we could continue to communicate. I asked him if he still wanted to do our spiritual geographying. When Park nodded yes, I asked him point-blank, "Okay, what's good about losing your voice?"

Park started working hard to get his answer down on his computer. He worked and worked at it; he was as determined and focused as a man running a marathon. At last, with a big grin on his face, he pushed the button to activate sound. A robotic voice said word by word, "Anything you say say say about God is a lie lie lie."

What was the blessing for Park in losing his voice? It took almost an hour to get to his bottom line: He could no longer speak, so he could no longer lie. The great mystics recognize that we are trapped by our own perceptions of God and reality. Park had come to the classical insight of mysticism: speculations about the spiritual life are a waste of time.

Soon after his voice went, Park lost the capacity to manipulate his computer. He no longer had muscle control; even tied to the computer, he flopped over, and he could not hold the stick to move the cursor and make words. His physical limitation meant he would not be able to express himself and his ideas. He no longer had the luxury of conversation or of research.

Park had previously set up a code system of communication with me. He knew his eye muscles would be the last to go. So he came up with a plan to spell out words with ocular movements and a system for signaling the basics. It was not enough to have one blink equal "yes" and two blinks equal "no." He added two other key expressions he wanted to be able to communicate easily: three blinks meant "thank you" and closing both eyes meant "amen."

Beat the Clock

It became a game of beat the clock. The challenge was to figure out, with every stage of his physical demise, what was left that was still essentially important to Park, or to discover something new that gave meaning to his life. Over and over, he asked himself, "How do I find a way with this new reality to still have purpose, still have hope?" And every step of the way, he found it.

In the end, Park became the profound spiritual leader he always wanted to be. Not a mystic in the sense of someone who levitates or has supernatural powers, but a kind of everyday mystic who could see beneath the surface of things to where everything is one.

Bedridden

Part of the cruel irony of ALS was that Park had been a fit man, who at one time had trained with the South Korean Olympic Team for discus and javelin throwing. At five foot six, he was well-built and stocky. This made it difficult work to transfer him to bed when he could not sit up any more. It was just a matter of time before he would have to move out of his place into a home and get twenty-four-hour care.

Park protested; he did not want to move from his apartment. The hospice team went to great lengths to respect his wishes. They found someone to coordinate a round-the-clock regime for him. They organized shifts of nurses so Park would never be alone.

A man who valued privacy above all, Park was totally dependent on others. Every one of his needs would have to be anticipated by someone else. Even the option of committing suicide was no longer available to him. Before, he could engage in a philosophical struggle of suicide; now he had to play out what was left of his life.

Morse Code Mantra

One time at this point when I went to see him, Park seemed agitated and ornery. He had a frantic look on his face. I tried to determine what was bothering him. "Do you need to be turned?" Two blinks; no. Are you hungry? Again, two blinks. He seemed to be staring toward his wheelchair. "Is it your wheelchair?" No. "The computer?" One blink; yes.

There was a message on the computer. Three words: "Morse code mantra." I knew that that meant it was time to start using the codified alphabet. I was also reminded of something else that was important to Park and part of our work together—centering prayer. Centering prayer is a monastic tradition of meditation using a mantra or single word or phrase in repetition.

I started seeing Park several times a week. It would take an entire visit to get out a couple of words, but he was still maintaining an amazing capacity to communicate, even with his body down to its last stages. He was fierce. His body could not do anything, but his mind was alert.

Using the alphabet communication code, Park got out the words, "the book." After much frustration, it turned out that he did not mean the Bible, but Thich Nhat Hanh's book. And not the book itself, but its title, *Be Still and Know*.

Be still and know. This would be the mantra to help him die well.

Centering Prayer

I had taught Park a simple form of prayer using Psalm 46, "Be still and know that I am God" (which was the basis of Hanh's title). The meditation shortens the phrase one word at a time, with several moments of silence in between each new sentence.

> Be still and know that I am God.
> Be still and know that I am.
> Be still and know.
> Be still.
> Be.

Centering prayer was a bridge between Christian and Buddhist traditions. By asking me to use Thich Nhat Hanh's title as a mantra, Park was orchestrating his own spiritual practice. The psalm was biblical. The final word, *Be*, was the epitome of Buddhist teaching. In the title of a book I happened to have with me on the day we first met was a practice we could do together.

Last Stage

The phrase in hospice is "actively dying." Park seemed nonresponsive. The nurses called me. It was just a matter of time. I went into his room and was pained by what I saw. A nurse was attending him, but lying in bed dying, Park seemed very alone. I hesitated only a minute, and then crawled into bed with him.

Park's breathing was shallow and rough; his pulse was racing. I could feel his heartbeat beneath my hand. Instinctively, I began the mantra we had practiced, pausing in silence between each shortened phrase. For half an hour or more, I repeated the prayer in its full cycle. Park's breathing evened out and became smooth and deep. Where before his breath was struggling and anxious, now it was calm.

The nurse was standing at the side of the bed, facing Park and watching this. I was behind him, on my side. By coincidence or synchronicity, Park's position was in keeping with Buddhist tradition. According to The Tibetan Book, the sacred position for dying is to be on the left, because that is the position the Buddha died in.

My arms were wrapped around Park, and my hand was on his chest when I got to the word Be. At that moment, I felt Park stop breathing, and I knew that he had died. The nurse saw his eyes glass over. I waited a minute or two. I was about to get up slowly when the nurse, who was facing Park, exclaimed, "Oh my gosh, he just blinked. Three times."

Park's Spiritual Diagnosis: Hopelessness Pain

Honor the Small Choices

Park's story is an important lesson about patient empowerment. Hopelessness is usually the result of helplessness. ALS is a particularly cruel disease that slowly destroys the body while leaving the mind intact. As Park's world shrank, it became all the more important to honor the small choices that he could still make.

Investigate Ways to Communicate

Hopelessness Pain is exacerbated by the inability to communicate. Park remained mentally alert throughout his disease process. By using his computer, creating his own Morse code, and speaking through his eyes, Park overcame the temptation of isolation and despair.

Let the Patient Be Proactive

It is important to defer to a person's need for some sense of control at the end of his or her life while providing appropriate support. Always let the patient lead the dance. Some concrete suggestions include:

+ Keep the patient in a familiar environment if possible

+ Be considerate of his or her need for privacy

+ Have familiar things around the patient

+ Respect the patient's timing and needs

+ Pay attention to the little signs of feedback that a person is always giving a caregiver

Suspend Judgment

In a real sense, Park became a mystic on his deathbed. But it was not without struggle. He needed space and freedom to explore every possibility open to him, including suicide. For Park, thoughts of suicide were not unreasonable in the early stages of his illness. Eventually his hopelessness was transformed into a remarkable commitment to continually discover life.

Spiritual Responses to Park's Pain: Spiritual Geographying and Meditation Practice

Analytical Appeal

Given Park's state of extreme spiritual pain, it took time and patience to discover which tool would be most helpful to him. The pain of hopelessness was alleviated by spiritual geographying, which also appealed to Park's analytical nature (see "Spiritual Geographying" in part III, "The Tool Chest"). As a Thinker personality type, Park needed something that would help him make sense out of his journey.

Discussion of Dichotomies

Park's work with spiritual geographying became a helpful framework for his own personal reflection as well as a jumping board for conversation. This practice supported Park's core Buddhist belief that there is no real separation between disease and wellness, dying and living, beginning or end. The Christian Beatitudes supported the same insights in terms of seeing blessing in what we try to avoid—sorrow, suffering, and illness. In other words, joy and sadness need not be separate realities.

Mantra as Provision for Calm

In the face of losing nearly all of his physical functions, Park used a form of centering prayer as a daily meditation practice (see "Meditation Practices" in part III, "The Tool Chest"). A simple mantra helped Park to be at peace with the world around him, to just be still.

Park discovered a form of centering meditation that bridged the Eastern and Western parts of his soul. Both traditions use the prayer of repetition as a way to support a contemplative state. Through the mantra, *Be still,* Park could meditate on the paradox that gave him comfort: A wave does not die to become water, she already is the water. Because Park had established a spiritual practice earlier on in his illness, a language for communication and support was in place during his final stages of dying.

Presumptions Surrounding Park

Assumptions were made in Park's case that appeared reasonable at first. But time clarified what he needed most at the end of life.

- We presumed that as Park's physical condition continued to deteriorate, he would attempt suicide.

- We presumed that being abandoned by his wife might be Park's greatest source of spiritual pain.

- We presumed that when Park was no longer able to speak, all significant communication would come to an end.

- We presumed that, given Park's upbringing, his spirituality would follow either an Eastern or a Western religious tradition.

- We presumed that an inventor and computer technician would have little interest in philosophy or theology.

- We presumed that a man who lived a very private life might not want a caregiver's intimacy at the end of life.

Lessons for the Anamcara: Supporting the Thinker Personality

In general, Thinker personality types prefer to observe and analyze life rather than fully participate in it. They experience spiritual pain according to their temperament. The anamcara can use the following guide as a way of supporting their friends.

Meaning Pain

Challenge: Thinkers have a strong need to make sense out of life. When facing a meaning meltdown, they tend to isolate themselves, trying to figure things out in their heads, rather than relying on relationships or the support of others.

Opportunity: A core issue for Thinkers is trust. The anamcara can invite them to face their fear of not understanding things when trapped inside themselves and encourage them to engage with the world rather than retreat from it.

Forgiveness Pain

Challenge: Rarely do Thinkers hold grudges against others. They can, however, severely beat themselves up with endless thoughts of self-doubt and hatred.

Opportunity: Self-absolution is necessary to set the Thinker free from the vicious cycle of not forgiving him or herself. Ironically, it usually takes an experience of compassion from the outside—or from others—to move the Thinker beyond such a lack of personal forgiveness.

Relatedness Pain

Challenge: Thinkers tend to live a detached existence, needing to figure out how things work by themselves. When the world seems unpredictable and insecure, relationships can feel threatening. This is when Thinkers typically retreat to their mental cave of isolation.

Opportunity: Those who truly love and support Thinkers in a time of crisis will give them plenty of space but refuse to abandon them emotionally. During times of extreme crisis, it is especially important to affirm the Thinker's warmth and humanity—qualities from which they often feel separated.

Hopelessness Pain

Challenge: The Thinker can appear to be emotionally challenged, especially during times of stress. Being cut off from others, however, is especially dangerous for this personality type, as it is impossible to think one's way out of hopelessness while alone.

Opportunity: When feeling overwhelmed, the Thinker often needs to hear about other options. A trusted anamcara can lead a Thinker to realize that even failures and struggles can be meaningful and rewarding.

Overarching Advice

Thinker personality types have an extraordinary ability to focus. The anamcara can support healthy thinking rather than obsessive analysis. Natural qualities such as a sense of humor, deep loyalty, and perseverance can deepen the Thinker's spiritual practice. The result will be an array of options in the face of life's challenges, rather than the paralyzing trap of limited possibilities.

HOSPICE — PATIENT CHART

NAME Sister Maria Elena

AGE 67   **GENDER** ☐ M ☒ F   **RACE / ETHNICITY** Hispanic

BORN IN Michoacan, Mexico

MARITAL STATUS Celibate   **CHILDREN** ☐ Y ☐ N   N/A

VOCATION Nun / Administrator

SPIRITUAL / RELIGIOUS ORIENTATION Roman Catholic

DIAGNOSIS Brain Cancer / Glioblastoma

PROGNOSIS 2 - 3 months

OBSERVATIONS Sister Maria Elena - hospital administrator and Mother Superior of her religious community for two decades. Terminal illness complicated by financial crisis of her motherhouse.

Maria Elena: the Loyalist

Will you love me even if I break the rules?

Sister Maria Elena, the former Mother Superior of a convent, had been diagnosed with a glioblastoma, an aggressive type of brain cancer. Every indication suggested she had only a few months left to live. The anticipated symptoms of this disease were that Maria Elena would either slip into a coma or a kind of dementia in which she no longer would be able to function in a normal way. This bright and powerful woman could soon be losing her mind.

You can imagine the fear, not only of Sister Maria Elena, but also that of the sisters who had depended on her. To add to the prevailing stress, Maria Elena's illness coincided with a financial crisis in the community.

The spiritual pain Maria Elena was dealing with was Meaning Pain. The tools that provided the breakthrough were guided visualization, sacred readings, and exercises to heal her image of God.

Maria Elena's Story

Sister Maria Elena lived by authority. She followed the Church's rules to the letter. A Hispanic woman in her late sixties, Maria Elena had spent over twenty years of her life as a religious superior, the spiritual and moral leader of a community of Catholic nuns whose ministry was primarily health care. She negotiated this group of sisters through turbulent years as religious life and health care ministry changed dramatically.

The sisters would soon have to make an important decision. The reduced number of working sisters, the diminishing number of vocations to the sisterhood, and ensuing economic considerations meant that the community needed to vote on a financial remedy. The motherhouse and the grounds around it had been the physical center of the sisters' community for nearly seventy years. Now the only way out, it seemed, was to sell it all.

More than just losing a beautiful piece of land and classic brick buildings, putting the property on the market symbolized a reality for the community: the community itself was dying. They were not getting younger vocations. The novitiate, the building where young sisters had formerly been trained for nursing ministry, had already been turned into a retirement home.

Richard went to see Sister Maria Elena in the convent infirmary at the request of several sisters from her community who were taking one of his workshops on death and dying.

Richard's First Visit with Maria Elena: A Gracious, Calm Lady

When I went to see Sister, I encountered a lovely older woman, who, in spite of her poor health, was apparently in control of her situation. She was charming and delightful. Madre Maria, as she was affectionately called, had celebrated fifty years of religious life, mostly in hospital ministry and eventually in hospital administration. She was fluent in both English and Spanish, but she said with a smile, "Most of the time I speak English, but when I talk to God, I still speak Spanish."

After a half-hour visit, I offered to pray with her in Spanish. As I left, she asked whether I would be coming to do more workshops, and if so, would I please promise to come to see her again? That was my only indication that this visit was more than casual, that it seemed to have some meaning for her.

When I went back to my seminar, the sisters were curious to know how the visit went. I told them that what I saw was a gracious lady very much at peace, not at all fearful as they had warned me she would be. They raised their eyebrows and told me that I had met her on one of her good days.

Second Visit: Maria Elena Is Agitated

A couple of months later, I was back at the same location for the course's next session and fulfilled my promised visit. This time, I found a person in a different state than she'd been in at our first meeting.

Maria Elena remembered me, but she was fidgety and uneasy. I could see a significant deterioration. She was not sleeping well, and she looked exhausted. Her eyes were wide open and staring. I wondered whether her state was due to the brain tumor or whether it reflected her emotional life or spirit.

I spent a couple of hours with her. During that time, she began to unload some of her huge fear and anxiety, questioning God, questioning what she had done with her life. Had her life been in vain? While listening to her, at one point I said by way of encouragement, "Good, tell me more."

Maria Elena looked at me wide-eyed and exploded. "Good! You're telling me this is good?!" That was the button. She started cursing like a sailor.

At first I was taken aback. Was this the other side of her that the nuns were talking about? In fact, at the sound of the shouting, one of the younger sisters ran into the room, frightened. I assured her that everything was okay and asked her to leave. The rough edge disappeared. "Lo siento mucho" (I am very sorry), she said. And then, "Tengo miedo" (I am so afraid).

Having finally admitted this, Maria Elena became emotional and started to cry. She confided that she had no sense of what her life meant anymore. She felt abandoned and in desolation. I agreed to stay in touch, to call her on the phone and have weekly contact with her, just as I would regularly visit one of my hospice patients. We made an appointment for Thursday evenings at five o'clock.

Telephone Visits: Two Different Personalities

I began my weekly calls. The telephone visits were unpredictable and revealed two sides of Maria Elena. Sometimes when she answered the phone, I was talking to a dignified woman who was sweet and grateful for my call. She was polite and friendly and said she felt fine, just fine, thank you. At those times, the contact was brief, not more than ten minutes. But when she was wound up and troubled, the calls tended to last an hour or more. Over the months, the latter type increasingly became the norm.

Whenever Maria Elena's situation seemed out of control, she was more frantic and also more verbal. One Thursday, I suggested using a form of guided visualization with her at these more difficult times. Guided visualization is a gentle process, a kind of meditation that can be calming and also can provide insights and direction. It can be a deeply spiritual process, a means of tapping into your higher self. The procedure involves imagining carrying on a conversation with someone you respect in a place where you feel comfortable.

When we did guided visualization during our phone calls, Sister Maria Elena used a speakerphone. I put on music in the background. Speaking in a soothing voice, I suggested to Maria Elena that she close her eyes and get into a comfortable position, then become aware of her breath and relax any tension in her muscles.

I asked her to imagine a place where she felt at peace. For her, this was the ocean. She could hear the sound of the waves breaking, smell the seaweed and the salty air. She could taste the salt on her tongue and feel the breeze, the water's mist on her face, and the sand under her feet.

The next step, when she got to that place, was to invite whomever she wanted to be there with her as a companion. It could be her guardian angel, a saint, a friend, someone who had died, anyone she trusted.

The person who usually came up for her was her grandmother, an old woman from Mexico who had raised her. She called her *Lita*, short for abuelita, which means grandma. Lita was someone she could talk to; she felt safe with her.

I invited Elena to enter into a dialogue with her grandmother and talk freely about whatever was most distressing or important to her. The dialogue was mostly interior, quietly inside her head, but sometimes Maria Elena started talking out loud. Then I became a kind of third party in the conversation, sometimes facilitating or repeating a word or phrase, but mostly letting her take the lead. After these sessions, Maria Elena reported that she felt less stressed.

Psalms Echo Despair

One week Maria Elena told me that she was getting nothing out of prayer anymore, so I asked whether she would be willing to pray out of her desperation. Instead of not praying because she was feeling so far from God, what would it be like to use the place of her despair as the foundation for her prayer? She was willing to try.

We started with Psalms first in Spanish, such as Psalm 22: "¡Dios mio, Dios mio! ¿Por qué me has abandonado?" In English this translates to: "My God, my God! Why have you abandoned me?" These Psalms allowed Maria Elena to curse, to scream out, to express herself out of the dark night of her circumstances. Instead of praying to make things better, I recommended that she shout out the words of the psalms, shake her fist at God, and repeat the verses that described what she was feeling. If she felt energy around a certain phrase, I told her to say it again, say it louder, to shout it from her gut.

I continued to call once a week. I gathered psalms that addressed the same kind of doubt and despair that Maria Elena was experiencing and prayed with her over the phone. The sisters put the speakerphone on in her room so we could talk. One week I read poem prayers that a Dominican sister had written for the terminally ill. Stark and raw, they got to the gut of what it was like to be in spiritual doubt.

Crisis Moment

The next time I visited Sister in person, I encountered Sister Corona, the current superior of the community. Sister Corona had doubts about the approach I was using with Sister Maria Elena. I invited her to accompany me—with Sister Maria Elena's permission—and experience a guided visualization process firsthand.

Sister Maria Elena was not very alert that day. One of the younger sisters was trying to pray the rosary with her, but she was nonresponsive. I asked Maria Elena in Spanish whether she was willing to pray in our own special way, that is, using guided visualization. I asked everyone but Sister Corona to leave the room.

I put on some soft music and led Maria Elena through breathing and muscle relaxation. I invited her to go to her favorite place on the beach and asked her whether she would like to invite God to come and talk with her this time. She struggled; I intensified the struggle. I asked her to tell me about this God she was frightened of.

After a pause and some resistance, she blurted out words in Spanish that described a fearful image of God. I realized from her choice of words that the God she was conjuring up spelled fear and doubt, not comfort.

I invited her to encounter the God she feared and speak from her heart. At this suggestion, Sister Maria Elena exploded. "¡No hay Dios!" (I don't believe in God!) In a violent gesture, to the horror of Sister Corona sitting by her side, Maria Elena took her rosary beads and flung them across the room. There was a moment of stunned silence. Then Maria Elena broke down sobbing. "Siento mucho." (I am so sorry.) While weeping, she confessed sorrow-fully, "¡Estoy seguro de que soy ateo!" (I am sure I am an atheist!)

Sister Corona was shocked, and she tried to reassure Maria Elena that she was anything but an atheist. She turned to me and said, "It's just the medication and the disease talking."

Sister Corona reluctantly agreed to let me stay in touch with Maria Elena on the phone even though she was concerned that I was feeding into Maria Elena's crisis of faith, rather than helping her. I left with a sense of doubt about whether leaning into the pain is always the best solution. Was I doing the right thing by trusting that code? Did that principle hold true in the case of a brain tumor?

Sister Corona answered when I called the following week. "Madre is resting nicely," she said. "Everything is fine here and in control, thank you. The doctors said her condition is worsening. She is not responsive at this point. It would be meaningless to talk with her." Suddenly, in the background, I heard Maria Elena screaming, "Just give me the phone!"

Sister Corona was whispering, yet Maria Elena knew who it was. For me, that loud belligerent demand was a confirmation that my approach was helping her. If I was hurting her, she would not want to talk to me. Sister Corona was a good person and wanted what was best for Maria Elena. She put on the speakerphone next to Maria Elena's bed so we could visit.

I encouraged Maria Elena to do what she needed to do. I told her not to judge herself on how she felt about God and faith. Sister Corona was famil-iar with the psalms, so I suggested that instead of praying the rosary with Maria Elena, she read the psalms, particularly the verses that allow being upset before God. Hearing these verses read to her would give Maria Elena permission to be upset and would allow her to continue to question her beliefs. These were the same verses used in the Celtic tradition to bring comfort. The laments became the prayer.

Healing Maria Elena's Image of God

Sister Maria Elena was getting weaker, but with Sister Corona's help, she could still do a guided visualization. Sister Corona would put on some music and sit by her side as, over the phone, I led Maria Elena through the familiar steps.

One week, once we got to the beach, I used the verses from Psalm 82: "You are gods, you are all gods." Inviting Sister Maria Elena to expand her notion of God, I suggested that she bring to mind anyone who was like God, who reminded her of God's goodness to walk with her. She invited Lita. "Talk to Lita about your struggle with God," I said. "Have a heart-to-heart talk." Eventually I heard Maria Elena's voice. "Ay Dios, ella es tan bonita." (Oh, my God, *she* is so beautiful.)

At the end of the meditation, Sister Corona told me that Sister Maria Elena was beaming with joy. It was a very emotional moment. Sister Corona said, "She is crying, but they seem to be tears of joy."

Community Crisis Comes to a Head

With the disease progressing rapidly, the physician said that Sister Maria Elena's death might be only days ahead. Her condition had deteriorated to a point where she barely seemed conscious.

All the sisters in the community would soon be coming together in a chapter meeting to decide about selling their property. Several of the nuns thought that the threat of selling the convent and grounds was what was killing Sister Maria Elena. They believed that she developed the brain tumor and willed herself to die, rather than face seeing the property be sold and witnessing the demise of her life's work. They decided not to have any conversations about the sale of the property within earshot of her.

The last time I went to see Sister Maria Elena, the nuns were in the middle of the chapter meeting. I sat down next to Maria Elena. Within moments of my sitting there, she opened her eyes. She stared at the ceiling with total composure and then she spoke, demanding to be taken to the meeting. The sister nurse sent word immediately to Sister Corona, telling her that Maria Elena was lucid and wanted to be brought to the chapel. At first, Sister Corona thought this would not be wise or appropriate. On reflection, she realized that Sister Maria Elena was asking to be heard, and they should respect that request. The constitution of the order said that every person in the community had a right to be at the meeting. The nuns wheeled Maria Elena in on a gurney. As soon as the vespers were over, Sister Maria Elena spoke in a low voice. "I have something to say to the sisters."

She was weak, and her voice did not carry, so they gave her a microphone. What she said, clear as a bell, was, "The time has come, sisters. You are more important than these old buildings. Just sell the whole *damned* place." That was it. That was her advice. There was a hush of silence, followed by a loud round of applause.

She had nothing more to say. They wheeled her back to her room. She lapsed into unconsciousness and died within a week. That was the last message that this spunky woman gave to her community.

Many of the sisters who were there felt they had witnessed an incredible vote of faith. Although struggling with doubt, the former Mother Superior had taken a firm, unequivocal stand, placing her faith in their mission, not the buildings and the property. Sister Maria Elena's declaration was a great credo. She was given permission to speak her truth.

Maria Elena's Spiritual Diagnosis: Meaning Pain

Create Space for Questioning

This chapter offers important insights into the delicate relationship among spirituality, religious and institutional faith, and healing unhealthy images of God. Maria Elena's story is an answer to an age-old question: Can doubt and insecurity be a path to faith?

Her story is a metaphor for what we put our faith in. After a life of faithful service to any institution, a struggle can show up at the end of life: Is this all there is? In the face of this "dark night of the soul," the task of the anamcara is to provide space to ask the courageous questions, even if it involves reexamining life's priorities.

Put Your Own Needs Aside

Maria Elena's spiritual pain was excruciating. A traditional religious environment exacerbated her ability to question her faith. Well-intentioned members of her community needed her to be okay for *their* well-being and security, leaving Sister no place to struggle with her own doubts and questions. The lesson is always to address what the patient needs.

Be Willing to Address Your Own Doubts

Facing spiritual pain makes us uncomfortable. It's okay to have doubts. But it is important to question whether the patient's discomfort may indicate something crying out for attention. Spiritual pain is often a sign that a person no longer wants to remain in denial of his or her feelings. Trust that this can be a window of opportunity for healing.

Listen without Judgment

The disease process brought forth another dimension to Mother Superior's personality—her personal doubt and conflict. Sister Maria Elena's outbursts expressed old inner demons regarding her relationship with God. The advice in such situations is to receive another's pain without being shocked or scandalized. Above all, trust the classical advice to do whatever is possible to help the patient *lean into, not away from the pain.*

Once Maria Elena faced her own demons, she could speak with a certain authority to the other members of her community. Supported by a new and courageous way of relating to God, Madre Maria's last act became her real spiritual legacy. In one sentence, she told her community what was most important.

Spiritual Responses to Maria Elena's Pain: Guided Visualization, Sacred Readings, and Healing Our Image of God Exercises

A Combination of Spiritual Therapies

Traditional approaches to prayer no longer served Maria Elena's needs during her terminal illness. She did not need to put on a pious front for others; she needed a place to express the doubts that were stealing her peace of mind. Find the spiritual practice that serves the patient's needs and desires, not those of the caregiver.

The therapies most useful to Maria Elena helped her face her crisis of faith rather than avoid it. Maria Elena needed a breakthrough and a larger context for what was meaningful to her. As is often the case, a creative combination of spiritual therapies provided the needed support.

Childhood Images of the Divine

The practice of sacred visualization allowed Maria Elena to face a long-feared, broken image of the sacred, which was crying out for healing. Often, our images of the divine are projections of our own limited understandings. She couldn't deal with a God who was harsh and judgmental, but her beloved childhood *Lita* became a symbol for the face of someone she could trust (see "Healing Religious Abuse and Images of God" in part III, "The Tool Chest").

Involving Family Members

It was important to invite Sister Corona into the guided visualization process (see "Guided Visualization" in part III, "The Tool Chest"). If some family members or friends are anxious about the use of certain therapies, everything possible should be done to address their concerns, or the effectiveness of the therapy will be compromised.

Prayer as a Cry for Help

By prescribing certain passages from the scriptures of her tradition, in this case the Book of Psalms (see "Religious Rites and Sacred Writings" in part III, "The Tool Chest"), Maria Elena's prayer became a genuine cry for help instead of pious pretending. The wisdom of the ancient sacred art of dying traditions encouraged any expression from the soul that was real. In the tradition of painful prayer, we leave behind the *thees* and the *thous* that often keep us separated from God, and dare to become real and direct.

Presumptions Surrounding Maria Elena

It is normal for caregivers to make assumptions when encountering the pain of others. It is important to be aware, however, that sometimes these assumptions can be misleading.

+ We presumed that Madre Maria would be a strong advocate *not* to sell the convent property.

+ We presumed that Sister Maria Elena's shift in personality was a tragic result of her cancer.

+ We presumed that the brain tumor caused Sister Maria Elena's outbursts.

• We presumed that facing fearful images of God might be harmful to Sister Maria Elena.

• We presumed that old forms of prayer might bring Sister Maria Elena comfort and keep her from cursing.

• We presumed that a crisis of faith is a bad thing.

Lessons for the Anamcara

Supporting the Loyalist Personality

The key dilemma for the Loyalist personality type is learning how to claim their own inner voice of authority, which can put them in conflict with outer authority. The Loyalist personality could encounter any of the four classical spiritual pains at the end of life. Here are some observations that may assist the anamcara if dealing with this temperament.

Meaning Pain

Challenge: Loyalists have a strong need to make sense out of life. Living primarily in their head, they are more comfortable in a world of black and white, knowing the rules of the game. When their world is turned upside down, their crisis of meaning is acute.

Opportunity: The anamcara can invite the Loyalist to explore the shades of gray they often overlook. Support the Loyalist in questioning unhealthy external voices of authority.

Forgiveness Pain

Challenge: A crisis of faith for a Loyalist does not necessarily involve faith or religion. Absolving oneself of self-doubt and self-contempt may be the most important forgiveness issue at the end of life.

Opportunity: An opportunity for a life review (see "Life Review Exercises" in part III, "The Tool Chest") can help Loyalists to see how healthy it is to trust their deepest truths, even when it places them in conflict with other persons or institutions.

Relatedness Pain

Challenge: Going against the grain or deviating from the rules can be threatening for the Loyalist. It is hard to admit that the very thing that we have been faithful to may have been the source of misplaced loyalty.

Opportunity: Support Loyalists in finding the courage to trust their own instincts about what really merits fidelity. A crisis of faith could be the doorway to deeper and more life-giving commitments.

Hopelessness Pain

Challenge: A profound dark night of abandonment occurs when old securities are swept away by the circumstances of life. The resulting hopelessness can be debilitating, threatening the Loyalist's very survival.

Opportunity: Any spiritual practice that can support Loyalists in getting out of their head will relieve moments of high anxiety. The practice of centering prayer or meditation (see "Meditation Practices" in part III, "The Tool Chest") is highly recommended as an antidote to the paralysis of fear.

Overarching Advice

Persons with a strong Loyalist personality tend to live in a world dominated by fearful expectations of what could go wrong. This demon of mistrust shows up in chronic worst-case thinking that undermines peace of mind and creates toxic inner tension. At the end of life, a problem that has been suppressed for years can become magnified. The anamcara can assist a Loyalist by creating space for them to express doubt and fear, followed by an invitation for them to trust at a deeper level of being that all shall be well. Ultimately, the Loyalist finds peace in the courage to trust his or her inner instincts as well as to challenge and even break the rules of unhealthy authority.

HOSPICE	PATIENT CHART

NAME ANDREW

AGE 22 **GENDER** ☒M ☐F **RACE / ETHNICITY** CAUCASIAN

BORN IN BOSTON, MASSACHUSETTS

MARITAL STATUS Single **CHILDREN** ☐Y ☐N N/A

VOCATION Chef, Entrepreneur

SPIRITUAL / RELIGIOUS ORIENTATION Agnostic

DIAGNOSIS AIDS (from blood transfusion)

PROGNOSIS Three months

OBSERVATIONS Andrew is a bright young man dealing with a rapidly advancing disease. In a wheelchair. Cared for by two devoted friends. Sense of urgency about this case.

Andrew: the Adventurer

Will you love me even if I cry?

Already in his young life, Andrew had had adventures that could fill several average lifetimes. Running away from home, he traveled cross-country. He created a rich and full life that amazed people twice his age. A blood transfusion compromised his immune system, and he contracted AIDS. A final New Year's Eve party provided an opportunity to release another kind of pain that had been stifling his spirit.

The spiritual pain Andrew was dealing with was Forgiveness Pain. The tool that provided the breakthrough was a "give away" ritual traditionally called a potlatch.

Andrew's Story

Andrew was born in South Boston, the son of a Northern Ireland expatriate. Andrew's father was a feisty guy, a prize-fighter and a fierce political activist in Ian Paisley's Orange Army. He brought his pregnant girlfriend, Andrew's mom, to the United States. They settled in Boston where Andrew was born.

Andrew did not have a lot of love for his Irish roots. Ireland represented his father's negative attributes. Andrew grew up with stories about the political hatred that divided Ireland, which gave him an intense religious dislike, especially of anything Catholic or Protestant. All his life, he heard stories about violence among the Irish factions. Ironically, though, Andrew had picked up some of his father's expressions and a bit of his dad's brogue.

His was not an easy childhood. He was raised in household of poverty, alcohol, and anger. At age fourteen, Andrew ran away from home and hitch-hiked to the West Coast, getting odd jobs along the way. By sixteen, he ended up with migrant workers in the San Joaquin Valley in California.

Andrew was a precocious boy who looked and acted older than his age. He was easily accepted in a labor camp community that was part Hispanic and part Chinese. He was the token white guy, the only American. He worked energetically round the clock. Everyone liked him.

The B & B Food Business

With no more than a grade-school education, Andrew taught himself about vegetable farming and Latin and Asian cuisines. He had two close friends, Joaquin from Columbia, whom everyone called Jack, and Lin Yee, who later became his fiancée. Both were older than Andrew.

As he earned a little money, Andrew got involved in sports betting through Jack. Andrew lucked out, and he and Jack wound up with a pot of money. They decided to invest their windfall in a food business. With Lin Yee, they became entrepreneurs, creating a catering service for the migrant camps, serving the kind of menu that would appeal to the Asian and His-panic laborers. They used to joke that theirs was "the world's first interna-tional fusion cuisine." Jack brought his Columbian experience with food; Lin Yee kept it healthy with her Oriental background. Andrew was one of the three cooks and doubled as the businessman who ran the show. Work-ing around farms, they had access to fresh produce, and the field workers were ready customers.

They named their mobile food station B & B—Bogotá to Beijing. Their venture was a huge success. It answered a need and did it with flair. The three friends and B & B were immensely popular, and they became relatively well-off. For Andrew, it was a heady experience, being an entrepreneur and achieving a level of financial independence at a young age, without an education. He was generous with his money, and he was always on the lookout for new adventures.

Birthday Trip to Boston

For his twenty-first birthday, Andrew had an idea for celebrating in a big way. He decided to return to Boston and take his two best friends with him. The Boston Red Sox were playing in the World Series, and there was a game in Fenway Park the week of his birthday.

Andrew's one fond Boston connection was baseball, the only thing he and his father had in common. However, the last time the Red Sox were in the World Series and lost, his father got into a fighting match after the game. Andrew's plan was to go back and replace that memory with a happy ballpark experience with his two good friends.

Following the Red Sox was an obsession with Andrew. Whenever Andrew got extra money, he spent it on a sports bet, whiskey, or sports memorabilia. He spent obscene amounts of money at collectibles stores for autographs or whatever he could get his hands on that had to do with baseball.

The three went to Boston. The Red Sox won the game and Andrew was ecstatic. Now the team was ahead 3–2; it looked like they had a good shot for winning the World Series. That night they went out to party.

Andrew had picked up his father's love of whiskey. Now here he was back in Boston, feeling free from his father's domination, shedding bad memories of Boston from his youth, showing off to his friends, and throwing his money around. He drank too much and got wasted. He told Lin Yee and Jack that he wanted to take them to the tenement house in the South Boston neighborhood where he grew up. When they got there, the building was abandoned and falling apart.

Impetuously, Andrew started climbing up the fire escape of the abandoned structure, trying to reach the eighth-floor apartment where he had lived. Jack and Lin Yee refused to follow. They screamed after him, "Andrew, get down. It's not safe." He made it to the landing. Feeling his oats, he balanced on the rail, showing off, whooping and hollering. From below, Jack and Lin Yee watched in helpless horror as Andrew lost his equilibrium and fell three stories into a metal dumpster by the curb.

Badly injured, Andrew was rushed to the hospital. He lost a lot of blood and was given a transfusion. He astounded the medical staff by announcing that he was ready to leave the hospital two days later. Against doctor's orders, he snuck out of the hospital in the middle of the night. The three went back to California. Youth was on Andrew's side. He bounced back, and soon the three friends hatched plans to expand and franchise their traveling restaurant idea.

But Andrew's energy was deceiving. Something had compromised his immune system. His red blood cell count was off. He contracted AIDS, and eventually the only way to keep his red blood cell count even was to remove his spleen. When that did not help, he was hospitalized in serious condition. Richard was teaching in San Joaquin Valley and had volunteered to help in a hospital in Ontario, California. He connected with Andrew there.

Richard's First Meeting with Andrew: The Tres Amigos

Andrew was a very noncompliant patient. The staff was on to his tricks—the reason he did not need morphine was that he had a secret stash of whiskey—but everyone was in love with him and with the other members of the trio affectionately called Tres Amigos. Jack, Lin Yee, and Andrew were inseparable. Over time, I became a friend and counselor to all three of them.

The first time I met them, they seemed like kids who had been through thick and thin with each other; they shared a level of commitment that bordered on the adolescent but had in fact matured them. Tres Amigos were an unlikely trio, and this crisis seemed to bind them even closer.

Their accents were heavy and hard to understand: the Boston Irish of Andrew, the "Beijinglish" of Lin Yee, and Jack's Columbian Spanish that most Mexicans could not understand. They spoke an English that was interspersed with phrases from all three native tongues. They completely understood each other, while those around sometimes scratched their heads, "What did you just say?" It was the most beautiful friendship I have ever seen, and was absolutely unconditional.

Bad News and Andrew's Response to It

Over the next few weeks, I continued to visit. Andrew's situation was increasingly desperate. The doctors tried every measure; nothing would turn his condition around. Finally it became apparent that he was going to die.

I was with them when the doctor came in to break the awful news. Lin Yee stayed with Andrew, but Jack couldn't stand it. He let out a howl and went running out of the room. I followed to console him. In the hallway, this short Columbian guy was pounding the wall and crying, "It's a fecking waste. It's a fecking waste." In the throes of great distress, he had taken on the borrowed Belfast speech of his friend.

Andrew's blood cell count had fallen to a dangerous point. White blood cells had taken over, and Andrew was hemorrhaging internally. They were going to put him on dialysis because his kidneys had shut down. The doctor wanted him to know that no more infusions were possible and the end was near. This was December 28.

While his two friends were beside themselves with grief, Andrew perked up, "I've got a bloody good idea. It's three days until New Year's Eve. We are going to party." He convinced the doctor to do a few more blood transfusions to keep his quality of life as high as possible for three days so he could make it to December 31.

Everyone Gathers for the Party

Andrew had been transferred to a nursing home. Everyone else there was in their seventies and eighties. The Tres Amigos talked the nurses and staff into letting them use the recreation room for their New Year's Eve party. The manager said, "You young folks can have the room. By evening, everyone here is sleeping. Nobody will be up at midnight." Andrew wanted the party to start earlier, though, and he wanted everyone to come. The manager agreed.

I have to admit I was not crazy about this plan. I felt sad that this was going to be about drinking lots of whiskey and getting blotto in the face of pain. Andrew could be within days of the end of his life, and I wanted to tell him that there is more to it than a party with no depth. It took him getting drunk to have the nerve to climb up the fire escape, and it was copious amounts of alcohol that braced him to return to his roots.

Everyone who knew Andrew knew there were buried issues under the extravagance of his life—under the excess, under the humor—unresolved issues with his family and with running away. When something was painful, Andrew's philosophy was to drink it, bury it, laugh it away, shrug it off. But Andrew was thinking about other things than booze. And it turned out that he had another reason, a profound and courageous reason, for wanting to start the party early.

The party started at six o'clock. Andrew went up and down the hall in his wheelchair, putting hats on old men's and women's heads. "Party time!" he said. "C'mon down." He wanted everybody to be there. Lin Yee and Jack brought in the most incredible spread of food. Andrew had insisted that the party not be funereal. He did not want any flowers around because they reminded him of a mortuary. The party went on for hours: extravagant food, music, and dancing. When it was getting close to nine o'clock, Andrew signaled to stop the music. He wanted to say something, to raise a toast, to address everybody there.

Andrew's Speech

First, Andrew asked Lin Yee to bring him one of the beautiful tomatoes that were part of the buffet. Taking a microphone, he started by thanking everyone for being there. "There are a few things I would like to say. There isn't a luckier guy on the face of the earth this New Year's Eve than me." He showed the tomato and talked about what it was like being a kid where there was no such thing as a tomato like this; vegetables in Boston did not look or taste like this.

"This is why I ran away from home. Those of you who have worked in the fields must think I am crazy. Who would come out here to pick vegetables? It's a hard life out in those fields. But the hot sunshine makes the tomato ripen. You can pick one of these and eat it off the vine." He took a bite, held the tomato up high, and let the juice run down his arm.

"I came out here and found real vegetables, real work, and real people. And I want to say the reason I am the luckiest guy in the world are these two people next to me tonight, Jack and Lin Yee. I don't think most people would ever in a lifetime have one friend like this; I've had two." Jack and Lin Yee smiled and looked at him with great affection.

Andrew went on, "I have spent a lot of my life running away. But sometimes you've got to stop running. There is no place for me to run anymore. I am very sick; I am not going to get the chance to become an old fart like most of you here." He stopped and looked around. Then went on, "There are three things I have to do tonight. First of all, I have to give away my Major League baseball collection."

At that, Andrew signaled to Jack, who followed him with a big box as he went around the room giving stuff to the people there. He didn't just hand things out; he accompanied each item with a story, a significance. He would take an autographed ball, for example, and say, "Do you know what this is? This is a baseball signed by Roger Maris. Man, you better take care of this, I spent a hell of a lot of money buying it."

Because I am from Detroit, he gave me a baseball autographed by out-fielder Al Kaline of the Detroit Tigers. "The damn Tigers won the World Series against the Boston Red Sox," he said, "and I want you to have this."

After the baseball memorabilia was gone, Andrew went through the box and gave out a whole pile of personal belongings: a boom box, a snazzy sports coat, anything that was valuable to him was in there. Then he wheeled himself back to the front of the room and took the microphone again.

"The second thing I've got to do tonight is to propose to Lin Yee." He took out a jade ring. "When I was in Chinatown, I bought this."

He tried to stand up, to get out of his chair, but he was too weak and she wouldn't let him. She took the ring, put it on her finger, and began crying. She did not say a word, but she accepted the ring.

Times Square at Midnight and the Third Thing

Andrew looked up at the clock on the wall. "Hey, someone turn up the volume on the TV. It's midnight in Times Square. They are singing 'Auld Lang Syne.'" Soon the strains of the song and the merriment on TV filled the room.

"The last thing I gotta do tonight is toast my old man. The only time I ever heard me father cry was when this song came on. He was usually tanked, but 'Auld Lang Syne' brought up some connection about the old country, and this tough bird prize-fighter let his family see him cry.

"It's midnight back on the East Coast, midnight in Boston, and I've been pissed off at that son of a bitch my whole life but, Pop, you did something for me." Andrew raised his glass. He was crying now himself. "You made me a fighter. That's what got me through here, and that's what makes me the luckiest man in the world tonight. In honor of you, Da, the weirdest little traveling restaurant in California is no longer B & B; it's B & B & B. Belfast to Bogotá to Beijing."

The people at the party were stunned. They did not know what to say. Then Jack broke the silence. Raising his glass in a toast to Andrew, he said,

"I'm not a religious guy, but I never heard a sermon as eloquent as that." The room was filled with applause, everyone crying and clapping all at once.

Andrew had tough days ahead; being taken off dialysis is not easy. His two friends lived by his bed; Lin Yee slept with him every night. He died on January 7, his two friends by his side.

Andrew's Spiritual Diagnosis: Forgiveness Pain

Look Beneath the Surface

Andrew was a survivor. Painful circumstances pushed the young adolescent out of the nest much earlier than normal. While no one would fault his adventuresome spirit, Andrew was also running away from his past life. Underneath Andrew's carefree exterior was a lifetime of disappointment, anger, and unforgivingness. Good friends know how to be there when the pain of life brings these demons to the surface.

Face the Facts behind the Father-Wound

This story is an archetype of the male journey. Andrew was more like his dad than he cared to admit. He was in a perpetual state of rebellion against his father's compulsive personality. The paradox is that in running away from pain, the pain often disguises itself in new and subtle ways. Eventually, the qualities Andrew hated most in his father became something he was able to see as a gift in himself.

Love the Addict Not the Addiction

Andrew had an addictive personality. In his elaborate attempts to create a life of enjoyment and success, he was haunted by what he was trying to avoid. In dealing with persons who struggle with addiction, trust that their reckless, impulsive tendencies stem from the energy of the very thing they are trying to avoid. Love the addict enough to help him face this truth.

Let Pain Be the Healer

Andrew's philosophy of life was that you can't hit a moving target. By keeping his options open, Andrew tried to keep pain at arm's length. But as death approaches, emotional pain is impossible to escape. If it is true that pain which is not transformed is always transmitted, then the job of friends and caregivers is to allow pain to have its voice, so it teaches us rather than controls us.

Address Anger and Regret When Death Is Untimely

Andrew died very young. He had an unusually vibrant spirit, which a cruel accident stole away. There are differences in how to support younger persons who are terminally ill. They may feel anger and regret for the parts of life that they will not live and resentment for unrealized dreams. In Andrew's case, his peers faced his untimely death and loss with him. At any age, however, death is a powerful teacher. Jack and Lin Yee's lives were forever impacted by Andrew's death.

Orchestrate Your Own Farewell

Andrew's final New Year's Eve party was an extraordinary event. Instead of cursing his situation, Andrew found an opportunity to celebrate his passing with those he loved. In many cultures throughout the world, this kind of farewell event for family and friends is commonplace. When the dying are honored as teachers, this venue can be a legacy to normalize death as a part of the rhythm of life.

Spiritual Responses to Andrew's Pain:
The Giveaway and
Other Deathbed Celebrations

Divestment of Material Possessions

Some Native American traditions call their giveaway celebration a pot-latch (see "Potlatch," in part III, "The Tool Chest"). The essence of a give-away ceremony is an opportunity to divest oneself of all material possessions, in this case while the giver is still alive. Generosity and detach-ment are the ideas behind the potlatch. Counterculturally, the potlatch teaches that, "He who dies with the *least* stuff wins." In Andrew's story, there were big rewards for everyone involved. The celebration was not so much about *the stuff* as it was an attitude of freedom. Perhaps in a culture that tends to emphasize material possessions, the potlatch is a tradition worth considering.

Deathbed Celebrations

Some people might be put off by the idea of an engagement or other sim-ilar events celebrated at the deathbed. For Andrew, proposing to Lin Yee was a way of expressing the depth of their friendship and love. It is not uncom-mon on the eve of death to hear of persons requesting baptisms, Bar Mitz-vahs, and the exchange of wedding vows. These ceremonies can be very profound as they constitute a kind of last wish for the dying person. Friends will honor the dying person by participating to the degree that they can.

Reconciliation Ceremony

Perhaps the most poignant deathbed celebration is granting absolution to a long-held grudge. At the stroke of East Coast midnight, Andrew was moved to toast his father from whom he had been seriously alienated. The cliché that there are no liars on deathbeds is true: Andrew needed to acknowledge the part of his relationship with his dad that he could sincerely honor. The change in the name of Andrew's food service business served as a final act of reconciliation with his hometown roots.

Presumptions Surrounding Andrew

It is a challenge for caregivers who enter into a dying person's life with no previous relationship. There can be a sense of urgency to learn all that there is to know about the person in order to provide the best support. The danger is that it is easy to fall into the trap of preconceptions and assumptions. Andrew's case was no exception.

+ We presumed that because of his youth, Andrew might succumb to bitterness after his diagnosis with AIDS.

+ We presumed that Andrew would take his ill feelings toward his father to his grave.

+ We presumed that Andrew and Lin Yee would remain just friends.

+ We presumed that Andrew's New Year' Eve party would include a drinking bash to numb the pain of his imminent death.

+ We presumed that Jack and Lin Yee might not have the capacity to walk through the pain of Andrew's final days.

+ We presumed that Andrew would consider his final days in a nursing facility to be depressing.

+ We presumed that Boston, a place that represented pain for Andrew, was the last place he would want to toast.

+ We presumed that an addictive personality like Andrew might not have the wherewithal to orchestrate a sober and inspirational celebration for himself and his friends.

Lessons for the Anamcara

Supporting the Adventurer Personality

Adventurer personality types are fun-loving, spontaneous, and adaptable; they can also be scattered, distracted, and superficial. The challenge for the anamcara is to support their highest qualities, since the shadow side of their personality is their source of spiritual pain. Adventurers require freedom to explore possibilities. At the end of life, limited options can be the source of their suffering. A lifetime of seeking pleasure and avoiding pain may also have undermined their commitments. On their deathbed, the work of the Adventurer is to stay sober and alert, admitting their broken promises without losing their innate sense of joy and forgiveness.

Meaning Pain

Challenge: Meaning for the Adventurer tends to be limited to the next attractive idea. The spiritual pain that can result is a fear of having lived life on the surface. The anamcara can support an Adventurer by helping him or her acknowledge the need for priorities, leaving other distracting plans behind.

Opportunity: Adventurers have a natural sense of idealism that can shine even in the darkest night. Believing that life is stronger than death, the Adventurer has a capacity to transform the most extreme pain into something hopeful.

Forgiveness Pain

Challenge: In their attempt to maintain freedom at all costs, Adventurers can leave important relationships in the dust when feeling constricted or threatened. Forgiving themselves for their lack of commitment is a dominant theme among Adventurers at the end of life.

Opportunity: The Adventurer is rarely able to hold a grudge. They can dispense joy and compassion more easily than any other personality type, even in the face of betrayal. The ease with which an Adventurer can let go is a blessing the anamcara can share.

Relatedness Pain

Challenge: Adventurers fear feeling trapped. The problem is they cover up this fear with a façade of smiles and levity. As a consequence, it can appear that they take no thing or person completely seriously, thus causing more pain and misunderstanding. The anamcara will challenge such behavior on the part of the Adventurer, which often brings about a necessary sober reaction.

Opportunity: When balanced, Adventurers can harness an amazing capacity for enthusiasm and focus. If they commit to a project or person out of this grounded energy, they become a source of joyful enrichment. The anamcara will encourage the discipline of regular, spiritual practice as an antidote to Relatedness Pain.

Hopelessness Pain

Challenge: The inner anxiety of the Adventurer usually shows up as distraction. If such persons have overindulged their appetite with too many adventures, the result can be a downward spiral of hopelessness and depression. The anamcara should not try to kid them back into their old personality, but instead can invite him to enter into the dark night in order to take stock of this destructive behavior.

Opportunity: The Adventurer is not just a daydreamer, but enjoys putting plans into action. At the end of life, support the Adventurer in taking concrete steps toward healing and reconciliation. The best spiritual practices for Adventurers include any form of contemplation-in-action, such as solitude, followed by engagement with the world around them.

Overarching Advice

Adventurers spend a lifetime trying to be all things to all people. They find it difficult to rejoice with the rejoicing and weep with the weeping. Anamcara need to be wary of feeding into behaviors that make light of a serious situation. Instead, provide space to express their often-denied emotional and spiritual pain. Like every other personality type, the Adventurer struggles with doubt, loneliness, and fear. These inner struggles are not easily shared, however, because the Adventurer's friends often unwittingly fall into the trap of always acting upbeat. Listen for a thread of reality underneath the joke or the platitude. It may be the key to the Adventurer's transformation.

HOSPICE — PATIENT CHART

NAME Dorothy

AGE 91 **GENDER** ☐ M ☒ F **RACE / ETHNICITY** Native American

BORN IN Manitoba, Canada

MARITAL STATUS Never Married **CHILDREN** ☒ Y ☐ N one adopted daughter

VOCATION Retired Attorney

SPIRITUAL / RELIGIOUS ORIENTATION Lutheran / Ogallala Sioux.

DIAGNOSIS End Stage Alzheimer's

PROGNOSIS Death Imminent

OBSERVATIONS Dorothy is close to death. She does not seem to be struggling, though her adopted daughter/caregiver Mariah is worried about her.

Dorothy: the Asserter

Will you love me even if I am weak?

Dorothy was an elderly woman whose life was sapping away. Three years earlier, she had been diagnosed with Alzheimer's. Her daughter stayed by her side, which made it possible for Dorothy to stay in her own home.

The spiritual pain Dorothy was dealing with was Meaning Pain. The tools that provided the breakthrough were bedside ritual and ancestor healing.

Dorothy's Story

Dorothy had a Native American look. Her father was a tribal elder in the Lakota tribe, part of the Sioux tradition. Her mother was white. Painfully for her, she was called a half-breed, and therefore was not fully accepted in the white world or the American Indian world. When her mother died in the 1920s, Dorothy's father put her in an American Indian school orphanage in South Dakota.

The Christian schools on the reservations in the '20s and '30s thought their mission was to "Americanize" the American Indian children. They cut off the children's hair, changed their names, and forbade them to speak their native language. Any reference to Native American custom was condemned as pagan and was cruelly punished.

Dorothy was an intelligent girl who studied hard, although her spirited nature got her in trouble. Reservation schools only went up to the fifth grade for girls (boys went to the seventh grade). After that, the youngsters were expected to work on the reservation. Dorothy had other ideas. After fifth grade, she ran away to Canada, where a farm family took her in.

The farmer and his wife saw Dorothy's potential. She was bright, a good reader, a smart student. She liked to go to the library and check out books. She was particularly attracted to issues of law and justice; from the start, Dorothey had a penchant for the underdog.

Dorothy's adopted parents encouraged her to enroll in a local high school. Later she won a scholarship to college in Minneapolis. It was unusual in those days for a girl to go to college, but Dorothy did not stop there. All those books about people's rights had unleashed a force that could not be held back; she went on to law school.

After receiving her legal degree, Dorothy created a law practice for herself and championed the little guy. She was a circuit-riding attorney in the 1930s and 1940s, known for her frontier justice. At four foot nine, she was a tiny woman, which was part of her legend. Dorothy took on cases that no one else would look at: women's issues, civil rights, domestic violence. If her clients couldn't pay, she helped them anyway.

Dorothy never married, but she had adopted a daughter, Mariah, who was now taking care of her in her last days. Although she had never been officially diagnosed, Dorothy, who was ninety-one, was being treated for end-stage Alzheimer's.

Richard's first encounter with Dorothy was by chance. He was not the hospice chaplain assigned to her. Her Lutheran pastor was sick and therefore not available to bring her communion, and Richard was asked to go in his place. The communion ritual had some meaning to her. Her daughter, Mariah, was insistent that her mother was not to miss communion. Mariah said the visits mattered to her mother.

Richard's First Meeting with Dorothy: Stern Not Confused

My visit was meant to be a one-time hospice call, in and out. There was not much I could do—say a prayer, give a blessing. For Dorothy, it was just a matter of time. She had, overall, what we call FTT, failure to thrive. A person does not always die from Alzheimer's. The mind shuts down, and then gradually the body shuts down. I did not expect to have a conversation with her.

I introduced myself as the chaplain. Dorothy was not in a coma, but she was nonresponsive. Mariah was not especially welcoming. It's not that she was rude, but she was not warm. She appeared to be Native American also.

The room seemed cold. As usual, I looked for the altars, reflecting what was important to Dorothy. There were not a lot of things around, but one item stood out: a judge's gavel framed and mounted on the wall with a hawk feather taped to the frame.

Normally with Alzheimer's, the patient has a blank, vacuous look. Dorothy looked present, but sullen, almost as though she was choosing not to share, not to talk. The impression was of a woman in control. Her face looked more stern than confused.

I sat by the bedside and asked if I could hold her hand. To my surprise, she turned her face away. Mariah intervened. "Oh Ma, this is the chaplain from hospice. He came to bring you communion. Pastor is sick." Dorothy kept staring out the window.

"Dorothy, I brought you communion." No response. "That's okay, we can just pray." I took out my book of psalms and recited one of them out loud. Dorothy said nothing; Mariah said nothing. I stood up and got ready to leave. Dorothy turned toward me and opened her mouth. Perhaps that was the signal that she wanted to take communion? I broke off a bit of the bread, gave it to her with a sip of water, and then left thinking, "I'm glad that's over." It was not a very satisfying encounter.

Second Meeting: Mariah's Story

Dorothy's pastor was still ill, and she was getting weaker. I decided to stop by and say hello again. This time, Mariah told me the whole story, how her mother was put in the orphanage and raised Lutheran. She said her mother carried the shame of being half-breed all her life. Dorothy's anger and resentment at the abuse she saw at the orphanage motivated her to become an advocate for those who suffered injustice and had no voice.

Mariah said her mom was very smart but never spoke much. It was partly because of her personality and partly a cultural characteristic; she kept her eyes downcast and was silent, but inside, there was a lot of rage. When Dorothy did act, she had a reputation for being a spitfire. She once attacked one of the mission school teachers who was hitting a little girl over the head; Dorothy bit the man on the arm.

I asked Mariah about the gavel, and she confirmed that for a short time Dorothy was a judge as well as an attorney; in fact, she was one of the first women appointed as judge in the Great Plains area. As a judge, she had a reputation for being what Mariah called "a mean son of a bitch" to those who were irresponsible and a fierce defender of children and women's rights. She had adopted Mariah because she had been abused.

Third Visit: Too Many Words

A few weeks later, I decided to make another follow-up call on Dorothy. I was actually surprised that she was still alive. Vital signs pointed to the likelihood that she was entering the last stages of her life, and she had stopped taking nourishment. When I went in the bedroom to see her, she was sound asleep. I did not touch her because she had pulled back before.

Mariah was skeptical at what she called the diagnosis of white men. She did not think her mother had Alzheimer's. To Mariah, Dorothy seemed more aware than an Alzheimer's patient. Alzheimer's metabolically robs a person's cognitive state. "My mother is not confused or disoriented. It is as though she is choosing to stay within herself. She's just tired of life." To support this contention, Mariah suggested that the fact that her mother had not spoken a word for two months, rather than being a sign of dementia, might be related to a comment she made before she went silent. The last thing Dorothy said was, "I have said too many words."

Mariah was disappointed that her mother wasn't more interested in Native American tradition. Raised in a white world, Dorothy seemed to have little connection to her cultural roots. Native American pride had been beaten out of her long ago.

I thought it might help if I knew something about the Sioux tradition, especially the Ogallala Sioux, which was Dorothy's tribe. I called Rosalee, a friend of mine who lived at the Rosebud Reservation in South Dakota.

Fourth Visit: A Prayer Stick

Right away, Rosalee had an idea for something that might help Dorothy. She sent a Lakota prayer stick, along with some instructions on how to use it. When the stick arrived, I opened it carefully, took it out of the box, and examined it closely.

It was a willow branch about two and a half feet long, with a small soft strip of rabbit's fur wrapped around its center, and four little leather sacks or bundles dangling from it. Each bundle was stuffed with herbs, and each one was a different color.

The instructions that came with the stick explained some of the symbolism of the herbs and the colors. Each color represented one of the four directions: north, south, east, or west. Different tribes might choose different colors to designate the compass points, but honoring the four directions is universal.

Hawk feathers and a blue band designated the top of the stick. Blue was for Grandfather Who Lives in the Sky, a traditional name for God. The bottom of the stick had a green band, pointing down to Mother Earth. Beads and horsehair decorated the bottom of the stick.

The essence of the written directions was that the stick was held in prayer in the morning, pointing one by one in the four directions. The fifth direction, then, was up; the sixth was down. The seventh and last motion pointed to the human heart, which contains all the colors of the rainbow.

Sunday, I went out to the house and showed Mariah the stick. She got excited when she saw it and immediately took it to her mother. Mariah shook her mother to wake her up and held the artifact in front of her. "See, a prayer stick. We could pray in the traditional way today."

Dorothy grabbed the stick from her daughter's hands. "Hecunsni."

It was the first time that I heard her speak. Mariah and I were shocked to hear her voice. It confirmed our suspicions that she was not out of it. But neither of us could make out the words. Dorothy spoke again. It sounded like, "Sha!" sharp and angry. I wrote down phonetically what she was saying. Was it possible she was speaking Lakotan? I called Rosalee on the reservation and repeated the words. "What are you doing?" asked Rosalee. "She is saying, 'Don't do that!'"

When Mariah heard the translation, she thought her mother meant, "Don't use that stick." Rosalee had a different interpretation. Maybe Dorothy knew the stick had to be used in a certain way, directionally. Maybe Mariah was holding it upside down. We went back to Dorothy and handed her the stick. Dorothy held it with the blue band up and started to speak hypnotically, almost chanting. Phrase by phrase, I repeated into the phone what she was saying, and Rosalee translated.

"Wakan Tanka (Creator God). Wi Yo. Hin Yan Pata." Dorothy was praying in the east, the sacred direction where the sun comes up, bringing light to the world.

The names of directions were prayers themselves, Rosalee explained.

Like a human compass, Dorothy said the prayers for each direction, turning the stick with her eyes closed. She knew where the directions were, and she was saying in Lakota what the instructions that came with the prayer stick spelled out in English.

Mariah and I could hardly believe our eyes and ears. Dorothy would not have been around anything like this prayer stick since she was a little girl. She hadn't heard these words for almost eighty years. Any exposure to this tradition would have had to be when she was small, before she was in the mission school and forbidden to pray that way.

In the middle of the prayer chant, Dorothy suddenly stopped praying and got excited. Eyes still closed, she cried out, "Cetan!" She became insistent that we open the window.

When we conveyed the dialogue to Rosalee, she explained that *cetan* means hawk. It was as if Dorothy was hearing a hawk cry as she was chanting the prayer. Normally a prayer stick is used outdoors.

She was deep in another world, in some other place and another time, and that part of her wanted to pray outdoors.

Cetan. The hawk. Open the window. Rosalee told us, "Perhaps the bird is calling her name."

These prayers went on for a while. Then Dorothy held the stick close to her, still praying. When her prayers were over, she seemed to be asleep.

The nurse came by that afternoon. When she saw Dorothy lying so still, clutching the prayer stick, she wondered if she were dead. In this somnolent state, without opening her eyes, Dorothy spoke to the nurse. "Ma Lakota" (I am Lakota), she said. These were the last words she said, and then she died.

Dorothy's Lakota Name

When I called Rosalee to tell her what a gift her prayer stick had been, mentioning Dorothy's name for the first time, it turned out she knew who Dorothy was, and her history. Rosalee said that an elder at the Reservation remembered that Dorothy's father had given her an American Indian name when she was a little girl, Wakinyan Cetan. Translated, the name he gave her was Thunder Hawk.

Dorothy had lived her life disconnected from her Native American tradition, not knowing her Lakota name, yet the essence of that name touched everything she did. It was as though in naming her, her father had predicted her life as an intense and passionate activist.

Mariah buried her mom with her gavel with the hawk feather taped to it. And on her tombstone, she engraved her American Indian name: Wakinyan Cetan. Thunder Hawk. The name summed up Dorothy's life as a fierce advocate of others and let her rest at last in the tradition that formed her.

Dorothy's Spiritual Diagnosis: Meaning Pain

Pay Attention to What Is Not Working

Dorothy was dying. She was old, but there was no physical evidence of disease. A failure-to-thrive diagnosis usually implies a loss of meaning and desire to live. So how do we help such persons? Dorothy's daughter had an intuition about what might help. Her mother had spent her life advocating for hopeless cases. Now she was feeling hopeless. If it was possible to get inside her mother's distress, there might be a more hopeful outcome.

Tell Your Life Story

Dorothy was not struggling against death, she was struggling over whether it was worth it to continue living. But Dorothy was no longer able to speak for herself; she needed her daughter, Mariah, to tell her story. Then we could consider a solution to Dorothy's spiritual pain. Each person's story is a rich drama of joy and suffering. We can trust that the spiritual pain being experienced at the present moment has its roots in the stories of our past.

Look for Unfinished Business

Dorothy's cultural wounds represented a lifetime of prejudice and rejection. Making sense out of who she was as a woman and a Native American was the only hope for her healing. Her case was extreme. As a young child,

Dorothy was rejected both by the white world and the American Indian world. This cultural distress motivated her to become a fierce advocate for other underdogs. But it also was the hole in her soul that begged for attention at the end of her life. Her daughter was willing to propose a radical-sounding solution—that she make a connection with the people of her ancestry. Mariah's instincts were right.

Check out Your Agenda

It is easy to speculate about what kind of unfinished business might be keeping a person from releasing her spirit at the end of life. But in our enthusiasm to diagnose spiritual pain, we need to be careful of making presumptions. Ultimately, even for someone in an altered state of consciousness, it is important to check our goals with the patient. Dorothy remained in control to the very end. No matter how well-intentioned the intervention of others, she decided what would—and would not—be helpful to her.

Beware of Religious Labels

In an effort to respect others' beliefs, we often identify people according to labels like their religious denomination. Initially all that Dorothy's chaplain had to go on was a one-word description of her spiritual belief: Lutheran. But now Dorothy seemed indifferent to receiving communion, and the prayers of her denomination. Once the prayer stick of her ancestral tradition was offered, however, she came back to life. Dorothy had not so much rejected Christianity as she needed to find a voice for her Native American heritage.

Spiritual Responses to Dorothy's Pain: Ancestor Healing and Bedside Ritual

Examining the Family Tree

The need for healing ancestral wounds is an end-of-life priority for many people. It can also be one of the more difficult issues to resolve. The persons involved in the original wounding are often dead. Frequently, the wounded person has given up hope that healing might be possible. The good news about ancestral healing (see "Healing and Assistance from Ancestors" in part III, "The Tool Chest") is that it doesn't matter who is dead and who is alive. In Dorothy's case, the issue involved her acceptance of herself. Sometimes, by respecting the language and customs of a person's heritage, a path to healing is opened.

Ritual Opportunities

Effective ritual cannot be forced. But a good ritual guide knows how to spot the right opportunity. Introducing a symbol and a ceremony does not so much create a meaning and faith as it celebrates a newfound sense of purpose. Use of a Sioux prayer stick was not in and of itself important for Dorothy. It symbolized her voice and power as a Native American woman.

Sacred Language

Not every culture or religion uses a traditional language. But those who do pray in a sacred tongue know that it can unlock many levels of emotion and history. When Dorothy reverted back to the language of her childhood, an undeniable sense of power came through her voice. Speaking in the language of her ancestors, she became Dorothy Thunder Hawk. Her story is a lesson that the caregiver need not necessarily be fluent in another language. Dorothy knew exactly what to say. The lesson is: no one should have to die in English.

Presumptions Surrounding Dorothy

When a person is noncommunicative, it is especially difficult to know how to provide him or her with support. It is all the more important, therefore, to be cautious when forming judgments about such a person's history or needs. Dorothy's situation generated numerous presumptions, many of which were proven to be wrong.

- We presumed that Dorothy had nothing more to live for.

- We presumed that Dorothy had long since resolved her conflict between the white and American Indian worlds.

- We presumed that because Dorothy was cut off from her tribal language and customs as a little girl, she no longer had a connection to anything that was Sioux.

- We presumed that given her diagnosis and lack of verbal response, Dorothy would never speak again.

Lessons for the Anamcara: Supporting the Asserter Personality

The Asserter personality type can be intimidating for others to deal with. Their decisive nature and confrontational style give the impression of control and confidence. But at the end of life, conflicts can arise that challenge the illusion of their control. An anamcara may be at a loss as to how to respond to the Asserter's spiritual pain. Stick with an Asserter, especially in times of weakness and vulnerability.

Meaning Pain

Challenge: Asserters prefer to be self-reliant. A crisis in meaning occurs when they are faced with an impossible challenge over which they have no control. The anamcara can help by simply receiving the Asserter's frustrations with compassion instead of with optimism.

Opportunity: Asserters are people of vision and action. Even at the end of life, their can-do attitude can overcome most obstacles, including the temptation to lose interest in life. An anamcara will support their natural sense of purpose.

Forgiveness Pain

Challenge: In the wake of an Asserter's life, overreaction and exaggerated passion often create enemies. Though the Asserter may not wish to overwhelm others, it is not uncommon for others to feel frightened by this energy. At the end of life, some form of confession may be essential for the Asserter to reconcile old wounds.

Opportunity: While Asserters often command a lot of attention with the sheer force of their personality, they do not intend to hurt others. The process of a life review may encourage the Asserter to make amends for past indiscretions, albeit unconsciously.

Relatedness Pain

Challenge: When an Asserter feels rejected, his or her initial response may be one of withdrawal or aggression. Stress eventually builds up, which can cause additional alienation from the persons and things that matter most to an Asserter. At the end of life, there may be a need to reconcile with these past ghosts.

Opportunity: Asserters possess an indomitable spirit. When healthy, they can bring both a natural strength and ability and an emotional vulnerability to a situation. An anamcara should support the Asserter's undying passion for life in an appropriate way.

Hopelessness Pain

Challenge: It takes a lot to get an Asserter down. This personality type is not prone to hopelessness. It is important, however, not to mistake belligerence with confidence. Sometimes such a strong demeanor is a coverup for a deep state of despair.

Opportunity: In the face of mortality and weakness, the Asserter can exhibit noble qualities of courage and strength. This is when their powerful presence in the world becomes a source of inspiration and healing to others.

Overarching Advice

Dying well is not an art that can be controlled. After a life of trusting their instincts, Asserters may become overwhelmed and disoriented by the chaos of illness and their approaching death. An effective anamcara will support the Asserter in trusting their underdeveloped, more vulnerable qualities. Old behaviors that kept people at a distance will be replaced with an enormous compassion for others. At the end of life, the transformed Asserter will be surrounded by loyal friends.

HOSPICE | PATIENT CHART

NAME
Larry

AGE
70

GENDER
☒ M ☐ F

RACE / ETHNICITY
Caucasian

BORN IN
Hannibal, Missouri

MARITAL STATUS
Married

CHILDREN
☒ Y ☐ N
(1) Son
(2) Daughters

VOCATION
Retired Military

SPIRITUAL / RELIGIOUS ORIENTATION
Evangelical Christian

DIAGNOSIS
Prostate Cancer

PROGNOSIS
6 months or less

OBSERVATIONS
Larry is retired life-time military. He is an easy-going easy-care kind of patient; a nice guy. He enjoys joking around, and seems to have no family issues.

Larry: the Peacemaker

Will you love me even if I disagree with you?

Larry was considered a good patient—compliant, amiable, not demanding—he did whatever the hospice workers asked him to do. He was a military man, retired from active duty, who had attained the rank of general in the army. At the caretaker meetings, the nurses and social workers nicknamed Larry a "five-star patient." Little did they know that Larry was wrestling with something deep, an issue that put him in conflict with his own hierarchy of obedience.

The spiritual pain Larry was dealing with was Forgiveness Pain. The tools that provided the breakthrough were nonlocal energy work and intercessory prayer.

Larry's Story

Larry was a diplomat. As an army officer, his mission was to be a warrior; he had served, however, as an attaché and negotiator, spending his career helping others avoid conflict. It was ironic that he was a mediator at a global level, yet in his own household there was a circumstance he could not mediate. Before he could die in peace, he needed to wrestle with his own demons.

Larry was not the kind of person who would have requested a traditional spiritual caregiver. He had little connection with his Protestant upbringing, and as a lifetime career military man, he was used to handling things on his own.

Richard has a background of experience in military chaplaincy, serving for several years on a variety of military bases. Military chaplains have a reputation for being regular guys. They will have a beer with you or go along to the pool hall. They often seem more like a buddy than your pastor. It is understood that there is no proselytizing, but they are there for you when you need help or counsel. Because of this background, and his cross-denominational training, anytime someone in hospice had been in the military, Richard was the one sent to see them. His experience with military chaplaincy was his calling card.

Richard's First Meeting with Larry: Detective Work— The Missing Son

Larry and I warmed to each other right away. We shared jokes and military stories. Larry had a great, earthy sense of humor, and he delighted in thinking he was scandalizing me. For my part, I loved to tease Larry, showing up with an Air Force jacket or with Annapolis Academy pennants, playing on the rivalry among the military services. We developed a camaraderie built on relentless ribbing and mutual respect. Underlying the earthy jokes was a sense of trust.

Sometimes a hospice worker needs to be a detective. There were hints that something was amiss: Larry's two daughters were often around and were frequently talked about. But the chart notes said that Larry had two daughters and a son, and the son was never mentioned. There were family pictures everywhere, but no pictures of a son. When I asked about the son, I was answered with silence. All I could find out was that his name was Tom. Was Tom in jail? Was he dead? Had he committed suicide?

One afternoon when I arrived, Larry was napping. I went to the kitchen and sat down over coffee with Larry's wife, Myra. We talked a bit about Larry's condition and treatment. And then I said, "Tell me about your son, Tom."

At first Myra did not answer. She got up, poured another cup of coffee, and silently went to the sink to rinse the dishes. When she spoke, it came out firm and angry. "Don't talk to Larry about his son. Don't go there; it makes his pain worse."

She wiped her hands on a dishtowel, sat down at the table, and sighed. Head down, her voice now almost a whisper, she spilled out the story. "Tom was a wonderful, gentle, loving child growing up. But he was different. I sensed that from the start. He was a disappointment to his father. Larry's only son, and he didn't want to play ball or get involved in sports. He bonded with me, but not with his dad.

"At the time of his high school graduation, Tom wasn't sure what he wanted to do next. Reaching out to him, wanting to create a shared experience between them, his dad suggested, 'What about joining the army?'"

Myra paused, twisting a paper napkin to shreds between her fingers. Looking up, she said, "It was the darkest day in this house in all our years of marriage when Tom answered, confirming what I had suspected but never wanted to admit, 'Dad, I can't join the army. I'm gay.'"

The news stunned Larry. He had no category for this, no way to solve it. His only son ought to be *like* him—no single issue went more to the core of his being. The revelation of his son's sexual orientation confirmed and explained their alienation. But Larry was a military man. Everything in his background and training taught him that when you have a problem, you seek advice and figure out how to fix it. So after the first shock, Larry's response was nonemotional and rational. For him, the focus was on how to get help and who to ask for advice.

To get some direction, Larry went to see the chaplain on the base, an old war buddy. For Larry, the military minister was the archetype of authority in moral matters. In addition, he was one of the few people Larry trusted.

The minister was unequivocal. "This is a serious moral predicament," he said. For the chaplain, *gay* equaled *predator*. "As harsh as it sounds," the minister told Larry, "you must demand that your son change or move out of your house. He could harm others, lead others to sin." But all was not lost. There was one avenue of hope. "Things can be done," the minister said. "These people can be helped."

Larry went back to his son and told him that as much as he hated to do it, they needed to talk about this sexual thing. "Whatever it costs, whatever it is, we can help you. We will spare no expense to find the program best for you." This did not sit well with Tom. He was insulted at the approach and its implied condemnation of him.

Myra recounted the scene, as clear to her as though it had happened yesterday. "One of the few times I ever saw Larry get angry was when Tom rejected his 'solution.' Mean words were said on both sides. Then Tom said, 'If you can't change me and make me what you want, what will you do, disown me?'"

Larry was conflicted. The chaplain's advice was that if he couldn't cure Tom, it was his responsibility to protect other innocents. Myra continued: "Tom said, 'I can't be "cured." If I leave, I'll be out of your life forever.' His father had no response. In the heat of emotion, Tom packed his bags and left."

After Tom left, Larry covered his pain by pretending that his son was dead or that he had never existed. Larry was not an angry or morose kind of person. He rebounded to his old style and put back on the mask of the peacemaker. It was a false sense of peace. Twelve years had passed. There was no contact with Tom. No Christmas cards or birthday wishes, no communication on either side.

Myrna reluctantly went along with her husband's wishes. Over the years, the two daughters challenged their father regarding their brother, and they urged him to try and contact Tom. But for Larry it was a closed door. The rule of the house was, It's over; he's gone. Whenever anyone brought up Tom's name, Larry had one stock answer, "We don't talk about that."

They later learned that Tom had left the country and become a Taoist. He went to Asia, studied energy healing, and became a Reiki master. He had changed his name; he did not want anything to do with the culture of his dad.

The End Is Near: A Shift

A hospice worker maintains regular contact with the dying person. By being there, you build trust and rapport, and get to know the subtle signs when something shifts. The work does not go by the book, but is an intuitive thing. One day you walk in, and there is a different look on the person's face. That gives you the leverage to ask, "What's going on?"

Larry's family, too, could sense that the end was near. For one thing, Larry had lost his sense of humor. That was hard on the family, but for the hospice workers, it was a signal that Larry was moving, appropriately, inside. The other thing that the family and the nurses noticed was that, using a self-administered pump, Larry was upping his morphine dosage.

I spoke to Myra privately. "Could it be that the reason Larry is in so much pain is about his son, the missing piece in his life? Could we try to contact Tom?"

"No. No, no, no. Larry would not want that. Besides, we have moved several times. We don't even know where he is."

I explained to Myra the difference between physical pain and spiritual pain. This could be a useful pain for healing. It was almost like a breech birth: Larry was *stuck*. This was an opportunity to be proactive, to help him lean into his pain. This was a moment to help him create a deep connection, a moment for truth. "Larry is dying. He needs to deal with the loss of his son, with some aspect of it, before he can die in peace."

I asked Myra if I could have time alone with Larry, and she agreed. Sometimes the caregiver can articulate what the patient already knows but everyone else is afraid to say. As soon as it was just the two of us, I spoke to Larry, point-blank. "You've only got a couple of days left. We've got a chance to make all the difference in the world here." I paused. "Let's talk about Tom."

At the mention of his son's name, Larry became emotionally distraught. He could not speak. Even without words, his response was a breakthrough. For once, Larry was acknowledging the pain of the separation, and that in itself could free Tom down the line. They had been disassociated for years. Physically, they did not even know where the other was living. I was convinced, however, that even though they were no longer together, they might be still somehow connected.

Internet Intercession: An Electronic Prayer Chain

The separation between father and son constituted such brokenness that neither man, neither the father nor the son, could fix it. It was a desperate situation.

I remembered reading on the Internet about a website dedicated to prayers for the sick and the dying. Although I had never used it, and confess my own misgivings about electronic prayer, I considered it now. The website asked for nothing except one request: After posting a name for prayer, you should return later and report what came about.

The network of prayers extended all over the world including monasteries of different faith traditions and such diverse places as the Wailing Wall in Jerusalem, Mother Teresa's hospitals, and Tibetan Buddhist communities.

I asked Larry if I could put his name on a prayer list. When he agreed, I went home, went online, and located the website for the terminally ill. I typed in Larry's name, and then, as an afterthought, asked for prayers for Tom, too.

Auras of Healing

One day soon after, the family summoned me: "Please come, Dad's dying."

The dying sometimes report seeing phenomena such as auras. When I arrived, Larry was muttering incoherently about seeing a purple glow around my head. In the language of energy workers, purple is the color of healing. But Larry was also writhing in excruciating pain. I encouraged the family to take a short break from their caregiving marathon. They went outside for a walk.

While I was silently praying for Larry, the phone rang in the corridor outside the room. I walked outside the room and answered the phone. When I heard the voice on the other end introduce himself, my hand started to tremble. I took the phone into the bedroom and handed it to Larry. "It's your son."

Tom, in Asia, on the other side of the world, had woken up with a nightmare. After twelve years of no communication, he felt driven to speak to his dad. He contacted the army authorities to track Larry down and get his telephone number.

As Larry held the phone, it wasn't even a struggle, it was more like a dam bursting. On both sides, "I'm sorry. I'm so sorry." The room was filled with the forgiveness, the "I love you's."

Looking to the upper corner of the room, Larry said, "Look, the purple light is moving. It's all white now." Larry died within moments.

Something had touched the son and made him call. He did not know his father was dying; he only knew he had to call. Tom had been trained in energy work, particularly the practice of Reiki. He knew how to help his dad release his spiritual pain. He was sending his loving-kindness energy through the phone line. The son's courage opened up the father's courage.

Larry literally died with the phone at his ear, looking toward the white light in the corner of the ceiling, his son talking him through to death.

Larry's Spiritual Diagnosis: Forgiveness Pain

Trust that Absolution of the Self and the Other Is Possible

Larry's story gives us courage to trust that eleventh-hour transformations are possible. Here was a conflicted father who did not want to die unreconciled with his son. Something extraordinary was needed, however, to break through years of conflict. Larry could have refused a last-minute phone call from Tom, but he didn't. He was ready for healing.

Most people are willing to forgive another on their deathbed, but self-forgiveness can be a more difficult challenge. For Larry, peace came at a great price. Rarely asserting himself, this gentle general spent a lifetime deferring to everyone else's expectations. The result was agonizing internal conflict. This story illustrates how self-absolution is possible when finally facing such personal conflicts.

Lean into Pain to Break through Barriers

Forgiveness work at the end of life is about removing barriers. The alienation between Tom and Larry was a huge source of Forgiveness Pain. Be sensitive to whatever creates anxiety between the dying person and others or between the dying person's mind and inner being. Uncertainty, tension, mistrust, and resentment are indications of a barrier that needs to be breached. Larry's story is a confirmation that leaning into the source of our pain is the only way through it.

Believe the Higher Self Will Emerge

As the body's energy wanes at the end of life, emotional and spiritual energy becomes more available. While Larry's illness was sapping his physical strength, other windows of opportunity were opening. Trust that as everyday, mundane concerns fall away, a dying person's higher self can see more clearly.

Respect Personality Changes

It can be distressing for family members to watch terminally ill relatives lose familiar aspects of their personality. Larry's usual sense of humor was replaced by seriousness and anxiety during his final days. Support the dying by allowing them space to move inside, otherwise their remaining energy may be spent trying to meet the expectations of family and friends.

Let Go of Temporal or Biological Expectations

Death is more than a biological event. Everything we have heard about how long a person can live without food or water, for example, has well-documented exceptions. In most cases, dying persons stay alive as long as it takes to complete their remaining unfinished business. Larry could not die in peace as long as his son stayed out of the picture. It was Tom's last-minute intervention that allowed Larry to release his spirit.

The death of a loved one or a friend is a time when neither the past nor the future has much meaning. Instead there is an amazing experience of the here and now. Those who witnessed Larry's death spoke about a sacred, transcendental quality to the experience. No wonder the books of the dead concurred that when extreme spiritual pain is finally relieved, death opens onto a fulcrum of eternity.

Spiritual Responses to Larry's Pain: Nonlocal Energy Work and Intercessory Prayer

The Power of Prayer

The synchronicity of Tom's telephone call to his father when Larry was dying could have been a coincidence. But Larry's family experienced something profound in the timing. Research data now exist on the effectiveness of intercessory prayers (see "Intercessory (Nonlocal) Prayer" in part III,

"The Tool Chest") or nonlocal healing. Just as importantly, phenomenal stories proliferate among those who have experienced a relationship between prayer and healing at the end of life. Dr. Larry Dossey encourages patients and caregivers to trust that "prayer is as effective a therapy as any other drug or treatment."

Auras and Other Energy Field Perceptions

It is not uncommon for a dying person to report visions that include rings of light, fields of color, or auras during the dying process (see "Auras" in part III, "The Tool Chest"). Many of us want to dismiss these phenomena as nonrational. But such sights can indicate enhanced energy field perceptions, which physical science is now able to measure. Presume that dying persons sometimes are able to perceive these higher vibrational frequencies. We honor their gift of deeper seeing by taking the extraordinary experiences of the dying seriously.

Channels of Healing and Receptivity

Larry's story offers two different but complementary perspectives on healing. Separated by thousands of miles, Tom became an integral part of what the family called a miracle of reconciliation. After years of training as a Reiki master, Tom trusted the intuition of a dream that indicated his father was in distress. Tom was convinced that the long distance or nonlocal energy work (see "Energy Therapies" in part III, "The Tool Chest") he sent to Larry created a channel of healing and receptivity for both father and son.

Bell's Theorem

The story of Tom and Larry poignantly confirms the principle of quantum physics called Bell's Theorem. Whenever two particles of matter have been connected, even if they are sent to the opposite ends of the universe, whatever occurs to one occurs to the other exactly at the same time and to the same degree. In spite of distances in geography and emotion, father and son were still connected. The spiritual tools of intercessory prayer and nonlocal energy work became instruments to reconcile and heal their connection.

Presumptions Surrounding Larry

In the great books of the dying, families often used the more objective services of an anamcara, or death coach, at the end of a loved one's life. The presumptions generated by Larry's story confirmed the need for another set of eyes on a difficult situation.

- We presumed that Larry would die without his son's knowledge.

- We presumed that on his deathbed, Larry would remain the same happy-go-lucky guy that he had been throughout his life.

- We presumed that Larry's visions toward the end of his life were hallucinations caused by medication or the disease process.

- We presumed that, given the degree of suffering experienced during the final hours of his life, Larry's final moments of death would be agonizing.

- We presumed that intercessory prayer and energy work might have only limited value in the face of extreme distances and suffering.

- We presumed that once a family system has been torn apart by years of painful disassociation, reconciliation is impossible.

Lessons for the Anamcara: Supporting the Peacemaker Personality

We value the Peacemaker personality type because they are easygoing, agreeable, nonconfrontive, and receptive. But herein also lies the dilemma for such persons. Rather than working to tame their ego, Peacemakers need to discover and assert their true self. At the end of life, it can be a challenge to finally wake up to what they are really committed to. The anamcara can be an invaluable support to this process depending on the nature of the Peacemaker's spiritual pain.

Meaning Pain

Challenge: A Peacemaker often suffers from a low-grade crisis of meaning because it is easy to get lost in someone else's agenda. In desiring harmony, Peacemakers sell out to what's not important to them, leaving them with a sense of purposelessness and cynicism.

Opportunity: Of all personality types, the Peacemaker has the capacity to live in the moment—an important quality for spiritual discernment. By taking a Peacemaker's current dreams seriously, the anamcara can unleash a passion for meaning and commitment.

Forgiveness Pain

Challenge: Peacemakers may come to the end of their life and realize how angry and resentful they are about having deferred their life to the demands of others. This kind of smoldering forgiveness issue may be directed both to another and toward the self.

Opportunity: It is never too late to "wake up." Support the Peacemaker by affirming his or her innate worth. The anamcara may discover a person who quickly moves beyond resentment to a renewed enthusiasm for life.

Relatedness Pain

Challenge: Peacemakers can easily shut down, thereby getting into conflict with others by being numb and emotionally unavailable. Inattentiveness and forgetfulness may compromise a Peacemaker's ability to remain committed to anyone or anything.

Opportunity: Don't let the Peacemaker off the hook. A primary spiritual question for the Peacemaker is, What are you willing to commit to in life and in death?

Hopelessness Pain

Challenge: Behind the Peacemaker's tranquil façade may lie a frighteningly apathetic person. If unhealthy, this personality type permanently escapes to a psychic inner sanctum where nothing or no one can harm him or her. But their overwhelming problems do not go away; instead they lead to despair.

Opportunity: The Peacemaker also has a natural capacity to be dynamic, be engaged, and be a healing presence for others. Chances are that such persons are not aware of the incredible source of blessing they have been to the world. Reminiscing and storytelling are good ways for the anamcara to remind the Peacemaker of their often understated contributions.

Overarching Advice

Peacemakers may have taken the advice, "Blessed are the peacemakers," too literally. Their spiritual work is to show up for life passionately, even in the face of conflict. For the Peacemaker, anger is not a destructive demon. In fact, it may be a healthy elixir that motivates their otherwise complacent personality. Family and caregivers at the end of life may be surprised at the Peacemaker's capacity to speak their truth. It is never too late to live fully, even in the face of death.

Story Archetypes

The authors of *The American Book of Living and Dying* selected nine stories that represent an ancient model for understanding the human personality called the Enneagram. Among many personality theories, the Enneagram is uniquely spiritual and nonsectarian in its approach. In the West, for example, Jews, Christians, and Muslims developed tools for spiritual discernment based on the wisdom of the Enneagram. The anamcara need not be familiar with this tool nor need care receivers understand the Enneagram at the end of life. Nevertheless, it may be reassuring to know that the stories at the heart of this book represent a classical approach to understanding human nature. Author Richard Groves has studied and taught the archetypes of the Enneagram for twenty-five years. The Enneagram archetypes provide invaluable insight in understanding the nature of spiritual suffering at the end of life. If you are interested in learning more about this extraordinary tool, please consult the bibliography.

Part III.

The Tool Chest

The Tool Chest offers a variety of traditional healing tools and therapies to support persons who are dying. Most of the following eighteen practices have a precedent in the ancient books of the dead and have been tested in contemporary clinical usage. You, the anamcara, may consider whether any one of these practices, or a combination of them, could be helpful for your end-of-life companion. *The American Book of Living and Dying* offers only a simple introduction to each of these tools. Consider using this part of the book in the following ways:

- To acquaint yourself with the extensive menu of spiritual therapies available

- To learn more about a particular practice from the Recommended Resource list following each therapy

- To locate someone who is a trained practitioner in one of the therapies

- To try some aspect of the practice yourself, as appropriate and as you are comfortable

Art Therapy

The artwork that dying persons produced in ancient times was highly valued. Even the most primitive drawings made by terminally ill persons were esteemed as portraits of the soul. The Swiss psychiatrist Carl Jung considered the dream mandalas created by medieval visionary Hildegaard of Bingen to be the most extraordinary mystical expressions in human history. Today therapists confirm the wisdom of our ancestors that the simple act of drawing can be a source of amazing insight and healing.

Applications for the End of Life

Terminal illness creates a natural opportunity for deeper contemplative exploration. Our ancestors observed the significance behind the use of colors, shapes, and symbols at the end of life. Today Jungian psychologists encourage bedside artistic expression as a powerful tool for healing. During the stress of chronic illness, encourage care receivers to paint themselves out of a corner through some form of artistic expression.

Basic Tools

A person does not need to be an artist to draw from the soul. In fact, there is an advantage to approaching creative expression with a beginner's mind. Consider a variety of media, including watercolor, tempera (poster paint), chalks, crayons, and finger paints. Find the medium that the patient finds most satisfying. Don't worry about composition and the finished product. In art therapy, the process is the product.

There are many creative styles and mediums; art therapy is not limited to drawing alone. Many people may not have played with art since childhood, so here are some ideas to get started.

+ *Mandala (The Sacred Circle).* The circle has been an important part of human culture since ancient times. Plato said the soul was a circle; in our time, Jung called the mandala a kind of sacred circle creating a longing for harmony within the heart when the soul is wounded.

  Have the patient begin by simply drawing a circle on a piece of paper. Then she can choose any color or design to fill in the circle. The placement and symbols of designs that emerge from the unconscious and appear in a mandala can have meaning. See books listed below for interpretations.

  Remind the patient to enjoy the process and consider giving her finished product a name.

+ *Doodling.* Doodling is the simplest form of creative expression. Some say that the unconscious and uncontrolled effort produces a snapshot of the soul.

+ *Art Journals.* An art journal is a record of our inner life based on spontaneous, creative designs, as opposed to verbal reflections. Give your friend these tips for keeping an art journal: Quiet the inner critic. Don't allow the editorial voice in. Respect yourself. Words are not needed to explain the person's images, but they might be part of the art therapy process.

+ *Clay Creation.* Working with clay is a soothing form of meditation. Put on one of the patient's favorite pieces of music. Have her breathe into the clay and warm it up. Tell her to allow her unconscious to direct its shape, rather than try to make something specific. Suggest that she spend at least fifteen to twenty minutes, with her eyes closed if she likes, modeling the clay in her hand. After the meditation, have her open her eyes. She might well be surprised by what her inner self has created.

* *Death Masks.* Masks are not a familiar part of American culture. In most tribal cultures, however, they are a significant way for the terminally ill person to put a face on their experience of death and dying. A death mask can express the person's anxiety or the fear they would like to keep at bay.

* *Sand Painting.* This art form is shared by American Navajo culture and Tibetan Buddhists. Creating a sand painting is a meditation. It draws forth the spiritual images hidden in the experience of illness.

Remember, you don't have to be an artist or a therapist to engage your patient in art therapy. Just play with shapes, symbols, and colors. Regarding color, be aware that ancient practice observed a correlation of colors to mood and emotion. Colors can indicate a connection between a person's inner state and the larger universe.

Level of Expertise

The term art therapy has a technical meaning among mental health professionals. In the context of death and dying, art therapy refers to an ancient spiritual tool available to anyone. There are many resources available for analyzing these therapeutic tools. Generally, it is the care receivers who are most qualified to interpret the deeper significance of their own work.

Resources for Art Therapy

PRINT AIDS

Bayles, David, and Ted Orland. *Art and Fear: Observations on the Perils and Rewards of Artmaking.* San Francisco: City Lights Books, 2001.
   An approach to the traps and pitfalls of entering into the artistic process. An enjoyable and insightful book.

Cappacchione, Lucia. *The Creative Journal for Children: A Guide for Parents, Teachers and Counselors.* Boston: Shambhala, 1989.

A collection of seventy-two exercises to help children express their feelings and deepest beliefs through art and writing.

Coles, Robert. *The Spiritual Life of Children.* Boston: Houghton-Mifflin, 1990.

An extraordinary book about how children express their inner life through art. Special segments focus on the religions of Judaism, Christianity, and Islam.

Cornell, Judith. *Drawing the Light from Within: Keys to Awaken Your Creative Power.* Wheaton, IL: Quest Books, 1997.

An approach to the healing arts in the light of physics, philosophy, and psychology.

—. *Mandala: Luminous Symbols for Healing.* Wheaton, IL: Quest Books, 1994.

A synopsis of the spiritual use of the mandala in many religious cultures.

Fincher, Suzanne. *Creating Mandalas for Insight: Healing and Self-Expression.* Boston: Shambhala, 1991.

A warm, direct, and practical explanation of the healing tradition of drawing mandalas.

Wilber, Ken. *No Boundary: Eastern and Western Approaches to Spiritual Growth.* Boston: Shambhala, 2001.

The different approaches to the psychology of the creative self, with specific exercises to lead the reader to greater self-awareness.

Breath Work

[*Note:* Richard Roech's book *To Die Well* (New York: HarperCollins, 1996), currently out-of-print, was helpful in preparing this section.]

In English, as in many languages of the world, the words that describe breathing and spirit are one and the same. When we speak of respiration, we literally are saying to take in spirit. As long as there is breath, there is life. To die is to cease to breathe. The ancients believed that the mingling of breaths, as they called it, was a critical physical and spiritual tool in stabilizing and directing the underlying energy of the body and the mind. Modern medicine has proven that regulating breath affects the body's internal organs and nervous system.

Applications for the End of Life

Breathlessness and other difficulties in breathing are common in people with serious illnesses, even if the primary symptoms of the disease are connected with other organs. Problems in breathing can worsen as an illness progresses. Patients with lung-related illnesses such as COPD (chronic obstructive pulmonary disease) and lung cancer understandably fear suffocation. When anxiety is high, breath work and breathing therapies help lessen the symptoms of breathlessness and create a more relaxed state of mind and body.

Basic Tools

There are a number of causes of breathlessness, many of which can be medically diagnosed and treated. In addition to medication, however, the conscious spiritual practice of breathing together with the care receiver is one of the most direct and accessible tools at the end of life. A few instructions from ancient and modern practice follow.

+ If the patient is conscious, talk about what you are going to do together and be sure you are in agreement.

+ The person should lie down or position himself as comfortably as possible. It is ideal to keep his spine in a straight position, with his arms resting loosely beside him.

+ It is important that the anamcara also be comfortable. You should sit near the person so he can feel your presence and hear you clearly when you speak.

+ When possible, ensure that the room is calm and quiet. Turn off overhead lights, especially fluorescent fixtures.

+ Before starting, take time to center yourself, balancing your energy. Close your eyes, relax your shoulders and chest, and breathe naturally. Calm your mind by engaging in a simple practice of meditation or prayer. One helpful practice is to become aware of the energy of the earth supporting you from below and the energy of light coming into the top of your skull.

+ Guide the person through a similar progressive relaxation exercise. Then tell him that you are about to begin a mingling of breaths.

+ Watch the person's breathing carefully. Notice whether it is deep, regular, and rhythmic or erratic and shallow. Follow along with it.

+ Begin synchronizing your own breathing with his. As he breathes in, you breathe in. As he breathes out, you breathe out.

- After a few minutes, you may invite the person to make the sound *ahhh* as he breathes out, as if sighing or expressing deep emotion. After several such breaths, have him return to silent breathing. You may continue to make the sound on your own, timed with the person's breathing out.

- If the patient was anxious, his breath may move from shallow, upper chest movements to deeper, abdominal rhythms. This can indicate physical relaxation and peace of mind.

- After about ten to fifteen minutes, invite the person to become more aware of his surroundings again, to feel his head, back, and legs where they rest. Have him open his eyes. Spend some time with the person afterward, first in silence, then inviting any comments, if he wants.

- You may find it helpful to maintain physical contact with the patient throughout the exercise, so he has a sense of your presence.

- Depending on the person's disposition or belief, you may conclude the exercise with a prayer of thanksgiving.

Level of Expertise

Mingling breaths requires little training and has minimal risk. If someone is in an acute state of breathlessness, medical attention should be sought immediately. But even in an emergency situation, such as an accident, you can help calm another person, as well as yourself, through this simple exercise. Especially during the final death vigil process, a number of people can take turns supporting a loved one through the mingling of breaths.

Resources for Breath Work

PRINT AIDS

Bernard, Jan Selliken, and Miriam Schneider. *The True Work of Dying: A Practical and Compassionate Guide to Easing the Dying Process.* New York: Avon Books, 1996.
    An exploration of the parallels between birthing and dying, with practical bedside advice for families and caregivers.

Levine, Stephen. *Guided Meditations, Explorations and Healing.* Garden City, NY: Doubleday, 1991.

A beautifully presented selection of texts that can be used by caregivers, dying persons, and others dealing with pain, intense emotional states, and conscious dying.

—. *A Gradual Awakening.* New York: Doubleday, 1989.

Guided meditations for opening body and soul to the mystery of life and death.

—. *Healing into Life and Death.* New York: Anchor Books, 1987.

A classic work for dealing with pain and grief through the use of ancient body-mind-spirit techniques.

Smith, Doug, and Marilu Pittman. *Tao of Dying: A Guide to Caregiving.* Washington, D.C.: Caring Publishing, 1994.

Helpful meditations for caregivers that reinforce the purpose of breathing therapies.

Stevens, Edward. *Spiritual Technologies: A User's Manual.* New York: Paulist Press, 1990.

A user-friendly manual with helpful approaches to breath awareness and contemplative practice. A great resource for bridging Western and Eastern spiritual traditions.

Coma Therapy

[*Note:* The authors are grateful to coma communication therapists Stan Tomandl and Ann Jacob, who are on the faculty at the Sacred Art of Living Center, for their valuable assistance in presenting this tool.]

Our ancestors knew that it was possible to support and communicate with persons in altered states of consciousness. Traditional Western medicine focuses on the physical condition of such patients. A new school of modern coma therapists believes that, even in the deepest coma, patients can have an incredibly rich inner life. Anamcara can lovingly support coma patients' inner lives. Coma work benefits patients, families, and staff, making periods of apparent unconsciousness more rewarding and, in some cases, shorter.

Applications for the End of Life

A significant number of persons will experience a coma in the process of dying. As people approach death, they often enter more or less remote states of consciousness for varying periods of time. These states may appear painful for the one dying and cause grief in loved ones. But coma therapists believe that altered states present opportunities, including a chance to complete unfinished business, explore meaning in life, and make spiritual connections.

Basic Tools

In order to support a loved one who is near death, family and friends should become acquainted with some basic tools of coma therapy. These easy-to-learn skills can help people in coma become more aware and communicate better with themselves, friends and relatives, and the larger world. Research with people who have been in a coma indicate that a person's greatest fear is not necessarily death; it is more often a fear of being trapped, either in an inner state that cannot be completed or in a negative state with no avenue of escape. A comatose state is symptomatic of a need for deep inner work. A person in coma is calling for a specific kind of supportive relationship; they are not necessarily requesting to be left alone or stimulated in nonuseful ways. Here are a few core principles of coma work.

+ Presume that persons in coma are always communicating to some extent. We need to be astute enough to pick up their cues and reactions.

+ Working with those in coma can be invasive if done thoughtlessly. It is important to: always introduce yourself, ask permission to communicate, and pay close attention to feedback.

+ If you attempt to communicate with someone in coma, they may show no change in their communication pattern. A lack of response indicates negative feedback. This means it is time to try something else.

+ Whatever is happening during your interaction with a comatose person is potentially meaningful, including small changes in breathing, eye movement, a tear, a swallow, or a twitch of the body.

+ Relating with people in altered states of consciousness, coma therapists find four categories, or channels of awareness, to pay attention to: visual, auditory, body sensation, and movement channels (see the following resource by Stan Tomandl for more information). In most cases, simply paying attention to a person's breath will indicate which channel of communication may be open.

- Since the comatose person rarely speaks, it is important to respond to any movements or cues with *blank access interventions*; that is, speak in an affirming way about what you observe without judgment or evaluation. For example, if a tear appears, instead of presuming sadness, simply acknowledge that there is water coming from the eye. It could be a tear of joy or a mechanical reaction to something environmental.

- Coma therapy takes time. Be persistent with your communications and sensitive to feedback from the patient.

- Trust that by doing coma therapy you are helping your loved one or client complete their inner work. If they do complete their inner work, they can use information from their inner and outer experiences to make important decisions, including coming out of coma, and life and death choices.

Level of Expertise

You need courage, awareness, and caution to communicate with someone in an extremely altered state. Trust your intuitions and body feelings. Consider purchasing one of the available excellent resources that teach basic communication skills with comatose persons. Be willing to experiment with interventions, but respect your personal comfort limits. If you feel uncomfortable and tired, you can assume that your care receiver feels the same. If after several attempts you receive no response, say good-bye for the time being. Be willing to check out your presumptions and experiences with a trained professional or coma therapy manual. For everyone's safety, coma therapy should be done with supervision and consent from family and medical staff.

Resources for Coma Therapy

Coma therapists owe their direction and commitment to American psychologist Dr. Arnold Mindell, who teaches internationally, including at the C.G. Jung Institute in Zurich and at his Process Work Center in

Portland, Oregon. Mindell teaches specific communication techniques and various interventions that support patients in coma. The following resources have been influenced by Mindell's work:

PRINT AIDS

The Journal of Process-Oriented Psychology. Vol. 5, No. 2. Portland, OR: Lao Tse Press. www.processwork.org

> A semiannual publication of the Process Work Center of Portland. This unique professional publication hosts regular contributions from experts in fields related to illness, coma therapy, and the end of life.

Mindell, Amy. *Coma: A Healing Journey: A Guide for Family, Friends, and Helpers.* Portland, OR: Lao Tse Press, 1999.

> A highly acclaimed, practical resource for the beginner dealing with persons in coma. Mindell's approach replaces the static image of a subhuman person in a vegetative state with a dynamic and hopeful vision of a healing journey.

Mindell, Arnold. *Coma: The Dreambody Near Death.* Portland, OR: Lao Tse Press, 2004.

> The groundbreaking work with comatose patients that offers new direction in psychotherapy and the study of near-death experiences. Mindell's process work shows how, far from being the horrific experience many assume, coma can be a time of ecstasy and remarkable transformation.

Tomandl, Stan. *Coma Work and Palliative Care: An Introductory Communication Skills Manual for Supporting People Living Near Death.* Victoria, B.C.: Great River Books, 1991.

> A comprehensive yet easy-to-use guide for the beginner in coma work. Highly recommended for family members and health care professionals.

TRAINING AND WORKSHOP OPPORTUNITIES

Coma Communication Therapy
annstan@islandnet.com
Phone: 250-383-5677
#502-620 View Street, Victoria, B.C., Canada, V8W 1J6

> An organization supporting the teaching and work of internationally acclaimed coma therapists Ann Jacob and Stan Tomandl.

Process Work Center of Portland
www.processwork.org
Phone: 503-223-8188; Fax: 503-227-7003
2049 NW Hoyt Street, Portland, Oregon 97209

Programs and workshops by coma work originators Arnold and Amy Mindell and colleagues.

Additional titles by the Mindells related to process and coma work are also available through Lao Tse Press at laotse@laotse.com.

Sacred Art of Dying National Education Programs
www.sacredartofliving.org

Courses include substantial training on coma therapy for health care professionals and family members. The program faculty includes coma workers trained by Dr. Arnold Mindell and/or coma associates Stan Tomandl and Ann Jacob of Victoria, B.C.

Dream Work

Ancient cultures took dreams seriously. Our ancestors were convinced that, especially at the end of life, the content of a person's dreams were the most direct path to diagnosing spiritual pain. Modern psychology affirms the significance of dreams. Carl Jung said, "Every dream is spiritual and it is always about death." The value of dream work is that our dreams help us get in touch with life's meaning and purpose. Dreams help us to risk confronting our nightmares in order to release energy for healing and courage.

Applications for the End of Life

Surveys of hospice patients indicate that dream work or dream therapy is generally well received and fruitful in exploring inner life. Dream content for terminally ill patients often parallels the most common end-of-life landmarks, such as closure on relationships, completing worldly affairs, accepting life's frailty, and surrendering to the unknown. When considered in a spiritual perspective, dream work is often successful in bringing hidden anxieties to the surface and helping patients find a deeper sense of trust and peace.

Basic Tools

Dreams are a language and an important link between our conscious and unconscious self. Sixty-nine percent of the general adult population does not remember their dreams with regularity. With the simple suggestion to pay attention to nightly dreams, 91 percent of the same group will have significantly improved dream recall.

There are four levels of recounting dreams:

- *Recalling.* Suggest that the patient attempt to recall a dream as soon as possible after awaking. You might suggest that the invitation to recall the dream be done with a simple prayer or ritual before going to sleep.

- *Sharing.* It is better if the patient share her dream with another. No matter how insignificant or irrational, encourage the patient to talk about her dream soon after awaking. She may be surprised at how much more detail she recalls simply by having this conversation.

- *Journaling.* It is even better to have the patient record the dream in a journal. Suggest that she keep pen and paper by her bedside. Have her write whatever comes forth, from random thoughts or feelings to full sentence insights.

- *Drawing.* The best way to evaluate a dream is to draw it. One need not be an artist to depict a dream. It can be quite a revelation to watch how a dream begins to self-interpret just by drawing it.

Basic rules of dream interpretation include the following:

- When the dreamer recounts a dream or writes about it, have her use the present tense.

- Instead of trying to figure out the symbols or meaning of a dream, first reflect on how the dream made her feel.

- When someone significant shows up in a dream, inquire, "What aspect of yourself does that person represent?"

- Pay attention to seemingly insignificant symbols such as color, smell, or location. These may provide a clue to the dream's deeper meaning.

+ Be aware that not all dreams have the same degree of importance. Dreams range from mental static to healing nightmares.

Level of Expertise

Psychologically trained dream analysts have developed clinical dream therapies. Some of the basic skills of observing dreams, however, are accessible to everyone and only require a few rudimentary concepts. Before attempting to help someone else understand their dreams, pay attention to your own. In most cases, it is more important to be a dream companion than a dream therapist.

Consider using the following dream work technique to record dreams in more detail.

DREAM WORK TECHNIQUE

TITLE

Give your dream a title (let it come spontaneously).

THEME

State the major themes or issues that surfaced in your dream.

_____

_____

_____

_____

AFFECT

What was the dominant feeling or emotion experienced during your dream?

_____

_____

_____

QUESTION

What question is the dream asking of you?

_____

_____

_____

Resources for Dream Work

PRINT AIDS

Kramer, Kenneth. *Death Dreams: Unveiling Mysteries of the Unconscious Mind.* New York: Paulist Press, 1993.

A treasure chest of stories and information on the relationship between dreams and the end of life.

Mindell, Arnold. *The Dreambody in Relationships.* Portland, OR: Lao Tse Press, 2002.

A focus on the therapeutic value of dreams. Mindell explores the relationship between body experience and dreaming during even the most difficult stages of life.

Salvary, L., and P. Berne. *Dreams and Spiritual Growth: A Judeo-Christian Way of Dreamwork.* New York: Paulist Press, 1984.

A helpful guide for Jews and Christians regarding the healing potential of dream work.

Sanford, John A. *Dreams: God's Forgotten Language.* San Francisco: Harper & Row Publishers, 1989.

Written by a Jungian analyst and Episcopal priest, a book that can help persons coming from biblical traditions to understand how dreams can reconnect us to the spiritual world.

—. *Dreams and Healing: A Succinct and Lively Interpretation of Dreams.* New York: Paulist Press, 1994.

A wealth of reflection on the creative and healing potential of dreams.

Von Franz, Marie-Louise. *On Dreams and Death: A Jungian Interpretation.* Peru, IL: Open Court/Carus Publishing Co., 1998.

A book that asks, What is there but dying? A scholarly and inspiring exploration of the ways in which our dreams prepare us for unimaginable transformations in and after life.

WORKSHOPS AND RESOURCES

Sacred Art of Dying National Education Programs
www.sacredartofliving.org

> Courses include instruction and experience in the practice of dream interpretation at the end of life from the perspectives of Jungian analysis and world religious traditions.

www.dreamworkshops.com

> A variety of workshops, training programs, and locations regarding dream work and dream interpretation from many religious perspectives.

www.jungiandreamworkshops.com

> Dream workshops in the Jungian tradition, found in many retreat house locations around the country.

Energy Therapies

In ancient times healing was associated with human touch and the laying on of hands. Today therapies like Reiki and Healing Touch are offered within mainstream medical institutions. The roots of these healing arts are deeply spiritual. Contemporary science confirms that at a measurable, physical level, human beings are a mass of energy that is alive and is the source of our vitality. Healing can occur when our life energy or vital force is flowing and unrestricted. Conversely, when energy is low or blocked, a person is more prone to illness. Eastern traditions have studied and honored the relationship between energy and healing more than the West. All spiritual traditions agree that, regardless of what this life force is called (*chi* in Chinese, *prana* in Sanskrit, *ki* in Hawaiian, or *God consciousness* in the West), there is an inseparable connection between the physical, emotional, and spiritual dimensions of this energy and health.

Applications for the End of Life

Whenever two human beings agree to support each other, in essence they are agreeing to do energy work. The sacred art of dying traditions encouraged healers to assist the dying person in cultivating energy, in the same way an athlete learns to conserve and sustain energy for long-distance competition. Both the caregiver and care receiver need stamina and patience to face the physical and emotional challenges of dying. Energy therapies ensure that our best resources are maintained for the important work of transition.

Basic Tools

There are tried and tested methods for sustaining energy in the face of life's stresses and difficulties. Certain practices are valuable for people who are dying or working with the dying. Even if you do not feel it is appropriate to engage in formal energy therapy, here are a few basic concepts worth considering.

- Gentle exercise can help promote well-being and can revitalize persons who are not capable of strenuous activity.

- Simple exercises inspired by Qi Gong or Chi Kung (meaning "internal energy exercise") can be adapted for bedridden patients. Likewise, Tai Chi offers some fundamental movements that support and relax the body's joints and muscles. Both of these Asian-inspired practices help keep the mind alert and the spirit relaxed.

- Metal Chinese handballs are widely available in craft shops and health centers. They are rolled in the hand to stimulate acupuncture points connecting the fingers to all major internal organs.

- Consider inviting a Reiki practitioner to offer a series of therapies for your patient. Many hospitals offer this service for free to pre- and post-surgery patients to reduce stress and, sometimes, to reduce the need for expensive medications and their undesirable side effects.

- Healing Touch, also known as Therapeutic Touch, is a holistic therapy that has a national network of trained practitioners available. Healing Touch providers use gentle, noninvasive touch to influence and support the human energy system within and surrounding the body. Results include the patient's enhanced ability for self-healing in body, mind, and spirit.

- For persons who relate to either the Jewish or Christian traditions, there are simple exercises to balance the body's energy in the context of scriptural texts (see the following resources list).

Level of Expertise

The ability to work with energy in quasi-medical therapies such as Reiki or Therapeutic Touch cannot be learned from a book. Training schools and certification programs are available for students wishing to become practitioners. Caregivers are encouraged to understand the basic concepts of energy healing, however, both for themselves and for their care receivers. Energy workers are available in most communities. You can find them at local medical institutions or listed as complementary health care practitioners.

Resources for Energy Therapy

PRINT AIDS

Addison, Howard, Rabbi. *The Enneagam and Kabbalah.* Woodstock, VT: Jewish Lights Publishing, 2002.

An inspiring meditation on bringing divine light to each of the human energy points.

Bates, Nancy. *An Introduction to Christian Yoga.* New York: Cowley Publishing, 2001.

A series of body-mind-spirit exercises using verses from the psalms as a point of reflection.

Brennan, Barbara. *Hands of Light: A Guide for Healing through the Human Energy Fields.* New York: Pleiades Books, 1988.

A book that Elisabeth Kübler-Ross describes as a must read for anyone involved in the important work of healing.

Fernandez, Carmen. *Reiki Healing: How to Channel the Power of Universal Love.* London: Lorenz Books, 2000.

McLaren, Karla. *Your Aura and Your Chakras: The Owner's Manual.* Boston: Weiser Books, 1998.

A collection of exercises, including both beginner and advanced techniques, by an expert in working with survivors of abuse and trauma.

Rand, William Lee. *Reiki: The Healing Touch.* Southfield, MI: Vision Publications, 1998.

A trainer's manual for first- and second-degree Reiki practitioners, demonstrating stress reduction techniques and promoting healing through the laying on of hands.

Seidman, Maruti. *Balancing the Chakras*. Berkeley, CA: North Atlantic Books, 2000.

A basic text for understanding the energy fields of the body called chakras. The author does a good job of describing the symptoms of imbalance and explores various modalities for healing.

White, Ruth. *Working with Your Chakras: A Physical, Emotional and Spiritual Approach*. New York: Barnes and Noble Books, 1993.

A book with simple prayers and exercises for the beginner to open subtle energy between friends and partners for healing.

VIDEO RESOURCES

Serrie, John, and John Saxon. *The Healing Workout Chi Kung: Experience the Beauty of Nature and the Healing Energy of Chi Kung*. PMN Distribution, 1996.

Stunning footage from nature accompanies the beautiful and accessible art of healing movement.

Watts, Alan. *The Art of Mediation*. Wellspring Media, 1994.

An inspiring and practical step-by-step guide to meditation.

TRAINING AND WORKSHOP OPPORTUNITIES

Healing Touch International
www.healingtouch.net

Offering and teaching the practice of Healing Touch as a therapy to complement traditional or allopathic medicine.

www.reiki.7gen.com

INFORMATION ON THE PRACTICE OF REIKI AND TRAINING

FOR PROSPECTIVE PRACTITIONERS

Sacred Art of Dying National Education Programs
www.sacredartofliving.org

Courses include comprehensive training on understanding and responding to issues of forgiveness at the end of life.

Forgiveness Exercises

More often than not, forgiveness issues are at the origin of a person's spiritual pain. Although cultures and belief systems express forgiveness in different ways, the underlying reality is the same. At the end of life, it is the responsibility of the caring community to do everything possible to assist in removing any barrier to the dying person's spiritual well-being that creates anxiety, mistrust, division, or resentment. A common barrier to forgiveness is a misconception regarding what forgiveness is and is not.

- Forgiveness is not condoning specific behaviors that may have caused irreparable damage in life.

- Forgiveness does not mean that we tolerate the wrong someone did to us.

- Forgiveness does not mean that we forget what happened to us.

- Forgiveness does not surrender our right to justice nor does it imply that we invite someone back into our lives to hurt us again.

- Forgiveness is a deep psychospiritual process that leads to freedom and relief, for the forgiver as well as for the one forgiven.

Applications for the End of Life

The world's sacred art of dying traditions concur that nothing is more important at the end of life than removing all barriers between ourselves and others. Recent work demonstrates the beneficial effects of forgiveness in terms of improved health and peace of mind. Our ancestors knew that forgiveness heals the spirit. The majority of persons who struggle with anxiety at the end of life cannot forgive themselves. They can no longer ignore a lifetime of repressed guilt or unresolved conflict. No one wants to live or die in agony, but sometimes life circumstances seem overwhelming. An invitation to privately engage in forgiveness work through a spiritual practice or exercise can be a first step toward relief of end-of-life suffering.

Basic Tools

Guilt and resentment are traps. Forgiveness is the only way out. The specific tool for forgiving is not as important as the attitude of one's heart. There is a treasure chest of practices to guide the process of reconciliation. Trust your own judgment as you discern which of the following exercises might be more appropriate for your patient's circumstances.

+ *Forgiveness List.* These lists are much like a review of life. Depending on a person's spiritual orientation, he can do this exercise in a profoundly prayerful context. Begin by inviting the patient to take all the time he needs and suggest that he makes two lists. On the first list, have him write the names of anyone who has ever hurt him. It doesn't matter whether the person caused the hurt intentionally or not. Have him walk through his life and name what has happened to him. Next have him make a parallel list with the names of those whom he has hurt. Tell him not to get trapped in judgments or rationalizations, just have the courage to put pen to paper and admit that certain relationships in his life have been wounded ones. Afterward, suggest that he consider how to respond to these lists. Are any actions called for? Is there a desire to ritually release these names? Admission is the first step in the process of forgiveness.

+ *Twelve-Step Process.* Twelve-Step programs are one of America's great contributions to spirituality. While developed for persons dealing with substance abuse, the Twelve-Step principles are psychologically and spiritually sound, and they include a remarkable way to deal with forgiveness. Following the step of life review, a person is invited to encounter those whom they have hurt with destructive behaviors. Such a confession can be an important step in leaving behind old guilt and fear and moving forward in life with genuine peace of mind. Twelve-Step coaches and sponsors are available in every community of the country to introduce this process of reconciliation.

* *Prayer of Gratitude.* A prayer of gratitude is a paradoxical way to address the spiritual pain of nonforgivingness. This practice is based on an ancient spiritual truism: It is not possible to hold feelings or thoughts of resentment and of gratitude at the same time. When stuck in a place of not being able to forgive oneself or others, a prayer of gratitude is a spiritual shortcut to forgiveness. A variation of this practice is to hold in prayer a person who has been the source of hurt. Suggest that the patient, instead of overlooking the misunderstanding, find something positive about the person for which they can be grateful.

* *Seventy Times Seven Practice.* Dr. Joan Borysenko articulates this forgiveness process. The term "seventy times seven" refers to a question and answer in the biblical tradition. The question is, "How often must we forgive another when we have been wronged? Seven times?" The answer suggests that we return to forgiveness, "Not seven times, but seventy times seven times." In other words, forgiveness is not a one-shot deal but may require several repetitions of the following cycle of seven steps: (1) take responsibility, (2) make a confession, (3) look for the good, (4) be willing to make amends, (5) look to God for help, (6) find meaning in what has been learned, and (7) offer a prayer of gratitude.

Level of Expertise

Anyone can forgive. Forgiveness requires no special technique or experience except a willing heart and open spirit.

Resources for Forgiveness Exercises

PRINT AIDS

Arnold, Johann Christoph. *Seventy Times Seven: The Power of Forgiveness.* Farmington, PA: Plough Publishing, 1997.

A book about real people scarred by betrayal, abuse, war, and bigotry.

Levine, Stephen. *Healing into Life and Death.* New York: Anchor Books, 1987.

A well-integrated and practical approach to body-mind-spirit meditations in dealing with the pain of forgiveness.

Linn, Dennis, Matthew Linn, and Sheila Linn. *Don't Forgive Too Soon: Extending the Two Hands That Heal.* New York: Paulist Press, 1997.

One of the finest resources for understanding and responding to issues of forgiveness from a spiritual perspective. Written from a Judeo-Christian perspective this book is delightful and inviting in presentation.

Smedes, Louis B. *The Art of Forgiving: When You Need to Forgive and Don't Know How.* New York: Ballantine Books, 1996.

AUDIO RESOURCES

Borysenko, Joan. *Seventy Times Seven: On the Art of Spiritual Forgiveness.* Sounds True, Audio Cassette Tapes.

A remarkable collection of stories and theory on the medical and spiritual benefits of forgiveness from one of America's leading psychoneuroimmunologists.

TRAINING PROGRAMS

Sacred Art of Dying National Education Programs
www.sacredartofliving.org

Courses include instruction and experience in the theory and practice of forgiveness work at the end of life.

Twleve-Step Programs

Consult your local telephone directory or go online for specific contact information.

Guided Visualization

Although the term guided visualization is relatively modern, all ancient end-of-life traditions encouraged some form of spiritual visualization practice. Visualization is a type of meditation that engages the active imagination, as if you were experiencing an external physical occurrence. An image may have the power to heal and to take you to a higher realm of experience. For many chronically ill patients, the practice of visualization can assist in controlling pain, alleviating physical discomfort, and bringing out deep desires. Guided visualization can be a source for healing body, mind, and spirit.

Applications for the End of Life

Of all the remarkable psychological and healing processes available, few seem to have the ability to transform pain at the end of life as powerfully as guided visualization. This kind of meditation begins with the belief that every moment of your life is infinitely creative. Visualization is more than the power of positive thinking. It draws on universal principles shared by both physical and spiritual sciences, such as the law of attraction. We tend to attract into our lives more of whatever we think about the most. When we are negative, anxious, or fearful, for example, we often reinforce the thing we are trying to avoid. By contrast, tapping into the benevolent flow of the universe, no matter what one's concept of the divine is, brings solace and healing even in the most painful situation.

Basic Tools

Creative visualization uses mental imagery and affirmation to produce positive change in the physical, emotional, and spiritual self. It incorporates a progressive relaxation technique, opening the mind and spirit to new and larger possibilities. If you are guiding someone through a visualization, it is helpful to remember that you are not the healer, rather your goal is to provide an environment in which healing can take place. The following principles refer to visualization in a spiritual context.

- It is important to discern who is *not* ready for guided visualization, including recent trauma victims, persons with thin ego boundaries or raw emotions, or cases where immediate family members have extreme anxiety. Visualization is inappropriate if there are philosophical or religious objections to the practice. Use your own intuition to discern who is ready.

- If you discern that a person is open to guided visualization, spend some time establishing trust and listening for cues to appropriate images for the exercise.

- Inquire what kinds of images in nature represent healing and relaxation for the care receiver. Later, you can suggest such a location during the visualization exercise.

- Inquire which persons from the care receiver's life represent trust and love and could act as a guide during the visualization process.

Use the following basic outline for facilitating a guided visualization process with your care receiver:

- Ensure a proper, distractionless environment: reduce obnoxious noise such as televisions, phones, and so on; keep lighting to a minimum; and consider using some recorded sounds of nature or nonrhythmic music such as white noise

- Then, begin with a simple conversation
- Determine whether there are any areas calling for healing
- Close your eyes and have the patient do the same; relax
- Pray for healing and illumination
- Speak slowly and softly with authority
- Initiate a breath awareness exercise, for example, breathing out all that is hurtful and distressing, and breathing in all that is life-giving
- Become more conscious of the presence of the moment
- Trust that wisdom will surface
- Help the care receiver to paint a mental picture that creates a supportive inner environment
- Evoke an image for the care receiver
- Allow the person to have a conversation with the image for as long as they want
- Suggest the prayer receiver express gratitude at the end of the visualization
- Return the care receiver to conscious breathing
- Open your eyes and have the patient open her eyes when ready
- Spend some time debriefing with the care receiver around her experience
- Consider concluding with a prayer or thanksgiving

Level of Expertise

Although there are sophisticated levels of training for visualization practitioners, family members and friends can draw on some of the basic concepts of guided meditation to assist care receivers. If you are not comfortable creating your own visualization process, consider using one of the many visualization programs available in print or audio format (see below). Some forms of visualization mediation can be self-guided. You may also inquire at your local hospice whether one of its professionals or volunteers has been trained in visualization techniques.

Resources for Guided Visualization

PRINT AIDS

Borysenko, Joan, and Miroslav Borysenko. *The Power of the Mind to Heal: Renewing Mind, Body and Spirit.* Carlsbad, CA: Hay House, 1994.

A treasure chest of meditation and mindfulness exercises especially for the chronically ill.

Droege, Thomas. *Guided Grief Imagery: A Resource for Grief Ministry and Death Education.* New York: Paulist Press, 1997.

A handbook of guided imagery exercises using the biblical psalms as sources of inspiration.

Fezler, William. *Creative Imagery: How to Visualize in All Five Senses.* New York: Simon and Schuster, 1989.

An analysis of visualization skills from a more psychological perspective; useful in understanding basic concepts and innovative techniques.

Gawain, Shakti. *Creative Visualization: Use the Power of Your Imagination to Create What You Want in Your Life.* Novato, CA: New World Library, 2002.

One of the best guides available for meditation exercises and techniques that tap into the power of imagination for healing.

Levine, Stephen. *Guided Meditations, Explorations and Healing.* Garden City, NY: Doubleday, 1991.

A beautifully presented selection of texts that can be used by caregivers, dying persons, and others dealing with pain, intense emotional states, and conscious dying.

Stevens, Edward. *Spiritual Technologies: A User's Manual.* New York: Paulist Press, 1990.

A book with many experimental approaches to contemplative practice, both practical and body-based. A great resource for bridging Western and Eastern spiritual traditions.

Vanek, Elizabeth Anne. *Image Guidance: A Tool for Spiritual Direction.* New York: Paulist Press, 1991.

A helpful resource introducing the practice of visualization based on case studies. A step-by-step introduction to the topic emphasizing the use of intuition.

AUDIO RESOURCES

The following audio resources (available on CD and tape) feature the work of author Richard Groves and are available through the Sacred Art of Living Center at 541-383-4179 or www.sacredartofliving.org.

The Golden Light: Guided Meditations for the Terminally Ill

A variety of meditations to ease emotional and spiritual pain with nonrhythmic harp music.

The Peaceful Journey: Guided Meditations for the Terminally Ill

A collection of specifically designed mediations for end-of-life care with soothing musical accompaniments.

The following audio resources feature Dr. O. Carl Simonton and are available through the Simonton Cancer Center at 1-800-338-2360 or simontoncancercenter@msn.com.

The Healing Journey Rhythms

A collection of music based on ancient percussion patterns that assist in shifting brain waves associated with deep relaxation and creativity.

Relaxation and Mental Imagery as Applies to Cancer Therapy

A classic tape that includes step-by-step instructions on the use of mental imagery exercises.

WORKSHOP OPPORTUNITIES

Sacred Art of Dying National Education Programs
www.sacredartofliving.org

Courses include comprehensive training on the theory and practice of guided visualization practice within a spiritual context.

Healing and Assistance from Ancestors

Previous generations believed that help is available from those who have traveled life ahead of us. Ancestors encompass, of course, those who have birthed us and all those previous generations of family that we can remember. They also, paradoxically, include children yet unborn. Ancestors also include deceased persons for whom we have great respect and admiration, including wisdom figures and saints. When a person carries a wounded relationship with someone who has died, it is consoling to know that healing may still be possible. Asking for help, forgiveness, or wisdom from those whom we no longer see, but sometimes sense "over our shoulder if we turn our head quickly" can be a powerful tool.

Applications for the End of Life

Spiritual traditions teach that life doesn't start at birth or end at death. This is not about reincarnation, but rather about continuity. Based on this premise, our ancestors play a vital role in our living and dying. For example, our birth family creates both blessings and challenges, and healing is sometimes needed. Unspoken family hurts and expectations can resurface as a person struggles with serious illness. Realities easily ignored during the hustle and bustle of living cannot be ignored when facing death. Many wisdom traditions draw comfort from the belief that the same ones who connected with us in life can support us during our time of death. Numerous deathbed visions of ancestors point to an affirmation that help from our ancestors is available.

Basic Tools

Consider the cultural and religious sensitivities of the care receiver when suggesting any form of ancestor assistance or healing. Certain traditions are comfortable with the language of intercessory prayer for the deceased. Intercessory prayer is the capacity for mutual exchange of love and healing energy. Other cultures have strict taboos about anything that could appear to welcome back the spirits of the dead. Most Native Americans, for example, do not invite ancestors back out of respect, not wishing to disturb their peace. Nevertheless, all spiritual traditions honor the continuity of life and encourage respect for ancestors, living or dead. Following are a few guidelines when introducing healing and assistance from ancestors to care receivers.

- Most persons can relate to a particular relative, friend, or wisdom figure who represents compassion and unconditional love. During the final stage of dying, encourage the care receiver to imagine that person as a source of support and strength. As caregiver, you might find it appropriate to suggest he repeat the ancestor's first name as a mantra or prayer of encouragement.

- Consider some form of guided meditation that includes a supportive ancestor (see "Guided Visualization"). Encourage the care receiver to have a conversation with the deceased person about whatever he fears in the dying process.

- When the care receiver has a wounded relationship with a deceased relative, consider facilitating a healing conversation or ritual. Even when the hurt involved physical or sexual abuse, trust that by bringing the issue from darkness to light (in the language of many spiritual traditions) healing is possible.

- Persons relating to the Judeo-Christian traditions can consult a biblical concordance for passages referring to ancestors as a starting point for prayerful reflection.

Level of Expertise

The principle criterion required for ancestor work is faith in the ability to welcome healing regardless of time or space. Certain skills can be useful in creating an environment for healing, using appropriate language, and so forth. Make sure you respect a person's belief system and temperament when mediating the profound work.

Resources for Healing and Assistance from Ancestors

PRINT AIDS

Finley, Mitch. *Whispers of Love: Encounters with Deceased Relatives and Friends.* Chicago: Crossroads, 1995.

A comforting book with stories drawn from the Judeo-Christian traditions.

Halifax, Joan. *Shaman: The Wounded Healer.* Chicago: Crossroads, 2001.

A classic in understanding the anthropology and spirituality of healing in the great lineage of the human family by a renowned Buddhist teacher.

Linn, Dennis, Matthew Linn, and Sheila Linn. *Simple Ways to Pray for Healing.* New York: Paulist Press, 1998.

A collection of practical exercises that integrates contemporary psychology, spirituality, and medicine. The chapter on "Healing Relationships with the Deceased" is especially relevant here. Based on the renowned healing ministry of the Linns.

—. *Remembering Our Home: Healing Hurts and Receiving Gifts from Conception to Birth.* New York: Paulist Press, 1999.

An excellent example of the wedding between theology and science. Based on Dr. William Emerson's leading-edge psychological research on human experience before birth, here is a collection of practical advice for those suffering from unresolved family-of-origin wounds.

Lyon, William S. *Encyclopedia of Native American Healing.* New York: W. W. Norton and Co., 1998.

A monumental volume exploring and honoring the healing practices of Native Americans including rituals, ceremonies, and the honoring of ancestors.

McLaren, Karla. *Your Aura and Your Chakras: The Owner's Manual.* Boston: Weiser Books, 1998.

A collection of exercises that include destroying negative images in order to open up new possibilities for healing by an expert on working with survivors of abuse and trauma.

AUDIO RESOURCES

Halifax, Joan. *Being with the Dying: Contemplative Practice and Teaching.* Chicago: Crossroads, 1997.

A master teacher voices some of her most insightful teachings in end-of-life caregiving.

TRAINING AND WORKSHOP OPPORTUNITIES

Sacred Art of Dying National Education Programs
www.sacredartofliving.org

Courses include comprehensive training on understanding and responding to issues of forgiveness at the end of life.

Using any search engine, search for *ancestor healing* to find numerous sites from many cultural and religious perspectives

Healing Religious Abuse and Images of God

For many people religion provides an important context and meaning for life. It is not unusual, however, to encounter persons who struggle from the harmful effects of negative religious experiences. Psychologists and theologians are in agreement that a person's image of God or the divine higher power is established by age four or five. People who encountered love and compassion from significant adult authority figures of early life are more likely to have a healthy sense of the divine. On the other hand, in the name of God or religion or authority, subtle or not so subtle, forms of spiritual abuse can occur. The end of life can exacerbate such a difficult problem.

Applications for the End of Life

A generation ago there was little distinction between spirituality and religion. Today most people understand that, while these two realities may overlap, there can be important differences. Sacred art of dying traditions assume that each person has a spiritual nature, though she may use different language to describe her beliefs. Formal religion may or may not be an essential part of someone's life. Nevertheless, at the end of life, our ideas about what gives life meaning and purpose are paramount. Toxic and shame-based belief systems about life, death, and the afterlife intensify spiritual pain.

Basic Tools

Not everyone who has been the victim of religious or spiritual abuse can name the experience. Boyd C. Purcell defines religious abuse as "the act of making people believe, whether by stating or merely implying, that they are going to be punished in this life and or tormented in hell fire forever for failure to live life well enough to please God and thus earn admission to heaven." No religion teaches this philosophy; however, this interpretation is all too common. The response to religious or spiritual abuse will vary according to the individual's personality, their belief system, and the degree of abuse. Here is some background information that can help the anamcara understand what is going on with the spiritual abuse victim.

- The underlying motivation of any abuse is control. In the case of religion, the control is over a person's inner life through an overly rigid system of rules and beliefs.

- It is not uncommon for religious abuse to be accompanied by physical and/or sexual abuse. The American clerical sex abuse crisis is symptomatic of a deeper issue of control and the abuse of authority.

- Once a person has been hooked by unhealthy religiosity, especially during early formative years, it can be difficult to disassociate from those beliefs no matter how much someone knows the beliefs are irrational.

- When religious abuse is extreme, for example, in the case of satanic ritual abuse, the support of mental health counseling is generally necessary.

- The only way out of religious abuse is to be spiritually reparented. A healthy religious experience, usually facilitated by a mentor or friend, must replace an unhealthy model of relating to the divine.

- When mild to moderate religious abuse is the issue, a person of the same religious institution may provide the therapy or antidote, but only if they are willing to listen to and accept the abused person's experience without judgment or defensiveness.

• Healing is always possible. Deathbed stories abound of individuals who encounter a great healing light or other sacred image that restores their confidence in God and in themselves.

Level of Expertise

Anyone can provide support to another human being in pain. In the case of religious or spiritual abuse, however, the assistance of a professional counselor may be required in addition to common sense companionship.

Resources for Healing Religious Abuse and Images of God

PRINT AIDS

Fowler, James H. *Stages of Faith: The Psychology of Human Development and the Quest for Meaning.* Cambridge, MA: Harper and Row, 1981.

One of the classics on the relationship between faith and psychology.

Linn, Dennis, Matthew Linn, and Sheila Linn. *Good Goats: Healing our Image of God.* New York: Paulist Press, 1994.

One of the finest books of its kind regarding fearful and broken images of God. Though written primarily from a Judeo-Christian perspective, the Linns' profound theology is readable and practical when dealing with religious wounds at the end of life.

—. *Healing Spiritual Abuse and Religious Addiction.* New York: Paulist Press, 1994.

Both respectful and insightful, a book that uncovers the subtle forms of abuse that occur in the name of religion and offers important perspectives for treating its victims.

—. *Understanding Difficult Scriptures in a Healing Way.* New York: Paulist Press, 2000.

A book for persons who have experienced religious abuse within a Christian tradition, this work by the Linns is sensitive in breaking through the kind of spiritual terrorism that is sometimes encountered due to passages from scripture that were presented in abusive ways.

Sattely, Lamont. *Tattooed in the Cradle: The Healing Journey from Family to Spiritual Wholeness.* NSW Australia: Search Foundation, 1993.

An important book about how persons inherit unproductive guilt and belief systems.

TRAINING AND WORKSHOP OPPORTUNITIES

Sacred Art of Dying National Education Programs
www.sacredartofliving.org

Courses include significant training components regarding religious and spiritual abuse based on the work of Dr. James Fowler of Emory University, the Linns, and other respected leaders of various faith traditions.

Intercessory (Nonlocal) Prayer

Modern physicians and scientists have challenged the distinction between faith and science by testing the thesis that prayer benefits the sick. Well-known research projects demonstrate that intercessory, or nonlocal, prayer is effective, even when the recipient does not know that she or he was being prayed for. A variety of so-called lower organisms, including plants and animals, likewise become healthier when they receive prayer. Larry Dossey, author of *Prayer Is Good Medicine*, quotes articles in leading mainstream medical journals, and he asks the prophetic question, Will the day come when patients will call the failure to prescribe prayer medical malpractice?

What is prayer? Prayers are as diverse as the people who pray. No one has a corner on prayer, and more prayer is not necessarily better prayer. You can even pray in your dreams. Every survey done in America in recent years indicates that when sick, more than 90 percent of us will turn to prayer. Prayer works, and that fact alone makes it an accessible and effective spiritual tool.

Applications for the End of Life

There is no best way to pray. Prayer is limited only by our imagination and willingness to help another. Intercessory prayer is a real and practical way to stay connected with dying persons who are often unconscious. Virtually every sacred art of dying tradition prescribes some form of nonlocal or intercessory prayer, acknowledging that time and distance do not matter at the end of life. Because prayer is often associated with hope, and because hopelessness kills, it follows that prayer can be a significant source of healing, even when the body is no longer expected to recover from illness.

Basic Tools

During the final stages of dying, inner healing becomes as important as the management of physical symptoms and disease. Prayer is not a last ditch effort, but an effective way of supporting a care receiver. The human person is made of energy more than matter, and so is the universe around us. Prayer calls upon and taps into the most positive, loving, creative life force, variously called God, consciousness, or the universe. You need not be a religious believer to pray. A follower of a faith tradition or not, when you feel the call to pray, pray.

- Trust that in the presence of chronic or terminal illness prayer is, in the words of Larry Dossey, "as valid and vital a healing tool as any drug or surgery."

- Don't be afraid to ask your care receiver whether they would mind if you prayed for them. In the vast majority of cases they will have no objection.

- Remember that intercessory, or nonlocal, prayer does not require your physical presence. Consider the gift of scheduling a regular prayer date or time with your care receiver, even if you are geographically distant.

- There is no right or wrong way to pray. Simply quiet your mind from other distractions and pray either with or without words. When you pray in the presence of the recipient, be sensitive to his comfort with religious language. For example, address the divine in a way that respects his belief system. When praying long distance, pray in whatever language fits you best.

Level of Expertise

As long as your intentions are pure, you cannot harm another human being with prayer. Granted, you are probably not a mystic or someone who prays professionally, but everyone has the capacity to be a conduit of loving-kindness, which is another definition of prayer. You may find one of the many following readings and resources about prayer useful and supportive in deepening your own commitment to pray for your beloved sick and dying one.

Resources for Intercessory (Nonlocal) Prayer

PRINT AIDS

Borysenko, Joan. *Minding the Body, Mending the Mind.* New York: Bantam, 1988.

A foundation for trusting the connection between healing, health, prayer, and science.

Dossey, Larry, M.D. *Healing Words: The Power of Prayer and the Practice of Medicine.* San Francisco: HarperCollins Books, 1993.

A thoughtful and eloquent collection of research and anecdotal evidence about prayer and its affect on cancer, spontaneous remission, and other important topics for caregivers and their patients.

—. *Prayer Is Good Medicine: How to Reap the Healing Benefits of Prayer.* San Francisco: HarperCollins Books, 1997.

A groundbreaking book that links prayer and health. Regardless of your faith tradition, Dr. Dossey's book can help you appreciate the healing benefits of prayer.

Linn, Dennis, Matthew Linn, and Sheila Linn. *Simple Ways to Pray for Healing.* New York: Paulist Press, 1998.

Based on eight simple ways of praying for healing, a widely acclaimed book that includes stories that integrate the worlds of spirituality and medicine.

Simonton, O. Carl, M.D., and Reid Henson. *The Healing Journey.* New York: Bantam, 1994.

An important book distinguishing between when it is appropriate to help a person prepare to die and when it is important to help them fight to live.

AUDIO RESOURCES

The following audio resources feature Dr. O. Carl Simonton and are available through the Simonton Cancer Center at 1-800-338-2360 or simontoncancercenter@msn.com.

Relaxation and Mental Imagery as Applies to Cancer Therapy
Easy-to-use tapes that include step-by-step instructions on the use of mental imagery exercises.

Hope, Hopelessness, Purpose and Trust
Designed to help cancer patients adopt a hopeful attitude to facilitate treatment.

VIDEO RESOURCES

The following videotape resources are available through the Simonton Cancer Center.

The Healing Journey. Ninety minutes.
A video presenting background on how our emotions affect our immune system and how we can impact the course of disease.

The Healing Process. Ninety minutes.
A video designed to help you access the body's natural healing wisdom. Dr. Simonton reveals how the purpose of facing death is to live more fully.

TRAINING PROGRAMS

Sacred Art of Dying National Education Programs
www.sacredartofliving.org
Courses include extensive instruction in the art and practice of intercessory prayer and related spiritual tools for healing at the end of life.

The Simonton Cancer Center
www.simontoncenter.com
Malibu, California
Patient programs for increasing the quality of life and decreasing tumor growth.

Journaling

Many people find keeping a journal a helpful way to reflect on life. During times of illness, journaling becomes a remarkable tool for exploring one's intuitions and tapping into one's natural wisdom. Psychologists observe that journaling uses both the right (creative) and left (analytical) hemispheres of the brain, thereby supporting a person's natural way of learning and processing information. Some journaling techniques favor the often less-used right brain, and therefore can relieve stress by accessing emotions and creative potential. Getting in touch with needs and feelings opens the door to finding solutions to problems and creating a more spontaneous approach to life.

Applications for the End of Life

Creative journaling is a profoundly spiritual tool that trusts the instincts and inner resources of each person. To write in the midst of a life crisis can be a boon for both the caregiver and care receiver. It is difficult for some people to express their values and beliefs in normal conversation. A journal is a place to vent when faced with the overwhelming experience of terminal illness. Writing can change negative beliefs into more life-giving opportunities for the future and can help make sense of what is happening.

Basic Tools

There is no right or wrong way to approach the exercise of creating writing. Tell the patient not to compare her results with others, and not to worry about making her journal perfect. Tell her, Just write. For those not accustomed to writing, a few guidelines and suggestions may be useful to get started.

+ *Confidentiality.* Make sure that the patient's journals are kept in a safe place, perhaps in a drawer, out of sight of others. Safety ensures greater honesty and depth of insight. Tell her that if desired, she may instruct a friend or confidant to destroy her journals after death.

+ *Environment.* Discover the best time and location for journaling, a quiet place where interruptions are unlikely. Have the patient go outdoors and if possible, get near water.

+ *Centering.* Teach the care receiver a breathing or meditation exercise to get grounded before journaling.

+ *The journal.* Purchase a bound volume that appeals to the care receiver, one which is easy for her to handle. Have her dedicate the pages just to journal entries. Suggest that she date each entry. To heighten mindfulness, have the patient include the location, the time of year, and her mood. Some people like to add a note about food, if they are eating and writing.

+ *Contents.* Instruct the patient to write about what is happening in her life and how she feels about it. Have her include her hopes, fears, dreams, and failures. Tell her to be honest and the lessons will come.

+ *Sacred time.* Journal time is like prayer or worship time. Have the patient mark its beginning and end by lighting a candle or performing some other ritual. The pages will begin to take on the soul's energy.

Some selected methods for journaling follow.

+ *Morning pages.* A traditional exercise for journaling is to record your thoughts first thing in the morning. Upon waking, the mind is less distracted and more open to listening deeply to the inner message. The morning is a good time to process fresh dreams. Julia Cameron, in the popular *The Artist's Way* (see resources below), recommends that a person allow random thoughts to drop from pen to paper.

+ *Prayer journaling.* This method employs traditional writing techniques within a more conscious spiritual perspective. The journaler may address her entries to God or a beloved intercessor as a way of writing from her soul.

+ *Life review.* A life review is a revealing task for many persons at the end of life. Instead of mere reminiscing, have the patient consider recording lessons she has learned. Have her notice the unique spiritual geography of her life's experiences (see pages 252–56).

+ *Portraits of the soul.* Suggest that the care receiver add a sketch, design, or color with her journal entries. A picture or doodle adds another layer of richness to the words.

Level of Expertise

Children and adolescents can journal as well as adults. Creative writing does not require formal training. Trust the truism: The more one journals, the more one comes to know one's soul.

Resources for Journaling

PRINT AIDS

Cameron, Julia. *The Artist's Way: A Spiritual Path to Higher Creativity.* New York: Tarcher/Putnam Books, 1992.

An empowering book that links creativity and spirituality, filled with many practical suggestions for journaling.

—. *The Vein of Gold: A Journey to Your Creative Heart.* New York: Tarcher/Putnam Books, 1996.

An encyclopedia of creative spiritual tools for healing through artful living.

Capacchione, Lucia. *The Creative Journal for Parents: A Guide to Unlocking Your Natural Wisdom.* Boston: Shambhala, 2000.

A book filled with simple and perceptive exercises that focus on parenting skills but also have universal application for all forms of journaling.

—. *The Creative Journal for Teens: Making Friends with Yourself.* North Hollywood, CA: Newcastle Publishing, 1993.

A rare resource for teenagers with applications for every stage of life in reaching the hidden depths of our dreams.

Klauser, Henriette Anne. *Put Your Heart on Paper: Staying Connected in a Loose-Ends World.* New York: Bantam Books, 1995.

A book by the coauthor of *The American Book of Living and Dying,* filled with inspiring and true stories of what happens when people write from their heart and share it with another.

—. *With Pen in Hand: The Healing Process of Writing.* Cambridge, MA: Perseus Books, 2003.

An explanation of why writing has the power to heal, with stories to illustrate various techniques. Includes a chapter on Ignation Discernment and learning to hold the light and darkness as one.

Klug, Ronald. *How to Keep a Spiritual Journal.* Minneapolis: Augsburg, 1993.

A resource for understanding how journaling is a mirror for the soul and an unparalleled spiritual practice for self-discovery.

Life Review Exercises

Testimonies from thousands of survivors of near-death experiences (NDEs) give insight into the psychospiritual process of death and dying. While each story is unique, there are clear patterns indicating universal shared experiences at the end of life. One of the most consistent reports concerns the life review. During the life-to-death transition, NDE survivors describe a sense of seeing the totality of their life events. The ancient books of the dead describe the same phenomenon. An NDE provides an opportunity to see one's life in context, as a whole. For most people, the review is neither frightening nor judgmental. Our ancestors believed that one of the jobs of the death coach was to help the dying with their life review.

Applications for the End of Life

Many spiritual traditions describe death as "a night between two days." They envision the period of dying as ripe for spiritual growth. In this context, the life review is more than just an inventory of past deeds; it is an opportunity to recommit old, or perhaps even establish new, life priorities. Stories of so-called eleventh-hour transformations are well-known. The life review often gives the care receiver clarity about unfinished business, especially regarding his core relationships.

Basic Tools

Why not regularly examine what gives our life meaning as carefully as we measure our blood pressure or cholesterol levels? Life becomes busy with distractions. Facing our mortality highlights what we truly love. Through life review exercises we face old fears, renew our deepest commitments, admit regrets, seek forgiveness, and complete our life's work. Meaningfulness makes us well; meaninglessness makes us sick. Here are some suggestions for life review exercises that have met with positive feedback from many hospice patients.

- *Ask a courageous question.* This life review exercise invites a person to examine their personal priorities. This ancient practice is based on the belief that whatever we pay attention to in life will grow more important to us as we near death. The process of formulating this kind of question involves an inventory of life.

- *Examine consciousness.* This activity is based on the Spiritual Exercises of Jesuit founder, Ignatius of Loyola. Rather than focus on what we have done wrong in life, this life review tool encourages us to hold the dark and light of our life together. At the end of life, this exercise could be as simple and direct as asking, without judgment, questions such as: Where have you most received love and compassion in life? Where have you least received love and compassion? Where have you most given love and compassion in life? Where have you least given love and compassion?

- *Sealed orders exercise.* This exercise is a metaphor for the belief that who we are and what we were created to be is in our spiritual DNA, encoded from birth. When we are faithful to our life's purpose, we feel joy and peace, no matter what obstacles we encounter. When we depart from our essential self, we suffer and become ill. There are many ways to reflect on our sealed orders. Check the resources below for specific ideas.

- *Deathbed confession.* Deathbed confession has been an important end-of-life ritual in many of the world's spiritual traditions. This particular life review invites the dying person to clear the slate of his past. The belief is that there is peace and freedom in naming past faults. Some traditions designate confessors for this role while others invite anyone who is willing to exercise this privilege.

- *Spiritual geographying.* This activity helps the terminally ill person to engage in a kind of life review while providing caregivers with insight into his spirituality. Invite the person to plot his life along a time line, indicating the three most challenging and life-giving moments. Often there is a correlation between the ups and downs of life. There are two possible approaches to this.

Spiritual Geographying Exercise 1

0 — — 10 — — 20 — — 30 — — 40 — — 50 — — 60 — — 70 — — 80 +

INSTRUCTIONS

1) Mark a slash through the time line at your present age.

2) Note with an X the five most defining moments of your life; give each a simple title.

3) Record a single adjective that best describes the full impact of each X'ed event.

4) Complete the five sentences on the following page. Fill in the blanks (for example, "I was _____") with your corresponding adjectives.

At age _____, I was _____

because _____

At age _____, I was _____

because _____

At age _____, I was _____

because _____

At age _____, I was _____

because _____

At age _____, I was _____

because _____

Another way to do it is:

Spiritual Geographying Exercise 2

0 — — 10 — — 20 — — 30 — — 40 — — 50 — — 60 — — 70 — — 80 +

INSTRUCTIONS

1) Indicate the three most challenging moments of your life with an X below the time line.

2) Mark the three most life-giving moments of your life with an O above the time line.

3) Assign a simple theme to each of these events.

MOST STRESSFUL EPISODES IN YOUR LIFE

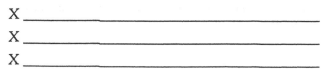

MOST LIFE-GIVING TIMES IN YOUR LIFE

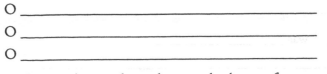

4) Reflect on the correlation between both sets of events.

Level of Expertise for Life Review Exercises

Most life review exercises only require a familiarity with the tool. Be sensitive to the fact that some persons may not be comfortable sharing intimate details of his or her life with close relatives or friends. Sometimes a clergyperson, hospice chaplain, or neutral party may be a better choice to engage someone in a life review.

Resources for Life Review

PRINT AIDS

Chopra, Deepak. *The Way of the Wizard: Twenty Spiritual Lessons for Creating the Life You Want.* New York: Random House, 1995.

Based on the mythical dialogues of King Arthur and Merlin, an entertaining and inspiring book that offers insight into the spiritual laws of purpose and desire.

Linn, Dennis, Sheila Linn, and Matthew Linn. *Healing the Purpose of Your Life.* New York: Paulist Press, 1999.

A gem of a resource that helps caregivers and receivers listen to their heart regarding life's purpose and meaning.

—. *Sleeping with Bread: Holding What Gives You Life.* New York: Paulist Press, 1995.

A little book that makes sense out of the practice of examining our consciousness.

Meditation Practices

Science can now measure the brain activity of persons in a meditative state; the benefits are both physical and emotional. Meditation and contemplation have become mainstream terms in our culture, but they include a wide range of definitions. Contemplative practices range from relaxation therapies to forms of prayer. Classically, the terms "prayer" and "meditation" are not interchangeable, though they can be related. For many persons at the end of life, it is not a choice of either prayer or contemplation, but a combination of both that supports them. There is a time and place for vocal and traditional prayer. But meditation can open another dimension of spirituality that is a refreshing contrast to the breakneck speed of normal life.

Applications for the End of Life

Observation shows that at the end of life most persons become naturally contemplative. The sacred art of dying traditions instruct caregivers to support the dying person as she moves from an active life to a more interior existence. Even though a person may never have had a contemplative practice per se, it is never too late to tap into the healthful benefits of meditation.

Basic Tools

Although schools of spirituality emphasize different forms of meditation practice, there is common ground among the traditions. All contemplative practice is a discipline of the mind. Today, Westerners are returning either to the roots of their own tradition or looking to the East to rediscover the healthful benefits of meditation. Here are a few of the contemplative practices that have been found to be especially helpful at the end of life.

+ *Centering prayer.* This type of prayer is a path to contemplation based on the tradition of early Christianity. It draws our attention away from the ordinary flow of our thoughts. Centering prayer repeats a sacred word or mantra over and over in harmony with our breathing. This practice does not negate further thought, but allows us to return to an anchor of calm in the midst of mental activity.

+ *Davvening practices.* This is a form of meditation based on Jewish spiritual practice. Simply put, davvening is a way to concentrate and focus on God's nearness by eliminating worldly distraction. Like most forms of meditation, the davvener, prayerer, may achieve an altered state of mind through traditional davvening techniques that include quieting mind and body and simple forms of blessing.

+ *Lectio divina.* This is an ancient contemplative practice using a short passage from scripture to guide the seeker. It has a three-fold structure: (1) become aware of the presence of Spirit, (2) listen to your inner self for ten minutes after reading a passage of scripture, and (3) select one word as a guide for the day and be grateful.

+ *Freedom meditation.* This meditation is a traditional end-of-life exercise that is useful for the patient who is overwhelmed by fear, anger, or anxiety. It has three parts:

   1. *Intention.* Get in touch with an incident that restricts her ability to be creative and loving.

   2. *Awareness.* Notice when she is stuck in patterns of negativity or judgment without putting herself down.

3. *Choice.* Shift into the present moment through grounded belly breathing. That is, drawing breath from deep in the abdomen, instead of high in the chest, which is indicative of anxiety.

Afterward, see if a new and creative path arises for her.

+ *Metta (loving-kindness meditation).* Metta has its roots in ancient Buddhist practice. *Metta* means empathy and compassion for all sentient beings. Metta meditation is an attitude rather than a feeling; as such, it can be the most emotionally fulfilling state we can know. Metta can be brought to another who is suffering or can be directed toward oneself. The method is as follows. First, have the patient relax by sitting quietly and paying attention to her body. Second, have the person notice her emotions. Tell her not to judge her emotions, as she cannot control them. Third, have the person bring loving-kindness to any area where she is suffering, either in herself or for someone else. Finally, invite the care receiver to return to normal consciousness when she is ready.

+ *Breathing meditation.* This meditation is one of the most fundamental tools for relaxation and reducing anxiety (see "Breath Work," earlier in this section).

+ *Walking meditation.* Walking is an invigorating way to involve the body in contemplative practice if the care receiver is able to ambulate. There are many kinds of prayer walking from different traditions. One Native American approach is called the Three-Step Meditation. To facilitate the patient in Three-Step Meditation, instruct her first to pick a place where there is privacy and beauty, preferably natural beauty. Then follow these instructions:

> STEP ONE. Make your first step into the world, noticing how the day is around you. Take as much time walking without a need to arrive somewhere.

STEP TWO. Make the second step into your own heart. Notice how you are within and be gentle with yourself.

STEP THREE. Make the third step back into the world with compassion for all living creatures. Step gently on the grass so it will bounce back for others after you have passed.

After the walking meditation is finished, take a moment to be grateful.

If a person is not ambulatory, she can do this three-step meditation with guided visualization.

Level of Expertise

There are many traditions and levels of contemplative practice. Most people in our society have not had formal training in the discipline of meditation, but the basics of contemplation can easily be taught and the results are immediate.

Resources for Meditation Practices

PRINT AIDS

Kaplan, Aryeh. *Jewish Meditation: A Practical Guide*. New York: Schocken Books, 1985.

A readable introduction to simple meditation practices based on the tradition of Judaism.

Keating, Thomas. *Open Mind, Open Heart: The Contemplative Dimension of the Gospel*. New York: Continuum, 1992.

An introduction to centering prayer by Father Thomas Keating, one of the world's foremost authorities on the practice of centering prayer.

Nhat Hanh, Thich. *The Miracle of Mindfulness: An Introduction to the Practice of Meditation*. Boston: Beacon Press, 1987.

A classic that introduces the Western mind to the rich contemplative practice of meditation.

Pennington, M. Basil. *Lectio Divina: Renewing the Ancient Practice of Praying the Scriptures.* New York: Crossroads Publishing Company, 1998.

A delightful invitation to rediscover a tried and true form of contemplative prayer.

VIDEO RESOURCES

Nhat Hanh, Thich. *A Guide to Walking Meditation.* VHS, thirty minutes, ASIN B000 2DQYHS. Order through www.amazon.com.

A video that features the popular Buddhist master teaching the simple practice of "making peaceful steps."

Novak, Jyotish. *Meditation Therapy for Health and Healing.* VHS, 2001, ASIN 1565891635. Order through www.amazon.com.

An encouraging approach to meditation for those who are dealing with illness.

Music Therapy

Death is a rite of passage. For people of all ages and cultures, music is a language that speaks strongly during times of transition. There is a clear relationship between music and healing. A thousand years ago, the monks at Cluny, France, developed elegant caregiving practices using different modes of music corresponding to human moods. Today, studies show the healing properties of certain instruments such as the harp. For many patients, the resonance from the strings often sets up a relationship between the sound and the listener, resulting in an enhanced quality of life for both patients and caregivers alike.

Applications for the End of Life

The sacred art of dying traditions believe that a total environment is necessary for the dying to do their inner work. Music therapy is one of the most primal and powerful tools to support persons in transition. Recent years have witnessed a renaissance in the field of music thanatology, or the therapeutic use of music at the time of death. Whether the needs are physical, emotional, or spiritual, certain kinds of music seem to provide a sacred and safe container for the work of healing.

Basic Tools

You do not have to be a musician to offer a friend or relative the benefits of music therapy. A few essential guidelines regarding the use of music at the end of life may be all that you need.

+ Ask the patient what kind of music he would enjoy. Do not presume at the end of life that the kind of music someone enjoyed when he was well is necessarily helpful now. Nostalgic music can sometimes be painful at this time.

+ Often the use of nonrhythmic or circular music allows the care receiver to turn inward as a necessary step in the process of dying. Circular music is repetitive, nonlinear music, sometimes called New Age music. In ancient times, the use of repetitive chants or melodies supported relaxation and deeper awareness.

+ Sometimes music can provide a pleasant white noise to drown out the more obnoxious sounds of oxygen machines or respirators. For example, recordings from nature, such as birds singing or ocean waves, may enhance a sterile institutional environment.

+ Pay attention to the effect that music is having on the care receiver. If it is causing agitation, turn it off or change the mood of the music. No matter how pleasant, music is best appreciated when interspersed with periods of silence.

+ Live music is generally more effective than recorded music. Many hospices and hospitals now have trained volunteers who are willing to play harp or other instruments at the bedside.

+ The skin is the largest and most sensitive organ of the human body. The vibration of certain instruments, such as the harp, often have a positive effect on care receivers, especially when played live.

* Music specialists sometimes offer the patient a small harp to play himself to further enjoy the benefits of music's healing vibrations. No prior skill is necessary. Children as well as the elderly often respond positively to this experience.

* Music therapy benefits caregivers as well as care receivers. Music can soothe the weary soul and break the somber mood of a household.

Level of Expertise

We cannot underestimate the power of music to heal. While it takes a certain level of expertise to play a musical instrument, all caregivers can access an array of resources to support a healing environment at the end of life. CDs can be purchased with appropriate music for the sick and dying (see below). Guilds of trained music professionals now exist around the country for the sole purpose of supporting the dying. Contact your local hospice regarding the availability of music volunteers.

Resources for Music Therapy

PRINT AIDS

Andrews, Ted. *Sacred Sounds: Transformation through Music and Word.* St. Paul, MN: Llewellyn Press, 1992.

A delightful introduction to music theory and therapy with a perspective on the spiritual nature of healing sound.

Benson, Stella. *The Healing Musician: A Guide to Playing Healing Music at the Bedside.* Seattle: New Grail Media, 1999.

A wonderful introduction to the art of healing music. The book includes a CD of selected pieces to be used at the bedside.

Campbell, Don. *The Mozart Effect: Tapping the Power of Music to Heal the Body, Strengthen the Mind and Unlock the Creative Spirit.* New York: HarperCollins, 2001.

A remarkable work that encourages caregivers to understand and explore the potential of music as a healer.

Gaynor, Mitchell, M.D. *The Healing Power of Sound: Recovery of Life-Threatening Illness Using Sound, Voice and Music.* Boston: Shambhala Press, 1999.

A worthwhile reference connecting the medical and spiritual aspects of healing.

VIDEO RESOURCES

Schroeder-Sheker, Therese. *Chalice of Repose: A Contemporary Musician's Approach to Death and Dying.* Sounds True, 1998, VHS.

A video introducing the inspiring, groundbreaking work of the widely recognized contemporary founder of the modern field of music thanatology.

DISCOGRAPHY

The following CDs are listed as a beginner's library of musical resources appropriate for the sick, the terminally ill, and their caregivers.

Benson, Stella. *The Healer's Way: Calming Music for Anxiety.* Seattle: New Grail Media, 1998.

Natural harmonic tones of the ancient harp that capture the healing potential to penetrate mental discomfort and muscle tension.

——. *The Healer's Way: Soothing Music for those in Pain.* Seattle: New Grail Media, 1998.

Solo harp music that includes medieval chant, ancient melodies, and Celtic music to create a serene and therapeutic audio-sensual experience.

Coon, Gail. *Luminous Journey.* Bend, OR: JourneySong Productions, 2001.

An inspiring collection of gentle and soft repetitive songs used for centuries in times of transition.

——. *Soul Journey: Tranquil Music from Antiquity for Healing and Peace.* Bend, OR: JourneySong Productions, 2001.

Music from the early Middle Ages re-created to illustrate the traditional modes or moods of healing melodies.

Enya. *Various New Age CDs.* Reprise Records, Time Warner Company.

Nonrhythmic music drawing from the Celtic tradition, suitable for easy listening and meditation by a popular New Age recording artist.

Schroeder-Sheker, Therese. *Rosa Mystica* and *In Dulci Jubilo*. Celestial Harmony CDs.

Two inspiring productions drawn from the Chalice of Repose repertoire of bedside harp music.

Taize Chants. GIA Publications.

Several CDs with popular interfaith chants acclaimed worldwide for their beauty, simplicity, and contemplative quality.

TRAINING AND WORKSHOP OPPORTUNITIES

International Harp Therapy Program
www.harprealm.com

An outstanding program to prepare musicians as specialists in end-of-life care. Program founder, Christina Tourin, is an acclaimed musician and teacher who has a passion for making music accessible to a wide range of audiences.

Sacred Art of Dying National Education Programs
www.sacredartofliving.org

Courses include an introduction to music theory and practice in end-of-life care. Program faculty includes nationally certified music thanatologists.

Religious Rites and Sacred Writings

We do not live in a homogenous society like those who produced the ancient books of the dying. Americans represent virtually every culture and spiritual tradition on earth. Data show that for a majority of people, some affiliation with a religious heritage is still significant. For them, the ceremonies and scriptures of a particular tradition may be an important source of comfort and continuity with their heritage. *The American Book of Living and Dying* does not include the details of each tradition. We acknowledge, however, the role of religion as a link between a person's individual life story and a larger or greater story, which faith traditions provide.

Applications for the End of Life

At the end of life, many people who have otherwise been disconnected from their religious heritage find comfort in its traditions. Families often call upon clergy from their faith community to offer specific prayers and rituals. As in other aspects of care, honor the requests of the dying regarding religious customs. Sacred scriptures address the great life-to-life transition and attempt to provide meaning and direction for the dying person.

Basic Tools

Religions describe death as a part of the unending cycle of nature, rather than as a dreaded enemy. Death is to be faced consciously and even embraced rather than avoided at all costs. Religious traditions can offer comfort at the end of life by acknowledging that every aspect of dying and living is sacred and deserves to be honored and celebrated. Some common ground perspectives shared by most faith traditions include the following:

- Death is a mystery so deep that sometimes only sacred ritual can express the fullness of its meaning both for the dying person and the caregivers.

- Like our ancestors who produced the books of the dead, our era also struggles to express the paradox of death. The disadvantage of our time is that modernity tends to distrust ritual and places its hopes in the rational and scientific. At the end of life, tapping into traditional culture and ceremony can address the spiritual hunger of our age.

- In the face of mystery, poetry and myth speak more powerfully than linear logic. The great scriptures of the world offer parables and open up sacred questions rather than trying to offer pat answers.

- Most religious systems are flexible and inclusive at the end of life. Even if a care receiver considers herself to be only culturally Jewish or nominally Catholic, for example, religious communities are normally very willing to respond to a person's request for guidance.

- Guidelines for celebrating the sacraments and other religious ceremonies—such as Anointing the Sick, Viaticum (Last Communion), or praying certain prayers and scriptures—are prescribed within the appropriate religious tradition. Consult the local clergy of the appropriate faith community for more information.

- Rituals can be meaningful. When you make an effort to customize rituals for the person and circumstances at hand, they have meaning even within the most orthodox religious traditions. Including children and family members in a ceremony turns a perfunctory and mechanical ritual into a meaningful celebration.

Level of Expertise

Faith traditions sometimes require clergy to perform certain religious ceremonies at the end of life. Aspects of these rites also may be adapted by family and laypersons who share the same religious belief system.

Resources for Religious Rites and Sacred Writings

PRINT AIDS

Bernstein, Eleanor, and Martin Connell. *Traditions and Transitions*. Notre Dame, IN: Notre Dame Center for Pastoral Liturgy, 1998.

A Roman Catholic perspective on contemporary relgious ritual.

Lamm, Maurice. *The Jewish Way in Death and Mourning*. New York: Jonathan David Publishers, 1989.

A thorough and painstaking effort to represent traditional Jewish practice in modern terminology.

Linn, Mary Jane, Dennis Linn. and Matthew Linn. *Healing the Dying*. Mahwah, NJ: Paulist Press, 1979.

A simple work to encourage and instruct those who are called to the bedside of a loved one.

Lyon, William S. *Encyclopedia of Native American Healing*. New York: W.W. Norton and Co., 1998.

An inclusive volume exploring and honoring the healing practices of Native Americans, including rituals and ceremonies for the end of life.

Ramshaw, Elaine. *Ritual and Pastoral Care*. Minneapolis, MN: Fortress Press, 2000.

A mainline Protestant perspective on the psychology and theology of ritual practices.

Rituals for Lay Persons: Holy Communion and the Pastoral Care of the Sick. New York: Catholic Book Publishing Co., 2001.

A complete outline of the sacraments of the sick and a variety of optional scriptural texts for clergy and caregivers.

Trungpa, Chogyam, and Francesca Fremantle (translators). *The Tibetan Book of the Dead*. Boston: Shambhala Classics, 2000.

An acclaimed translation of the extraordinary Buddhist text traditionally read aloud to the dying person, with helpful commentary.

Rituals for the Bedside

When people died in ancient or preindustrialized cultures, a belief structure that transcended death equipped them. Our ancestors realized that people needed ritual throughout the life cycle. Traditionally, during the process of dying, the role of the community ritualizer was as important as that of the physician. The situation of modern American is in sharp contrast—we tend to be a culture devoid of ritual. It is particularly important, therefore to consider ritual at the bedside during the end-of-life processes. Especially when recovery seems unlikely, rituals can address our urge to understand existence in a meaningful way and provide marked pathways as we move from one stage of life to the next. Good ritual has the power to translate the truth of a difficult situation into a memorable celebration of the experience.

Applications for the End of Life

Various stages mark the process of terminal illness. In the Celtic Books of the Dead, for example, there was a potential for forty stages to be observed, each of which was marked by a corresponding ritual. Today, last rite rituals tend to be associated with a one-time final blessing when a person is at the edge of death. Good ritual is more than mere ceremony or obligatory rite. You know when you're in the presence of effective ritual when it turns loss and fear into an affirmation of life. As a general rule of thumb, as normalcy decreases during the dying process, the need for ritual increases. Following the death, as normalcy returns to the family system, the need for ritual decreases.

Basic Tools

Sacred ritual is powerful at the end of life because, in the words of Jean Houston, "In times of suffering, when you feel abandoned, perhaps even annihilated, there is occurring at deeper levels than your pain, the entry of the sacred." While there are certain essential elements in every authentic ritual, the truth is that every human being has an innate capacity to create a ritual experience. Trust your own instincts to create ritual. Following are a few basic guidelines.

If you look back on a positive ritual experience, you consistently will find the presence of five essential ritual elements:

1) *Story.* Something is crying out to be acknowledged; the patient's story yearns to be connected with the larger story of creation.

2) *Community.* Ritual is a shared experience that more than one person must witness; for example, ancient rituals called upon the lineage of the entire human family.

3) *Space.* Ritual occurs within sacred time and space that needs to be marked; for example, a chime is sounded or a candle is lit.

4) *Symbol.* Something tangible can represent the vast wonder of the intangible; for example, oil may become a metaphor for healing.

5) *Action.* A symbol and the community connect to tell the story; for example, bread is eaten or water is poured.

Before initiating a ritual, pay attention to three rules of discernment:

- LISTEN and accept the truth of the care receiver's experience
- TRANSLATE the care receiver's truth into ritual elements
- ENCOURAGE the appropriate community participation in the celebration

Level of Expertise

There are programs that teach the basics of rituals for the bedside. But, in a pinch, anyone can spontaneously create a meaningful ritual. Handbooks and resources on ritual abound. Consider learning from the experience of others, then tailor the ritual for the bedside to your experience.

Resources for Rituals for the Bedside

PRINT AIDS

Anderson, Megory. *Sacred Dying: Creating Rituals for Embracing the End of Life.* Roseville, CA: Prima Publishing, 2001.

With a forward by Thomas Moore that sings its praises, a practical guide for assisting others at the end of life and making sure that the caregiver's needs are not confused with the needs of the dying.

Biziou, Barbara. *The Joy of Everyday Ritual: Spiritual Recipes to Celebrate Milestones, Ease Transitions and Make Every Day Sacred.* New York: Golden Books 1999.

A delightful and practical aid for the beginner ritualist.

Feinstein, David, and Peg Elliott Mayo. *Rituals for Living and Dying.* San Francisco: HarperCollins, 1990.

A collection of provocative exercises to assist the terminally ill in designing meaningful ritual.

Some, Malidoma Patrice. *Ritual: Power, Healing and Community.* New York: Arkana/ Penguin Publishing, 1993.

A book acclaimed by scholars, including Michael Meade and Robert Bly. Bly calls this "the greatest and most detailed book about ritual I have ever read."

Van Gennep, Arnold. *The Rites of Passage.* Chicago: University of Chicago Press, 1960.

One of the classics in this field. The author was the world's first anthropologist to note the parallels of rites during times of transition between world cultures.

WORKSHOP OPPORTUNITIES

Sacred Art of Dying National Education Programs
www.sacredartofliving.org

Courses include extensive instruction on and experience with the art of making rituals from diverse cultural and spiritual traditions.

Rituals of Release

Death is not our only experience of dying. Before our heart stops beating, there are many deaths to self, ego, and identity along the way. The wisdom of our ancestors was to mark and even celebrate these important times of transition, rather than simply to endure them. Rituals of release provide an opportunity to acknowledge these moments, especially as physical life comes to an end. Such rituals acknowledge the reality of change, especially the paradoxical mystery of life and death. It is often difficult for the person enduring critical transitions to do more than survive the experience. Family, friends, and caregivers can support their loved ones by witnessing these changes with some kind of simple ritual.

Applications for the End of Life

The person who is dying often feels isolated in his or her experience. Creating a ritual that acknowledges the reality of what is happening reinforces intimacy and community. Many of the rituals recommended here have their origins in the world's great spiritual traditions. The job of the caregiver is to tailor release rituals to the particular circumstances at hand. Rituals of release are an affirmation of support for the dying person. The result is often a deeper sense of peace and acceptance.

Basic Tools

Rituals of release should draw on the same principles of all good bed-side rituals (see pages 270–72). The following recommendations are a few classical examples of rituals of release.

+ *Potlatch.* A potlatch or "giveaway" is inspired by many Native American traditions. The principle behind the potlatch is that none of us really owns anything, rather, every thing we have is a spiritual gift. Done either before or after a person's death, a complete inventory is taken of every-thing that a person owns. Then a conscious effort is made to offer each item to another person, along with an explanation of the history and meaning of the thing being given away. When done in a spiritual context, a giveaway ritual can be a powerful witness to the temporary nature of life; it can also assist the anticipatory grief process by making a more con-scious connection between the dying person and those facing bereavement.

+ *Permission.* Giving someone permission to die can be an important step in the dying process. Often there is a point before death when the dying person finds himself trapped in a struggle to continue living. He may believe he needs to continue living for others, to look after dependents, or to complete unfinished parts of his life's work. Our ancestors knew that some people need to be given permission to die. A ritual or cere-mony may include reminiscing about a person's life and acknowledging his gifts and failures. The ritual may include any form of creative expres-sion, such as a poignant piece of music and a blessing.

+ *Litany or mantra.* A litany is a sacred text or short phrase that is repeated over and over as a kind of verbal meditation, or mantra. Most religious or mystical traditions have created such prayers of mercy and peace for the end of life. The essence of the practice is to help a person center himself or stay grounded by eliminating distracting thoughts and focusing on what is compassionate and life-giving. A chant sometimes accompanies the process or repetition. Other traditions use prayer beads. Some exam-ples of litany and mantra are:

Hear, O Israel, the Lord our God is One (the Shema)

Kyrie Eleison ("Lord have mercy," from the Greek Orthodox liturgy)

Holy Mary, Mother of God, pray for us sinners, now and at the hour or our death (the Hail Mary)

Lord Jesus, Son of David, have mercy on me (from the Gospel according to Mark)

Whatever may come to pass is the Will of Allah, the Merciful and Compassionate (from the Koran)

Om (the Hindu chant of supreme spiritual power)

May the Great Buddha of Compassion be my guide, the embodiment of enlightened, limitless love (a universal Buddhist prayer)

The nature of these prayers is to be accessible to all. Caregivers need to find a tradition that does not conflict with their own beliefs. The second caveat is to select the phrase that is most helpful to the care receiver.

- *Family ritual of release:* An opportunity for a family system to acknowledge that death is imminent. A family spokesperson can lead the following litany and invite everyone present to respond:

*Spokesperson:*_____ , in knowing that you are returning home to the place where you came from [use appropriate language],
Family: We release you.

*Spokesperson:*_____ , in knowing that you have led a good and complete life,
Family: We release you.

*Spokesperson:*_____ , in knowing that we care for your total well-being,
Family: We release you.

*Spokesperson:*_____ , in knowing that we are doing what is best for you,
Family: We release you.

*Spokesperson:*_____ , in knowing that we are not angry with you,
Family: We release you.

*Spokesperson:*_____ , in knowing that you have all our love,
Family: We release you.

*Spokesperson:*_____ , in knowing that we are doing what is best for you,
Family: We release you.

*Spokesperson:*_____ , in knowing that your pain will soon be relieved,
Family: We release you.

*Spokesperson:*_____ , in knowing that you are held safe in the hands of
God [use appropriate language],
Family: We release you.

Level of Expertise

No training is necessary to facilitate rituals of release. It may be useful,
however, to review the basic structure of good ritual (see pages 270–72).

Resources for Rituals of Release

Devotional materials and prayer books from various religious traditions
often include texts for special occasions such as the end of life. Most hospices and hospitals are excellent resources for interfaith libraries.

TRAINING AND WORKSHOP OPPORTUNITIES
Sacred Art of Dying National Education Programs
www.sacredartofliving.org
Extensive coursework regarding the use of ritual in end-of-life care.

Vigil Rituals and Rituals for Remembering

The ancient books of dying distinguished between care for the chronically ill person and care during the final stages of dying. During the latter state, the community did everything possible to establish a special kind of presence known as the vigil. The commitment to the dying person and their family during the vigil period was sacred and unconditional. Traditional vigil rituals were unique in light of the imminence of death. Today many hospices offer some aspects of this important dimension of end-of-life caregiving.

Applications for the End of Life

Historically, special end-of-life caregivers called midwives tended death vigils. Parallels to the birthing process are evident in the final stages of dying. For both caregivers and care receivers there is a sense of quickening and urgency. Physical, emotional, and spiritual changes are noted in the final stages of dying. Vigil rituals can create a sense of support and comfort for everyone involved. This can be the most important time in the dying process to consider the use of rituals.

Basic Tools

The death vigil should be initiated once the final stages of dying arrive. As the body and spirit of the dying person change, be aware that each shift requires a different kind of caregiving attention. Each change is also an invitation to include ritual in the process. Be creative in your use of ritual. Remember that a ritual does not have to be something that looks religious. Just think of ways to honor and mark the steps along the way. The following three stages, based on Jan Bernard and Miriam Schneider's *The True Work of Dying* (see page 283), show the similarity of dying to giving birth and clarify the physical, emotional, and spiritual work involved in each stage of the dying process.

STAGE 1: PRE-ACTIVE LABOR. This is the initial stage of the dying process that begins at the time of physical demise due to illness or aging. The time spent in this stage will vary greatly, from days to weeks. Allow your loved one to follow his or her own schedule.

PHYSICAL LABOR INVOLVES THE FOLLOWING CHANGES:

- a decrease in eating and drinking
- a change in breathing patterns
- an increase in weakness or confusion
- temperature fluctuations
- varied sleeping and waking patterns
- a heightened sensitivity to sight, sound, smell, and activity

CONSIDER THE FOLLOWING SUPPORT MEASURES:

- provide food and fluids as desired
- offer medications to relieve pain
- supply cool cloths on the body
- assist with physical needs
- offer gentle massage and touching
- employ slow, mindful actions

EMOTIONAL AND SPIRITUAL LABOR INVOLVES THE
FOLLOWING CHANGES:

- withdrawal
- more frequent crying
- a fear of being alone, especially at night
- restlessness and agitation
- anger or impatience with loved ones
- the need to discuss their death and the death of others who have died
- depression
- a need to say good-bye to loved ones
- a need to complete business issues and funeral plans

CONSIDER THE FOLLOWING SUPPORT MEASURES:

- keep the dying in touch with the current time and place
- honor their dignity by maintaining privacy
- begin a vigil attendance if appropriate
- notify support persons of changes
- be honest with the care receiver about changes
- express your feelings
- provide calm and reassuring statements
- listen quietly
- reevalute extraordinary life-support measures
- continue to laugh and play with the care receiver
- continue making physical contact with the patient
- assist with prayers and rituals

STAGE 2: ACTIVE LABOR. This stage may be as short as a few hours or as long as a few days.

PHYSICAL LABOR INVOLVES THE FOLLOWING CHANGES:

- withdrawal
- cooling and mottling skin
- extreme temperature fluctuations
- lung congestion
- changes in skin color
- an increase in irregular breathing patterns
- changes in awareness, an inability to close their eyes, respond verbally, and so on
- a deterioration of body functions (such as odors or loss of bladder and bower control)

CONSIDER THE FOLLOWING SUPPORT MEASURES:

- keep her warm and dry if cool
- use light covers and a cool cloth in case of fever
- elevate the head of her bed if tolerated
- continue to provide medications for symptom relief
- turn to a support group for continued help
- ask yourself what you want or need
- honor your feelings, both the negative as well as the positive
- contact those who provide spiritual support
- nurture yourself; take a nap, a bath, or a walk or meditate

EMOTIONAL AND SPIRITUAL LABOR INVOLVES THE
FOLLOWING CHANGES:

- relaxing when loved ones are near
- out-of-body events
- intermittent fear
- an intensified sense of their spiritual source
- the calmness of acceptance

CONSIDER THE FOLLOWING SUPPORT MEASURES:

- continue to talk, touch, and pray with the patient
- continue to provide comfort, support, and care
- talk about beloved people or pets who have died
- give them permission to let go
- trust what your heart directs you to do

STAGE 3: DEATH. The moment of death is a long one. Just as the moment
of birth, it contains an eternity of meanings and sensations. It is time to
say our last good-byes.

PHYSICAL LABOR INVOLVES THE FOLLOWING CHANGES:

- a need to push as if birthing
- gradually discontinued breathing
- the absence of a pulse
- skin color changing to gray
- an involuntary loss of stool or urine
- the mouth and eyes possibly remain open

CONSIDER THE FOLLOWING MEASURES OF SUPPORT AND RESPECT:

+ remove any tubes
+ cleanse the body

EMOTIONAL AND SPIRITUAL LABOR INVOLVES THE
FOLLOWING CHANGES:

+ a complete disconnection from physical life
+ an occasional sense of lingering spiritual presence

CONSIDER THE FOLLOWING SUPPORT MEASURES:

+ honor your needs for rest, time alone, and time away
+ listen, hold, and hug others quietly
+ allow your feelings to surface
+ accept assistance if that is what you want
+ if you desire, ask for time alone with the one who has died and to bathe
  or dress the body
+ pray and spend time reflecting quietly

Rituals for Remembering

At the time of death, consider ways to mark this life transition.

+ Light a candle near the bed. Candles symbolize illumination and clarity.
  Choose one that is special to you or the one who has died.
+ Place a passage quilt on the person's body. Put a favorite blanket or quilt
  over him. The special covering can be buried with the person or used
  during the memorial service.
+ Toast the one who has died. Give a glass to each person in the room.
  Form a circle around the bed. A prayer may be shared aloud in accom-
  paniment with the toast. The drink is a symbol of new life.

+ Bathe and prepare the body. This is a sacred moment of ritual. Oils can be applied after the body is bathed. This ritual symbolizes cleansing and invites a final moment of physical connection with the person.

+ Place a flower on the person's bed. After the body has been removed, a favorite flower is comforting as a symbol of new life.

Level of Expertise

Dying is as natural a process as birthing. At both ends of life, a certain amount of experience and know-how can be useful. Trust your instincts, but be willing to consult others who may provide important insights into a person's physical and emotional changes at the end of life.

Resources for Vigil Rituals and Rituals for Remembering

PRINT AIDS

Bernard, Jan Selliken, and Miriam Schneider. *The True Work of Dying: A Practical and Compassionate Guide to Easing the Dying Process.* New York: Avon Books, 1996.

An exploration of the parallels between birthing and dying with practical bedside practices and rituals for families and caregivers.

Callahan, Maggie, and Patricia Kelley. *Final Gifts: Understanding the Special Awareness, Needs and Communications of the Dying.* New York: Bantam Books, 1992.

One of the simple classics produced from the American hospice movement based on stories to encourage caregivers at the end of life.

Feinstein, David, and Peg Elliott Mayo. *Rituals for Living and Dying.* San Francisco: HarperCollins, 1990.

Exercises and stories to assist caregivers in the final stage of dying.

Ference, Dennis. *Keeping Vigil with the Dying: Helpful Insights and Prayers.* Liguori, MI: Ligouri Press, 2000.

Spiritual exercises to comfort the family of the dying.

Miller, Sukie. *After Death: How People around the World Map the Journey after Life.* New York: Touchstone, 1997.

A fascinating exploration of the parallels of how different cultures and religions explain what happens in the journey between life and death.

Nhat Hanh, Thich. *No Death, No Fear: Comforting Wisdom for Life.* New York: Riverhead Books, 2002.

A book that could provide immense comfort to caregivers at the end of the dying process.

Sapienza, Jerral. *Urgent Whispers: Care of the Dying.* Eugene, OR: LLX Press, 2002.

A handy spiral-bound personal reference manual for friends and family assisting a loved one at the end of life.

Smith, Doug, and Marilu Pittman. *Tao of Dying: A Guide to Caregiving.* Washington, D.C.: Caring Publishing, 1994.

Helpful meditations for caregivers to keep the process of dying in a spiritual perspective.

Wolfelt, Alan. *How to Care for Yourself While You Care for the Dying and the Bereaved.* Fort Collins, CO: Companion Press, 1996.

Necessary advice for caregivers from one of America's leading grief therapists.

Yates, Elizabeth. *A Book of Hours: Embrace the Ordinariness of Everyday Life and Make it Holy.* New York: Walker and Co., 1984.

A universal prayer book for caregivers and care receivers with creative and consoling reflections attuned to each hour of the day.

Bibliography

In addition to the resources listed in part III, "The Tool Chest," *The American Book of Living and Dying* is also indebted to the remarkable and courageous contributions of the following scholars and caregivers on whose work this book stands.

Print Aids

CAREGIVER SUPPORT

Halpin, Marlene. *Caregivers: Reflections on Coping with Caregiving.* Dubuque, IA: Islewest Publishing, 1998.

Hover, Margot. *Caring for Yourself When Caring for Others.* Mystic, CT: Twenty-Third Publications, 1993.

Kuebelbeck, J. *Caregiver Therapy.* St. Meinrad, IN: Abbey Press, 1995.

Larson, Dale. *Helper's Journey: Working with People Facing Grief, Loss and Life-Threatening Illness.* Champaign, IL: Research Press, 1993.

Meyer, Charles. *Surviving Death: For Those Caring for the Dying and Bereaved.* Mystic, CT: Twenty-Third Publications, 1991.

Wolfelt, Alan. *Healing Your Grieving Heart: 100 Practical Ideas.* Ft. Collins, CO: Companion Press, 1998.

—. *How to Care for Yourself While You Care for the Dying and the Bereaved.* Ft. Collins, CO: Companion Press, 1996.

CULTURAL PERSPECTIVES

Carter, James, M.D. *Death and Dying among African Americans: Cultural Characteristics and Coping Tidbits.* New York: Vantage Press, 2001.

Clancy, Padraigin. *Celtic Threads: Exploring the Wisdom of Our Heritage.* Dublin: Veritas, 1999.

Coward, Harold. *Life after Death in World Religions.* Maryknoll, NY: Orbis Books, 1997.

Iofiinan, Yed. *Japanese Death Poems: By Zen Monks and Haiku Poets on the Verge of Death.* Boston: Tuttle Publishing Co., 1986.

Kramer, Kenneth. *The Sacred Art of Dying: How World Religions Understand Death.* New York: Paulist Press, 1988.

Lasky, Kathryn. *Days of the Dead: Mexico's Celebration.* New York: Perion, 1994.

Luenn, Nancy, and Robert Chapman. *A Gift for Abuelita: Celebrating the Day of the Dead.* New York: Rising Moon Books, 1998.

—. *Un Regalo Para Abuelita: En Celebracion Del Dia De Los Muertos.* New York: Rising Moon Books, 1998.

Lundquist, Irish, and V. Jenkins Nelson. *Ethnic Variations in Dying, Death and Grief: Diversity in Universality.* London: Taylor & Francis, 1993.

Nhat Hanh, Thich. *No Death, No Fear: Comforting Wisdom for Life.* New York: Riverhead Books, 2002.

Oaks, Elizabeth. *Death and the Afterlife in Pre-Columbian America.* Genealogy Publishing Co., 1975.

Schachter-Shalomi, Zalman, Rabbi. *From Age-ing to Sage-ing: A Profound New Vision for Growing.* New York: Warner Books, 1995.

Smith, Doug, and Marilu Pittman. *Tao of Dying: A Guide to Caring.* Washington, D.C.: Caring Publications, 1997.

Trungpa, Chogyam, and Francesca Fremantle. *The Tibetan Book of the Dead.* Boston: Shambhala, 2000.

White Deer of Autumn. *The Great Change: A Native American Perspective on Dying.* Hillsboro, OR: Beyond Words Publishing, 1992.

DEATH AND DYING

Albom, Mitch. *Tuesdays with Morrie: An Old Man, A Young Man, Life's Greatest Lesson.* New York: Broadway Books, 1997.

Bernard, Jan Selliken, and Miriam Schneider. *The True Work of Dying: A Practical and Compassionate Guide to Easing the Dying Process.* New York: Avon Books, 1996.

Byock, Ira, M.D. *Dying Well: Peace and Possibilities at the End of Life.* New York: Riverhead Books, 1998.

—. *The Four Things that Matter Most: A Book About Living.* Free Press, 2004.

Hallock, Daniel. *Six Months to Love: Learning from a Young Man with Cancer.* Farmington, PA: Plough Publishing, 2001.

Kübler-Ross, Elisabeth. *Death: The Final Stage of Growth*. New York: Touchstone, 1986.

—. *On Death and Dying: What the Dying Have to Teach Doctors, Nursus, Clergy and Their Own Families*. New York: Touchstone, 1997.

—. *The Tunnel and the Light: Essential Insights on Living and Dying*. New York: Marlowe and Co., 1999.

Levine, Stephen. *Healing into Life and Death*. New York: Anchor Books, 1987.

—. *Who Dies?* New York: Anchor Books, 1982.

Sherwin, Nuland B. *How We Die: Reflections on Life's Final Chapter*. New York: Vintage Books, 1995.

THE ENNEAGRAM

Addison, Howard, Rabbi. *The Enneagram and Kabbalah: Reading Your Soul*. Woodstock, VT: Jewish Lights Publishing, 1998.

A beautiful introduction to the Enneagram within the biblical tradition, including prayerful meditations.

Almaas, A. H. *The Diamond Approach: An Introduction to the Teachings of A. H. Almaas*. Boston: Shambhala, 1999.

An advanced book with insights into the Enneagram drawn from Sufi sources by a master of psychology and spirituality.

Hurley, Kathleen, and Theodore Dobson. *My Best Self: Using the Enneagram to Free the Soul*. San Francisco: Harper Books, 1993.

A worthwhile history and insight into how the Enneagram works.

Hurley, Kathy, and Theodorre Donson. *Discover Your Soul Potential: Using the Enneagram to Awaken Spiritual Vitality*. Lakewood, CO: WindWalker Press, 2000.

A concise and practical guide for personal transformation and spiritual development.

Palmer, Helen. *The Enneagram in Love and Work*. San Francisco: Harper Books, 1995.

A handbook that describes every possible combination of relationships from the perspective of the Enneagram.

Riso, Don Richard, and Russ Hudson. *Discovering Your Personality Type*. New York: Houghton Mifflin Co., 2003.

A basic primer on the Enneagram with an easy-to-use personality test included.

—. *The Wisdom of the Enneagram: The Complete Guide to Psychological and Spiritual Growth for the Nine Personality Types*. New York: Bantam Books, 1999.

Perhaps the most comprehensive study of Enneagram theory from the perspective of emotional and spiritual growth.

Rohr, Richard, Fr., and Rev. Andreas Ebert. *The Enneagram: A Christian Perspective.* New York: Crossroad Publishing Co., 2002.

A remarkable history of this ancient spiritual tool in early Christianity from two widely acclaimed Catholic and Lutheran scholars.

ETHICS

Callahan, Daniel. *The Troubled Dream of Life: In Search of a Peaceful Death.* New York: Touchstone, 1993.

—. *What Kind of Life: The Limits of Medical Progress.* New York: Touchstone Books, 1991.

Hardwig, John. *Is There a Duty to Die? And Other Essays in Bioethics.* New York: Bruenner-Rutledge, 2000.

FUNERAL AND MEMORIAL PLANNING

Carlson, Lisa. *Caring for the Dead: Your Final Act of Love.* Hinesburg, VT: Upper Access, 1998.

Cochrane, Don S. *Simply Essential Funeral Planning Kit.* Ontario, Canada: Self-Counsel Press, 2002.

Farmer, Stephen. *Sacred Ceremony: How to Create Ceremonies for Healing, Transitions and Celebrations.* New York: Hay House Publishing, 2002.

Wolfelt, Alan. *Creating Meaningful Funeral Ceremonies: A Guide for Caregivers.* Ft. Collins, CO: Companion Press, 2000.

—. *Creating Meaningful Funeral Services: A Guide for Families.* Ft. Collins, CO: Companion Press, 2000.

GRIEF AND LOSS

About Grief. South Deerfield, MA: Channing L. Bete Co. Scriptographic Booklets.

D'Arcy, Paula. *Gift of the Red Bird: A Spiritual Encounter.* Chicago: Crossroads Publishing, 1996.

—. *Song for Sarah: A Young Mother's Journey through Grief and Beyond.* Colorado Springs, CO: Waterbrook Press/Shaw Books, 2001.

Katafiasz, Karen. *Grief Therapy: Out of Pan Can Come Profound Transforming Healing.* St. Meinrad, IN: Abbey Press, 1993.

Lewis, C. S. *A Grief Observed: A Masterpiece of Rediscovered Faith.* New York: Bantam, 1961.

Miller, Robert J. *Grief Quest: Men Coping with Loss*. St. Meinrad, IN: Abbey Press, 1996.

Mundy, Linus. *Grief Therapy for Men: How to Grieve Like a "Real" Man*. St. Meinrad, IN: Abbey Press, 1997.

Wolfelt, Alan. *Death and Grief: A Guide for Clergy*. London: Taylor & Francis, 1988.

—. *Healing the Bereaved Child: Grief Gardening and Other Touchstones for Caregivers*. Ft. Collins, CO: Companion Press, 1996.

—. *Healing the Grieving Heart: Practical Ideas for Families, Friends and Caregivers*. Ft. Collins, CO: Companion Press, 1998.

HISTORICAL PERSPECTIVES

Aries, Phillipe. *The Hour of Death: The Classical History of Western Attitudes Toward Death Over the Last One Thousand Years*. Oxford: Oxford University Press, 1991.

—. *Western Attitudes Toward Death: From the Middle Ages to the Present*. Baltimore, MD: Johns Hopkins University Press, 1991.

Binski, Paul. *Medieval Death: Ritual and Representation*. Ithaca, NY: Cornell University Press, 1996.

Cameron, Ron. *The Other Gospels: Non-Canonical Texts*. Philadelphia: Westminster Press, 1982.

Camille, Michael. *Master of Death*. New Haven, CT: Yale University Press, 1996.

Evans, G. R. *A History of Pastoral Care*. London: Cassell Publishing, 2000.

Geary, Patrick J. *Living with the Dead in the Middle Ages*. Ithaca, NY: Cornell University Press, 1995.

Golden, Thomas R. *Swallowed by a Snake: The Gift of the Masculine Side of Healing*. Gaithersberg, MD: Golden Healing Publishing, 1996.

Kramer, Ken. *Sacred Art of Dying: How World Religions Understand Death*. Mahwah, NJ: Paulist Press, 1988.

McCall, Andrew. *The Medieval Underworld*. New York: Barnes and Noble Books, 1979.

Menocal, Maria Rosa. *The Ornament of the World: How Muslims, Jews and Christians Created a Culture of Tolerance in Medieval Spain*. Boston: Little, Brown and Co., 2002.

Paxton, Fredrick. *Christianizing Death: The Creation of a Ritual Process in the Early Middle Ages*. Ithaca, NY: Cornell University Press, 1989.

Powell, James M. *Medieval Studies: An Introduction*. Syracuse, NY: Syracuse University Press, 1992.

Walker Bynum, Caroline, and Paul Freedman. *Last Things: Death and the Apocalypse in the Middle Ages*. Philadelphia: University of Pennsylvania, 2000.

MEDICAL PERSPECTIVES

Borysenko, Joan, and Miroslav Borysenko. *The Power of the Mind to Heal.* London: Hay House, 1995.

Byock, Ira, M.D. *Dying Well: Peace and Possibilities at the End of Life.* New York: Riverhead Books, 1997.

Chopra, Deepak, M.D. *Quantum Healing: Exploring the Frontiers of Body-Mind Medicine.* New York: Bantam Books, 1989.

Dossey, Larry, M.D. *Meaning and Medicine: Lessons from a Doctor's Tales of Breakthroughs.* New York: Bantam Books, 1991.

—. *Prayer Is Good Medicine: How to Reap the Healing Benefits of Prayer.* San Francisco: Harper Books, 1996.

—. *Recovering the Soul: A Scientific and Spiritual Search.* New York: Bantam Books, 1989.

Kearney, Michael, M.D. *A Place of Healing: Working with Suffering in Living and Dying.* Oxford, UK: Oxford University Press, 2000.

Rosenfeld, Arthur. *The Truth about Chronic Pain.* New York: Perseus Books, 2003.

Siegel, Bernie, M.D. *Love, Medicine and Miracles: Self-Healing from a Surgeon's Experience.* New York: Harper & Row, 1998.

PHILOSOPHY

Basta, Lofty L. *A Graceful Exit: Life and Death on Your Own Terms.* New York: Plenum Press, 1996.

Becker, Ernst. *The Denial of Death.* New York: Free Press Paper Books, 1997.

Bolen, John Shinoda. *Close to the Bone: Life-Threatening Illness and the Search for Meaning.* New York: Touchstone, 1996.

Carmody, John. *Cancer and Faith: Reflections on Living with Terminal Illness.* Mystic, CT: Twenty-Third Publications, 1995.

Levine, Stephen. *Who Dies?: An Investigation of Conscious Living and Conscious Dying.* New York: Double Day, 1982.

Van Gennep, Arnold. *The Rites of Passage.* Chicago: The University of Chicago Press, 1960.

Wilber, Ken. *A Brief History of Everything.* Boston: Shambhala, 1996.

PRAYER AND RITUAL

Brener, Anne. *Mourning and Mitzvah: A Guided Journal for Walking the Mourner's Path through Grief to Healing.* Woodstock, VT: Jewish Lights Publishing, 2001.

Buxbaum, Yitzhak. *Real Davvening: Jewish Prayer as a Spiritual Practice and a Form of Meditation.* Flushing, NY: The Jewish Spirit Publishing Co., 1996.

Childs-Gowell, Elaine. *Good Grief Rituals*. Barrytown, NY: Station Hill Press, 1992.

Douglas-Klotz, Neil. *Prayers of the Cosmos: Meditations on the Aramaic Words of Jesus*. San Francisco: Harper Books, 1990.

Ference, Dennis. *Keeping Vigil with the Dying: Helpful Insights and Prayers*. Liguori, MO: Liguori Press, 2000.

Gabriele, Edward Francis. *From Many, One: Praying Our Rich and Diverse Cultural Heritage*. Notre Dame, IN: Ave Maria Press, 1995.

Halpern, Marlene. *Right Side Up: Reflections for Those Living with Serious Illness*. Dubuque, IA: Islewest Publishing, 1995.

Merrill, Nan. *Psalms for Praying: An Invitation to Wholeness*. New York: Continuum, 2002.

Rinella, Maureen. *Be with Me: A Book of Prayers to Comfort Dying Persons and Their Loved Ones*. St. Meinrad, IN: Abbey Press, 1997.

Walker, Elizabeth Yates. *A Book of Hours*. New York: Walker and Co., 1984.

PSYCHOLOGICAL PERSPECTIVES

Bullis, Ronald K. *Spirituality in Social Work Practice: A Look at the Whole Picture*. London: Taylor & Francis, 1996.

Lair, George S. *Counseling the Terminally Ill: Sharing the Journey*. London: Taylor & Francis, 1996.

Rando, T. A. *Grief, Dying and Death: Clinical Interventions for Caregivers*. Ottawa, ON: Research Press, 1981.

Worden, J. William. *Grief Counseling and Grief Therapy: A Handbook for the Mental Health Practitioner*. New York: Springer Publishing, 1991.

SPIRITUALITY AT THE END OF LIFE

Arnold, Johann Christoph. *I Tell You a Mystery*. Oxford, UK: Plough Publications, 1996.

Berman, Phillip. *The Journey Home: What Near Death Experiences and Mysticism Teach Us about the Gift of Life*. New York: Pocket Books, 1996.

Brooke, Avery. *Healing in the Landscape of Prayer: Contemporary Understandings of Healing*. New York: Cowley Publications, 1996.

Carmody, John Tully. *Meditations on the End of Life*. Harrisburg, PA: Trinity Press International, 1997.

Dossey, Larry, M.D. *Prayer Is Good Medicine: How to Reap the Healing Benefits of Prayer*. San Francisco: Harper, 1996.

Guroian, Vigen. *Life's Living toward Dying*. Grand Rapids, MI: Wm. B. Eerdmans Publishing Co., 1996.

Nowen, Henri. *Our Greatest Gift: A Meditation on Dying and Caring*. San Francisco: Harper Books, 1993.

Rinpoche, Sogyal. *Tibetan Book of Living and Dying*. New York: Touchstone, 1993.

Rohr, Richard, O.F.M. *Job and the Mystery of Suffering: Spiritual Reflections*. Chicago: Crossroad, 1996.

Tolle, Eckhart. *The Power of Now: A Guide to Spiritual Enlightenment*. Novato, CA: New World Library, 1999.

Vince, Ken R. *Visions of God: From the Near Death Experience*. Burdett, NY: Larson, 1994.

Whipple, Barbara. *I've Got Cancer, But It Doesn't Have Me! A Survivor's Book of Poems*. Westmont, IL: Full Moon Press, 1995.

Wicks, Robert J., and Thomas E. Rodgerson. *Companions in Hope: The Art of Christian Caring*. New York: Paulist Press, 1998.

THERAPIES

Please refer to part III of *The American Book of Living and Dying*, where a separate resource list is provided for each modality or healing therapy.

Audio Resources

Pinkola Estes, Clarissa, Ph.D. *The Radiant Coat: Myths and Stories About the Crossing Between Life and Death*. Boulder, CO: Sounds True, 1991.

The following resources featuring author Richard Groves are available for purchase on CD or audiocassette at www.sacredartofliving.org.

The Art of Discernment: Wrestling with Sacred Questions. 2002.

A three-hour program.

The Sacred Art of Dying: Living with Hope. 2000.

A two-hour program.

The Ten Commandments of Grief Ministry. 2001.

A one-hour program.

Groves, Richard. *The Contemplative Enneagram: The Sacred Art of Living and Dying*. Bend, OR: SAL Resources, 2001. Audiocassette, eight hours.

The only resource produced to date on the Enneagram and end-of-life care. Series is based on life-changing stories from the hospice together with spiritual insights from the Enneagram.

Rohr, Richard, Fr. *An Enneagram Evening with Richard Rohr*. Bend, OR: Spirit Records, 2001. Audiocassette, sixty minutes.

A good introduction to the Enneagram by an extraordinary spiritual teacher, includes helpful historical and practical perspectives.

Contact www.sacredartofliving.org for a complete list of Enneagram-related programs from a spiritual perspective.

Video Resources

The Eternal Now: A Celebration of Life. Pan Image Inc., 1997.

516-569-6884.

A remarkable film that features interviews with residents of an actors' retirement home. Humorous and insightful reflections on the meaning of life and death.

Letting Go: A Hospice Journey. DVD or VHS. Films for the Humanities and Sciences, 1996.

1-800-257-5126 or 609-275-1400.

An inspiring ninety-minute special HBO production featuring the lives of terminally ill persons and their families.

Monsen, Maren, M.D. *The Vanishing Line*. New York: 52-minute film. First Run/Icarus Films, 1998.

212-727-1711.

Winner of the 1998 Award for Excellence in Documentary Filmmaking, a video that chronicles one physician's exploration of how to try and meet the needs of the dying and their families while balancing compassion and care.

Palmer, Greg. *Death: The Trip of a Lifetime*. 4-part video series. New York: Ambrose Video Publishing, Inc.

An extraordinarily well-produced series with footage from every part of the globe depicting practices and customs at the end of life.

About the Authors

PHOTO BY MARY L. GROVES

RICHARD F. GROVES is the founder of the internationally renowned Sacred Art of Living and Dying educational series, which teaches participants how to alleviate spiritual and emotional distress at the end of life. A hospice chaplain for nearly thirty years, Richard has attended the deaths of more than five hundred people. He speaks nine languages and has earned graduate degrees in theology, ethics, law, and pastoral counseling. Richard and his wife, Mary, established the Sacred Art of Living Center in Bend, Oregon, twenty-five years ago, where he still resides today.

Visit www.sacredartofliving.org

PHOTO BY KEVIN R. SMITH

HENRIETTE ANNE KLAUSER, Ph.D., is the author of four books, including the best-selling *Writing on Both Sides of the Brain* and *Write It Down, Make It Happen*. She is the president of Writing Resources, a seminar and consulting organization, as well as an active lecturer, workshop leader, and freelance writer. Henriette Anne is dedicated to helping people use the power of the written word to build relationships, bring families together, and heal emotional wounds. She lives in Edmonds, Washington.

Visit www.henrietteklauser.com